CHRIST

CHRIST FOR US

Sermons of Hugh Martin

THE BANNER OF TRUTH TRUST

THE BANNER OF TRUTH TRUST
3 Murrayfield Road, Edinburgh EH12 6EL
P.O. Box 621, Carlisle, Pennsylvania 17013, USA

★

First Published 1998
ISBN 0 85151 741 2

★

Typeset at The Spartan Press Ltd,
Lymington, Hants
Printed and bound in Great Britain by
MPG Books Ltd, Bodmin, Cornwall

CONTENTS

BIOGRAPHICAL INTRODUCTION

Dr Hugh Martin was born in Aberdeen on 11 August 1822, the son of Alexander Martin of that city. Like his later friend and colleague Dr John ('Rabbi') Duncan, he was educated at the city's Grammar School before going on, at an early age, to Marischal College to pursue an arts degree.

Little is recorded of his early spiritual experience, but the late Professor G. N. M. Collins of the Free Church College, Edinburgh, tells us that Martin 'feared the Lord from his youth', and that 'his early conversion was followed by the call to devote himself to the ministry of the Gospel.'[1] 'His higher studies, from the beginning,' Collins continues, 'were directed to that end.' Despite his youth – he cannot have been more than fourteen or fifteen years old when he first attended Marischal College – these higher studies were exceptionally brilliant. He carried off numerous prizes, including the highest award in mathematics granted by the College, the Gray bursary. He graduated MA in April 1839, when he was not yet seventeen, and shortly after began his theological studies. At that time, Aberdeen students of divinity attended classes in both Marischal College and King's College, since neither by itself was able to provide a complete theological curriculum. The two colleges did not unite to form the University of Aberdeen until 1860.

[1]Biographical Introduction to *The Abiding Presence*, the Knox Press edition of Martin's work originally published as *Christ's Presence in the Gospel History* (Edinburgh, 1865), p.15.

This was a momentous time to study for the ministry of the established Church of Scotland. The long conflict over patronage, as well as the underlying tension between the Moderate and Evangelical parties in the Church, was approaching its climax. A parting of the ways was not far distant. During most of his divinity studies, Martin was unsympathetic to the position of the 'non-intrusion' party, then struggling to assert the spiritual independence of the Church from the interference of the civil courts. The attempts of the Court of Session to force unwelcome ministers on congregations against their wishes brought the struggle to a head. On 23 May 1842, Martin heard Dr William Cunningham speak in the General Assembly on the subject of patronage. According to an eye-witness, Cunningham 'arrayed against the whole system of church patronage the combined authority of scripture, of ecclesiastical history, of right reason, and [of] the nature of things.'[2] It was enough to convince Hugh Martin.[3] He was completely won over to the principles of the non-intrusionists.

At this Assembly, too, the Claim of Right, the most important single document of the Ten Years' Conflict (1834–43), was approved. This was a petition to the Queen and the Government claiming protection from the encroachments of the courts on the rights of the Church. Its adoption set the non-intrusionists on a course which led directly to the Disruption of the following year. Martin now belonged to the band of divinity students who

[2]Robert Buchanan: *The Ten Years' Conflict*, Glasgow, 1854, vol. ii, p.354.

[3]Martin's warm attachment to Cunningham in later years can be seen in a reference to him after his death as 'the beloved and ever-to-be-lamented William Cunningham' (*The Atonement*, p.195).

were willing to renounce the security of a position in the Established Church in order to maintain, along with some 470 serving ministers, 'the Crown Rights of the Redeemer'.[4] He later recalled this period with gratitude: 'I remember those days, and witnessed some of their grandest scenes.'[5] To his student days Martin also traced the influence of Dr Robert S. Candlish whom he first heard preach in 1840. Candlish, he says, 'awoke my young enthusiasm'.[6]

Licensed to preach on 19 May 1843, the day after the Disruption took place, Hugh Martin was called in the following year to Panbride, near Carnoustie, in the newly established Free Church Presbytery of Arbroath. The congregation was formed immediately after the Disruption, but had to endure considerable opposition from the local landowner, Lord Panmure. He let it be known that no member or adherent of the Free Church would be allowed on his estates. All tenants who joined the new church would be evicted, unless they returned to the Established Church. Undeterred, the congregation at Panbride met at first in the barn at Westhaven Farm. Then, in the year of Martin's arrival among them, a wooden church was built in a field. The farmer had a lease and could not be evicted, but he had to defy threats of future expulsion when the lease came up for renewal. A lady in a neighbouring parish who built a wooden meeting-place in the garden of her cottage was evicted in

[4]This phrase was adopted on the eve of the Disruption as a conscious echo of the watchword chosen by the Covenanters of the seventeenth century (Thomas Brown: *The Annals of the Disruption*, Edinburgh, 1893, p.5).
[5]Sermon on the death of Candlish, preached in Dingwall, 2 Nov 1873.
[6]ibid.

1844. Another tenant of Lord Panmure's who spoke of acting according to his conscience was 'sharply told to pocket his conscience if it were opposed to Lord Panmure'.[7] This was the rather daunting setting in which the young preacher, aged only twenty-one, was called to begin his labours. He was to remain in Panbride until 1858, exercising what must, judging from surviving manuscript sermons, have been a remarkable and powerful ministry. Some of the sermons now published are from the Panbride period. We know little of the results, though it is recorded that in 1848 the membership of the church stood at 202.[8]

In 1846 Martin married Elizabeth Jane Robertson. Their son Alexander, later Principal of New College, Edinburgh, and four daughters were born at Panbride. Towards the end of his life, Martin published a *Letter to My Daughter on the Prophetic Office of Christ* (Montrose, 1880).

He was content to labour in this quiet parish for fourteen years. During this time aristocratic hostility to the Free Church appears to have cooled, since, in 1854, Lord Panmure's successor gave a site for the construction of a permanent church building, together with a donation of £100 and free use of his stone quarries. The church was opened in May 1855. A permanent manse was built only in 1859, after Martin's departure.

Invitations to larger and more influential charges were not lacking in this period. At least one vacant city congregation was interested in securing his services.[9] He was already known as a gifted writer as well as a preacher.

[7]*Annals of Disruption*, p.452.

[8]W. Ewing (ed.): *Annals of the Free Church of Scotland*, Edinburgh, 1914.

[9]Sermon on the death of Candlish, 2 Nov 1873.

As early as 1845, his sermon *The Manifestation of the Son of Perdition* was published at Aberdeen, while the sermon *Precept, Promise and Prayer* in the present volume was thought worthy of inclusion in the *Free Church Pulpit* in 1847 when Martin was only 25. But it was not until April 1858 that he accepted a call to Free Greyfriars Church in Edinburgh. He was inducted to the charge on 10 June.

Although the potential of this enlarged sphere of influence seemed great, his time at Greyfriars was destined to be short. He suffered a breakdown in health in 1861 which interrupted his ministry there for six months. Recurrence of ill health eventually caused his early retirement from the charge in June 1865. A note in the periodical *The Watchword,* edited by Martin's friend Dr James Begg, of Newington Free Church, Edinburgh, refers to this as 'a mysterious Providence', removing him 'from the place where he was confidently expected to exert a mighty and extensive influence for good.'[10] Perhaps, in retrospect, we can see part of the providential reason for his early retirement in the literary labours he was able to pursue in his later years. Following his recovery, he dedicated to the members of his Greyfriars congregation, *Yea and Amen: A Sermon on the Steadfastness of God's Promises,* as a memorial of his labours among them. Originally printed for private distribution, this work was soon published with an added preface in defence of the Westminster Standards. A comment in *The Watchword,* probably from the pen of Dr Begg, declared, 'We have seldom read a sermon in which strength of argument and fervency of appeal are more happily united. It is itself a refutation of the idea that definiteness of creed, and an earnest appreciation of the doctrines of the Bible, are

[10] *The Watchword,* May 1, 1866.

incompatible with earnestness in the Christian life and depth of Christian experience; the idea that there is any necessary connexion between strength of mind and coldness of heart.'

After his retirement, Martin moved to Greenhill Cottage, Lasswade, near Edinburgh. During the remainder of his life, though not engaged in pastoral ministry, he continued to preach throughout Scotland and further afield as occasion arose and to take an active part in the affairs of the Church, despite recurring periods of illness. He regularly attended the General Assembly where he was a frequent and able speaker. He also maintained an interest in mathematics and in music. 'He was one of the foremost home-bred and original mathematicians that Scotland has produced,' says Dr John Macleod.[11] As such he regularly contributed to the *Transactions of the Mathematical Society of London,* as well as acting as Examiner in Mathematics to the University of Edinburgh. He is even identified as a Member of the Mathematical Society of London on the title page of his book *The Atonement,* published in London in 1870, while another of the works published after his retirement was *A Study of Trilinear Coordinates* (Cambridge, 1867). In addition, he lectured on science in relation to the biblical doctrine of creation to the Lasswade and District Science School in 1871.[12]

But it is as a penetrating theologian and warm-hearted expounder of themes lying at the heart of the Christian gospel that he is chiefly remembered today. His literary output, particularly after his retirement, was large. In recognition of his achievements, Edinburgh University

---

[11]*Scottish Theology,* Edinburgh: Banner of Truth Trust, 1974, p.325.
[12]The lecture appears in *The Watchword,* Nov. 1, 1871.

conferred a Doctorate of Divinity on him in 1872. Much of what he wrote appeared in periodicals, particularly the *British and Foreign Evangelical Review*, and *The Watchword*, edited by his friend James Begg between 1866 and 1873. Martin was Begg's principal helper in the running of *The Watchword* and a major contributor to its pages. This magazine was produced largely to give a voice to those opposed to union between the Free Church and the United Presbyterian Synod – a union regarded by Begg and those sharing his outlook as a betrayal of basic Free Church principles. Martin defended these principles, which were both ecclesiastical and theological, with directness and vigour. His other occasional writings on matters of church and state included *Where Will the Free Church be Found?* (Free Church Tract No.4, undated), *Christ's Headship over Church and State* (1859), *Christ's 'Own House'* (1859), *The Ten Years' Conflict Misread by Historians* (1869), *National Education: A Reply to the Lord Advocate's Speech at Stranraer* (1872), and *The Connexion between the Headship of Christ and Revival in the Church* (1875). His *Westminster Doctrine of the Inspiration of Scripture* (1877) and *Letters to Marcus Dods* (1877) both concerned the views of the younger Dods, whose theological wanderings greatly grieved him.

Other works whose continuing value is still recognised include his commentary *The Prophet Jonah* (1866), still available from the Banner of Truth Trust in the Geneva Series of Commentaries. Of this book C. H. Spurgeon remarked in his *Commenting and Commentaries*, 'A first-class exposition of Jonah. No one who has it will need another.' Then, lastly, there is what Professor Collins regarded as 'a quite remarkable trilogy'[13] on themes

[13]Biographical Introduction to *The Abiding Presence*, p.16.

central to the gospel: *Christ's Presence in the Gospel History*
(1865), *The Atonement: in its Relations to the Covenant, the
Priesthood, the Intercession of Our Lord* (1870) and *The
Shadow of Calvary* (1875). The first of these was reissued
by Knox Press as *The Abiding Presence*. It contemplates
the life and ministry of Christ, recorded in the gospels, in
the light of his promise to be with his people always, even
to the end of the world, and relates this theme to present
Christian experience. *The Shadow of Calvary* is still
available from the Banner of Truth Trust. In this work,
based on discourses preached during his ministry at
Panbride, Martin leads the reader through the closing
scenes of the life of Christ prior to his crucifixion,
interpreting the events recorded in the light of the benefits
which flow to believers from his death. Characteristically,
Martin called this eloquent book 'a feeble contribution
towards the elucidation of this wonderful theme'. *The
Atonement* has long been out of print. In it Martin defends
'the Catholic Doctrine of the Cross', viewing the sub-
stitutionary nature of the atonement as being grounded in
the covenant of grace. Broad-Church evasions of true
substitution, such as that of F. W. Robertson of Brighton,
are thoroughly demolished. While acknowledging all that
was amiable in Robertson's character, Martin regards his
sermons as 'a lamentable compost of unintentional
blasphemy and theological ignorance'. John Macleod
believed that Robertson 'came very limp indeed out of his
grips'.[14] Of this volume Spurgeon wrote: 'Something like
theology. We wish our young divines would feed on such
meat as this. Dr Martin teaches a real substitution and an
efficient atonement, and has no sympathy with Robertson
and his school.'

[14]*Scottish Theology*, p.325.

Biographical Introduction

Hugh Martin died at Lasswade on 14 June 1885. His wife, his son and two daughters survived him. The sermons in this book are taken for the most part from the unpublished manuscript notes he left behind. One of those included, *The Eternal Priesthood of Christ, and the Father's Oath,* was previously published in a limited local edition, while *The Righteousness of Faith* was published by the Religious Tract and Book Society of Scotland. *The Hidden Life* was printed in a series called *The Modern Scottish Pulpit,* and *Precept, Promise and Prayer* originally appeared in the *Free Church Pulpit,* Volume III, 1847. All are long out of print. The Publishers are indebted for the remaining sermons to the late Principal James Mackintosh of the Free Church College, Edinburgh, who painstakingly prepared typescripts from Martin's hand-written notes. They were preached at various times during Martin's ministry – those which can be dated range from 1847 to 1877 – but the doctrine expressed remains the same throughout. All Martin's teaching and exhortation centre on Christ's office as Priest, consisting in 'his once offering up of himself a sacrifice to satisfy divine justice, and reconcile us to God, and in making continual intercession for us' (*Shorter Catechism*, Answer to Question 25). He maintained 'the Westminster and Puritan theology' on these points in an age when, as he put it, ' "other gospels" are already rife, and in many quarters the covenant of grace seems to be forgotten.'[15] In recognition of this central theme, and prompted by a passage in the sermon *Crucified with Christ,* we have adopted the present title. The passage reads:

[15]Preface to *The Shadow of Calvary*, Edinburgh: Banner of Truth Trust, 1983, p.9.

[xv]

Observe then . . . that the Scriptures in explaining the scheme of redemption make frequent use of expressions of this general form: 'Christ for us'. 'He was made sin for us.' 'He was made a curse for us.' 'He gave himself for us.' 'He gave himself a ransom for many.' He is set forth manifestly crucified for us. He died for us. He appeareth in the presence of God for us. These, and many other similar expressions, are grounded on the fact that, according to the counsels of the everlasting covenant, Jesus was by the Father appointed, and of his own free and joyful will became, our Surety, our Representative. The scheme of redemption is founded on a marvellous exchange of places between Christ and his people, he taking theirs, they being translated into his. He became their federal Head. He became Christ for them.[16]

Even when Martin is expounding other scriptural emphases, this theme frequently comes to the fore. 'How ashamed we should be', he writes to a friend towards the end of his life, 'of our low and superficial views of that blessed mystery into which even angels desire to look!'

What was said by an anonymous reviewer in the periodical *The Rock* of his book *The Atonement* is also abundantly true of these sermons: 'The author brings to bear extraordinary powers of reasoning, warmed and animated by a soul that has felt the blessedness of an interest in the blood of the atonement.'

---

[16]Martin also expounded this theme in a helpful way towards the end of his life in an article published in the *British and Foreign Evangelical Review*, 'The Exchange of Places' (*31*, 1882, p.460).

∾ I ∾

The Righteousness of Faith

*'The righteousness which is of faith speaketh on this wise,
Say not in thine heart, Who shall ascend into heaven?
(that is, to bring Christ down from above:) or, Who shall
descend into the deep? (that is, to bring up Christ again
from the dead.) But what saith it? The word is nigh thee,
even in thy mouth, and in thy heart: that is, the word of
faith, which we preach'* (Rom. 10:6–8).

The righteousness which is of faith is here represented
as a person speaking, arguing, expostulating, advising. And this not by a mere figure of speech. It is not a
mere 'personification' that sets the righteousness of faith
a-speaking; though regarded even in that way, it casts an
uncommonly beautiful light upon the passage. But it is
more. There is more than personification here – there is a
Person. Little wonder if the righteousness which is of
faith can speak, and actually speaks, seeing it is none
other than the Word – the Word which was in the beginning, which was with God, and was God. It is none
other than the Second Person of the Godhead, God incarnate, the Christ of God. For Christ crucified is the
righteousness of God to every one that believeth. Christ
is of God made unto us righteousness. As is said in a
preceding verse of this chapter, 'Christ is the end of the
law for righteousness to every one that believeth.' He is

'the Lord our Righteousness'. And because he becomes ours by gift on God's part, and by simple reception, or, in other words, by faith, on our part, he is 'the righteousness which is by faith'.

What has he, in this capacity, to say? When he would act and speak as the righteousness of faith, what has he to say?

Right wisely, right powerfully, right tenderly he speaks. He speaks to sinners, who would be the better of him as the Lord their Righteousness, infinitely the better of him, and who never will be the better of anything till they have found and been pleased with him. And he speaks to them, first, in a double dissuasive; and, second, in a double persuasive.

FIRST, A DOUBLE DISSUASIVE.

i. Say not in thine heart, Who shall ascend into heaven? (that is, to bring Christ down from above): for that would imply that no Saviour has as yet come down from heaven. But, behold! we bring you good tidings of great joy, which shall be to all mankind, for to you is born a Saviour, which is Christ, and his name shall be called Wonderful, Counsellor, the mighty God, the everlasting Father, the Prince of Peace. 'This is a faithful saying, and worthy of all acceptation, that Christ Jesus came into the world to save sinners.' Never say anything 'in thine heart' that is at variance with this. Never be in any state of mind or frame of heart at variance with the blessed fact that, 'when the fulness of the time was come, God sent forth his Son, made of a woman, made under the law, to redeem them that were under the law, that we might receive the adoption of sons. And because ye are sons, God hath sent forth the Spirit of his Son into your hearts, crying, Abba, Father.'

ii. Say not in thine heart, Who shall descend into the deep? (that is, to bring up Christ again from the dead): for he is risen again, in very truth. Death could have no permanent dominion over him, no dominion at all. He conquered death by dying. He was not made a victim. He became a conqueror. And his resurrection is the proof of it. Never think of him as an incomplete Redeemer. His redemption work is perfect. And his resurrection proves it. He died for our offences, and was raised again for our justification. He finished the work given him to do. He left none of it for his weak and weary people. Said he to his Father, 'I have glorified thee on the earth: I have finished the work which thou gavest me to do.' And in token that the Father is of one mind with him on this, the very basis of his people's faith and joy, he raised him from the dead and gave him glory, that our faith and hope might be in God.

Say not anything in thine heart which it would be right and reasonable to say only on the supposition that Jesus was still the prisoner of death. He is risen. He is ascended. He is within the veil in glory – able to save to the uttermost them that come unto God by him. Let not thine heart ever for a moment be in a state or frame that would be reasonable only on the supposition that Christ were not raised from the dead.

Say not then, 'Who shall go down into the deep?' – any more than, 'Who shall go up into heaven?' Say neither the one thing nor the other. Speak neither of going up nor of going down, as little the one as the other. I bring near my salvation, and you have no journey to take to reach it – neither up nor down – neither to the right hand nor to the left. Your attitude is that of waiting, not working: waiting as those that watch for the morning, which, behold! how it dawneth, and cometh on, not a whit aided by any works or journeys of yours, but breaking in omnipotent glory in the east, being itself master of the day: yea, itself the day-spring from on high.

SECONDLY, A DOUBLE PERSUASIVE.

i. 'The word is nigh thee . . . that is, the word of faith.' Now this implies, O sinner, that, Christ's redemption-work being perfect, and sealed as such by his resurrection, your salvation-work is a work done at a 'word'. That is clearly implied in this persuasive. It has no meaning at all if it does not imply, first of all, and above all, that salvation is by grace, seeing all the redemptive work is done already. Ye are saved by grace, through faith. And it is of faith that it might be by grace. But faith needs a word to go upon. 'Be merciful unto me according to thy word.' 'Remember the word unto thy servant, upon which thou hast caused me to hope.' The promise, accordingly, is the word of faith, the word which faith receives, the word which the Spirit uses to generate faith. This is the word on God's part which answers to faith (or, rather, to which faith answers) on man's part, in that great transaction in which reconciliation between the offended God and the alienated sinner is effected by the word of the truth of the gospel.

Now this 'word', which is all that is needed to thy salvation-work (because redemption-work is a finished work) – this 'word' which is required to be taken home in faith in order to the taking home of a perfected redemption-work (unto the resulting work of our actual individual salvation) – this 'word', intended of God to be so received in faith unto our actual salvation, and, in point of fact, so received by every one that believeth, is therefore very properly called the 'word of faith'. It is the word which faith proceeds upon as true, the word which kindles and calls up faith itself, and then trusts itself to the faith

[4]

which it has kindled: this word is nigh thee; even in thy mouth and in thine heart.

Such is the testimony of the 'Righteousness which is of faith'. And none can be so deeply interested in the word of faith as the Righteousness which is of faith. By the word of faith, he, the Righteousness which is of faith, puts himself into the possession of every one that believeth, and sees of the travail of his soul. And this word is nigh thee, even in thy mouth and in thy heart.

ii. Oh! says the sinner, I can understand how this word should be in my *mouth*. I can, of myself – alas! only too easily – take it in my *mouth* and utter it. But that it should be in my *heart*, that I should know and love the joyful sound, that I should willingly receive and be in actual possession by faith of the great redemption – this is another matter altogether, and not competent to this depraved and sinful heart of mine. How can it be true that the word is 'in my heart'?

Very good, dear fellow sinner. Very good and very true. Who can bring a clean thing out of an unclean? Very true. But consider!

Who, indeed, if *he* cannot, who here speaketh? And is it not in and by *speaking* that he does it? He who here speaketh is the All-Powerful Word, who speaks and it is done. He said, 'Let light be', and light was. He 'calleth those things which be not as though they were.' He *brings* into being by *calling* into being. His call *gives* the being to which it *calls*. His people are a willing people in the day of his power. If he says that the word is not in your *mouth* only but in your *heart*, have you any interest to question and gainsay him? He can *make* it true, in *saying* it is true. Is it too wonderful, think you, to be true, though *he* say it who came to bear witness of

[5]

the truth? He can *realise* that as the case in *describing* it as the case.

For he is acting here as a *prompter*. Yes, as a *prompter*. That's the edge and joy of it. And it is faith's part, and faith's nature, and faith's inward instinctive prompting, to act on *his* promptings, not to gainsay and resist them. 'When thou saidst, Seek ye my face; my heart said unto thee, Thy face, LORD, will I seek.'

If you were a pupil, and a trusted master was prompting you, you would 'out with' the word with which he was furnishing, urging, and prompting you at that moment. Just as you would, in such a case, 'out with it', from your *mouth*, so remember Christ's almighty power over the *heart* in prompting it – even as complete as that which an earthly master has over the mouth in prompting *it*. And see that you 'out with' the word from your heart, even the word of faith which is preached unto you. Be it yours at once to cry: 'My Lord, and my God', or 'Lord, I believe; help thou mine unbelief.'

Yes, go not about to construct, or establish, or find a righteousness. Go not up to heaven. Go not down into the deep. Go neither up nor down. Go neither to the right hand nor to the left. But here, where you are, this moment – here and now – listen to another righteousness, the Lord your Righteousness, the Righteousness which is by faith, which comes by faith, which is yours by faith. Is there never to be a first time? If there is, let it be *now*. For what advantage is there to be *gained* by *loss* of time? And let it be *here*, for what advantage is there to be gained by change of place? This righteousness (and all the salvation that depends upon it) is yours here and now, because it is yours at a word. And 'the word is nigh thee' – nigher than you think. Let the Righteousness of faith itself tell you how nigh: 'even in thy mouth and in thy heart.' Oh! doubt not.

Say not, 'It is too good to be true'. If that's the only style of objection you have to what Jesus Christ says, it's a very poor one. For grace is poured into his lips, and his words are so good that, just on that ground, the Father, in infinite admiration of him, hath done every thing possible to make him most blessed for ever more. Say not that anything is too good to be true, when Jesus Christ, the ever blessed 'delight' of the Godhead, hath said it. Rather, try and see if it be not thoroughly true indeed. Try and 'out with it': 'My Lord and my God.' 'Lord, I believe.'

In the rich full flow of his goodness, so great as to be telling the things to which thou canst have no objection, except that they are too good to be true, 'out with' the word from thy very heart, prompted by him, yet uttered by you – you, the travail of his soul. He, thy regenerating Lord and Saviour, making thee willing in the day of his power. 'Saved by grace through faith' – *his* grace. Grace on his part, faith on your part: *your* faith in the sense that it comes from your believing heart, but *his* gift in that it is wrought by his Spirit there and prompted by his Word there. Yet altogether such that this other glorious utterance may take place in terms of it, and because of it, sealing eternal espousals between him and you: 'My beloved is mine, and I am His'. 'My Lord and my God.'

Aye, truly: 'Hearken, O daughter, and consider, and incline thine ear; forget also thine own people, and thy father's house; so shall the king greatly desire thy beauty: for he is thy Lord; and worship thou him.'

Yes, and then just proceed upon the truth of it. Try and see if those things be not true, which are and ought to be true because of this. 'Being justified by faith, you have peace with God' – have you not? – 'through Jesus Christ our Lord.' Yes, and have you not 'access by faith' into an estate of grace, not merely an occasional and fortuitous blessing, but an entire estate of grace, 'the grace wherein ye stand'? Are Christians always careful to do justice to this? This, at least, is what you have to do justice to. This is what you have to be thankful for. Try if you don't *get* access, just by *taking* access into 'this grace wherein ye stand', this gracious right and title to all blessings of the everlasting covenant. This 'grace wherein ye stand' is to you a 'status' and 'estate of salvation by a Redeemer', as truly as formerly you were in an 'estate of sin and misery'. 'And not only so, but we glory in tribulations also.' Do you not? Would you not rather suffer affliction with the people of God, than have all the pleasures of sin to all eternity? You 'glory in tribulations also: knowing that tribulation worketh patience; and patience, experience; and experience, hope: and hope maketh not ashamed; because the love of God is shed abroad in our hearts by the Holy Ghost which is given unto us.' Put all this to the proof by proceeding in faith upon the truth of it: and so you find it true. You get access into what of Christ's fulness you need just by taking access to it by faith, taking your way by faith to the very blessing that you need, asserting that in Christ it is yours, maintaining your assertion against all efforts of the enemy to deny it. Who, or what, is he? A damned and vanquished foe! And the Lord, in such case, gives his fainting, faithful soldier – fainting through the very efforts of his fidelity – to find that he is not fighting for the wind, for a fancy, for a shadow, but for the faithfulness of God, and thus he finds that the faithfulness of God is in the heavens, and is also a shield and buckler to himself upon the earth.

Oh, to bow the head of the soul, to bend the knees of the soul, to set the silent smiling face of the soul steadfastly towards heaven, and let God speak! Oh, to follow, fearless, where his Word leads the way! Oh, to follow, and to follow on, nothing doubting, cherishing neither a proud unbelief, nor, what is even worse, a humble unbelief, but cherishing just the Word itself, because it is 'the Word of faith'. Thus we would think nothing of our faith, but all things of the Word. Dwelling in a realm in which we had learned to silence every voice, save the voice of our heavenly Teacher, as he speaks, by his Word and Spirit, the will of God for our salvation, our joy and our duty, we should have the blessedness of the people who in that case truly know the joyful sound, and walk, O Lord, in the light of thy countenance!

The Eternal Priesthood of Christ, and the Father's Oath

'The Lord hath sworn, and will not repent, Thou art a priest for ever after the order of Melchizedek' (Psa. 110:4).

Concerning this wonderful divine oracle it may well be said, as of heaven, 'The glory of God did lighten it, and the Lamb is the light thereof.' In these marvellous words there is a whole heaven of grace and glory. In them Jehovah the Father puts himself rejoicingly on oath to attest to Jehovah Jesus, the Son, the perpetuity of that office which deals with sin for the purpose of expiating, forgiving and eternally abolishing it, to the glory of God in the redemption of a people that no man can number. 'Jehovah hath sworn, and will not repent, Thou art a priest for ever after the order of Melchizedek.'

I need not enter at any length on the nature of our Lord's priesthood. No better statement could be given than that with which we are intimate from infancy: 'Christ executeth the office of a priest, in his once offering up of himself a sacrifice to satisfy divine justice, and reconcile us to God; and in making continual intercession for us.'[1] Nor do I require to point out to one that has tried to understand

---

[1] *Shorter Catechism*, Answer 25.

it that it is on this office that our redemption most directly and immediately depends, inasmuch as Christ could have nothing to reveal as prophet, nor rule as king (except to destroy), were it not that he is primarily a priest. It is from the priestly office that all the grace overflows to the kingly power and prophetic revelation, so that what he reveals as prophet is for our welfare because he is a priest, and the gentleness of his kingly power arises from his being the Lamb of God who was given over for our offences and rose again for our justification.

The prophetic office is promised and prophesied without an oath: 'The LORD thy God will raise up unto thee a Prophet from the midst of thee, of thy brethren, like unto me' (*Deut.* 18:15). The kingly honour also is conferred on Jehovah Jesus without an oath: 'The LORD said unto my Lord, Sit thou at my right hand' (*Psa.* 110:1). But in the case of the priesthood Jehovah interposes the solemnity of his sacred oath: 'The LORD hath sworn, and will not repent, Thou art a priest for ever after the order of Melchizedek.'

The kingly office is embraced in the stability of the oath as reward for his priesthood. Every function roots in the priesthood, partakes of its stability, and comes under the full sweep of this wondrous office. Speaking of that kingly office, here made to unite with the priesthood in the person of Jesus, we find a union which is not exhibited in Aaron's priesthood. In the Messiah, kingship and priesthood are combined, because he is priest after the order of him whose name is King of Righteousness, and who by designation was King of Salem, that is, King of Peace. No less obvious is the harmony of divine attributes and divergent interests, for mercy and truth are met, righteousness and peace have embraced each other, in a priest faithful and merciful, who is at once a king of righteousness and a king of peace.

[11]

We are not to suppose that Melchizedek was without father or mother literally. If he was, he did not belong to our race, but was really a second man, and the Lord from heaven would then be the third man. What we are led to understand is that the narrative brings him before us without speaking of father or mother, without mention of genealogy, without anything about the commencement of office, or retirement from office, thus presenting him as priest without predecessor or successor, beginning of days or end of life, made in this respect (according to the literal aspect of the story) like unto the Son of God, so that Jesus might be made like him, not having his priesthood transferred to him from another, or by him to another. So is Jesus a priest after the order of Melchizedek.

In attempting to open up a little the wonderful contents of this verse, feeling our need of the light and teaching of God's Spirit, we may consider

1. The call to the priesthood which it constitutes.
2. The commandment it involves.
3. The constitution of office it effects.
4. The pledge of success it implies.
5. The congratulation it expresses.
6. The testimony it bears.
7. The oath by which it is sealed.

1. *Christ's Call to the Office*. Hereby God the Father calls him, saying, 'Thou art a priest'. Such a call was necessary. A call from God is necessary to all office in the service of God, especially to the office of priesthood, for priesthood is with a view to the worship of God. The High Priest is minister of the true sanctuary. On his shoulders rests the responsibility of the worship of God. All will-worship is abhorrent to the mind of God and injurious to the divine glory. Whatever is according to these must stand the test

of this divine rule, 'of him, and through him, and to him, are all things.' First, 'of him', originating with him, before it can find a place among the all things 'through him, and to him'. God's worship stands pre-eminent in this. All will-worship is peculiarly offensive to him. Christ's priesthood, intended to take the lead and headship of worship to the Father throughout all eternity, must pre-eminently find its origin in the will of God, and come into existence at his call. Hence the divine expositor in Hebrews, speaking of the priesthood, says, 'No man taketh this honour unto himself, but he that is called of God, as was Aaron.' The general principle thus exemplified was not violated or dispensed with in the case of Christ; even God the Son would not assume office without the call of God the Father. 'So also Christ glorified not himself to be made an high priest; but he that said unto him, Thou art my Son, today have I begotten thee.' 'Thou art a priest for ever.' Behold, then, the fountainhead of salvation, the divine origin and authorization of the priesthood of Christ in the call of God.

That call springs from the love of God, and carries the authority of God; it is a call which came from God, as sovereign in grace, in authority and in government too. Now is verified that word in which the Father, addressing the Son, says, 'I the LORD have called thee in righteousness, and will hold thine hand, and will keep thee, and give thee for a covenant of the people.' What magnificent help this consideration affords to the poor and needy soul struggling under a conviction of the guilt and strength of sin, when wondering whether sin can possibly be forgiven, vanquished and expelled, whether conscience, perishing under the shame of sin and its matchless perplexity and confusion, can ever be cleansed and brought to bask in the sunshine of self approbation!

What help it is to such a soul, when ready to strike sail and to be driven before the wind helpless, to be told that there is One called of God waiting on this continually, to be told, I say, that there is a great responsible office-bearer, whose very call of God is to make an end of sin, to make reconciliation for iniquity, and to bring in everlasting righteousness, to cleanse confused, polluted, self-affronted souls to a delightful purity, whiter than snow, God himself being judge! What an aspect of precious-ness Christ's priesthood assumes, having the approbation of God, and originating in his authority, his love and his call.

'May I draw on the services of this great High Priest?' the soul asks. 'Have I a warrant to solicit his services?' Is not his call to the office warrant enough for you to present yourself before him, that he may have an opportunity to exercise his office? This opportunity he cannot have without having poor sinful souls to trust in him and commit their case to him. Besides, is this call the only call you ever heard about? Is not Christ's call to the priesthood the great root call, the parent of many more? Even now a branch shall grow out of its roots. To whom shall it bend, and into what bosom shall it seek to deposit its clustered fruitfulness? To thine here, if thou wilt have it. Every branch call comes from the root call, partaking of the root and fatness of that call. Strong in the might of the Father's oath, and love to the Son, comes the call to thee, 'Incline your ear and come unto me: hear, and your soul shall live; and I will make an everlasting covenant with you, even the sure mercies of David.' The gospel call comes to thee in spirit and in truth, in presence of God the Father, as he swears and will not repent, 'Thou art a priest for ever'. Hear him as he goes on to call thee to come boldly to a throne of grace, that thou mayest obtain mercy. Take thy call as coming out of Christ's call. Remember, thou never hadst been called had he not been called. Out of his and its glorious vitality springs the call to thee; and dost thou not feel as if such a call, so grounded upon and springing out of Christ's call to his priesthood, were grappling with thine inmost heart-strings, and bringing thee effectually to taste and see that the Lord is gracious?

2. *The Father's Commandment.* Christ's priesthood is the fruit of divine commandment. The Father speaks as sovereign, and in the language of command: 'The Lord sware'. As Lord he contemplates the Son as incarnate, calls a servant, and gives commandment: 'Behold my servant whom I uphold; mine elect, in whom my soul delighteth.' In intimate relation with his character as God's elect, but also as servant, it is true that 'a bruised reed shall he not break, and the smoking flax shall he not quench.' Such, however, is not the service to which he has been called. He has finer work to do than that. Great as his love for his office is, it is as the servant of the Father, strictly under commandment, that he fulfils all that his office requires of him. 'I lay down my life . . . This commandment have I received of my Father.' It is by commandment that he offers himself to God to satisfy justice, that the Father may freely forgive. It is by commandment he rises again from the dead and makes intercession, that other great department of the priest's office; for, listen, 'Ask of me, and I shall give thee the heathen for thine inheritance, and the uttermost parts of the earth for thy possession.' The Mediator has to obey the commandment first, 'Ask of me', and he obeys through intercession for his people. Blessed be the condescension of the Son of God, for he has been pleased to come to circumstances in which it is his duty to relieve sin-

burdened souls, when they come to him. It is not only his call: he will attend to it. It is not only his profession: he will not be above it. But it is his duty: he has to perform it. He received commandment to this effect, and now that it is his duty, 'him that cometh to me I will in no wise cast out.' Why? Because it would be a violation of his duty, as well as against his loving disposition. He made it his duty to receive weary perplexed sinners, 'for I came down from heaven, not to do mine own will, but the will of him that sent me. And this is the Father's will which hath sent me, that . . . every one which seeth the Son, and believeth on him, may have everlasting life.' If you have cause to bless God that his call to Christ is his commandment, are you to forget or be less thankful that his call to you is his commandment: 'This is his commandment, That we should believe on the name of his Son Jesus Christ.' And if the commandment to Christ to be priest involved all that it did to Christ, shall it, to escape from shame, sorrow and death, be burdensome to you? Surely this is not a grievous yoke. 'My yoke is easy, and my burden is light.'

3. *The Constitution of the Priesthood.* The oracle that calls the Son constitutes him a priest. Nothing more is needed to his being a priest, or to the constitution of his priesthood, than this call. This call makes him what it calls him. In short, it is an effectual call. This is not a minute or superfluous distinction. 'The word of the oath . . . *maketh* the Son' a priest. Again, 'Inasmuch as not without an oath he was made priest', and again, 'Who is made, not after the law of a carnal commandment.' What is the proof that he is made a priest? Nothing but God appealing to the oracle of call, 'For he testifieth, Thou art a priest for ever.' The call made him what it called him, and that for ever. Such is the power of the Word of God: it gives being to

that to which it gives expression. It brings what it calls into existence, even though it calls things that be not, for being called, they begin to be. The supreme instance is in the priesthood of the Son. As soon as God calls him to the priesthood the office exists, for Jesus is not disobedient to the heavenly message. He says, 'I come to do thy will, O God.' And is not this supreme case intended to be in the church of God the ruling case, an example to all others? Is not this glorious effectual call of Christ to the priesthood the model of every effectual call God gives forth? Shall not God's Word be always credited with power to give being to that to which it gives expression? 'Behold, what manner of love the Father hath bestowed on us, that we should be *called* the sons of God.' Called! Is it merely nominally? Does it not *make* those souls whom it *calls* the sons of God? Brethren, whether is it easier to account for the call of God being effectual or ineffectual? Which is more likely to be regarded as the probable result of God giving a call: that it should be effectual or ineffectual?

Concerning effectual calling, then, are there two gospel calls, the one effectual and the other ineffectual, totally distinct? No, the gospel call is one and the same to the saved as to the lost. The difference is not that there is a different call, but that there is in the one case efficacy which is not in the other. Again, I ask, whether is it easier to account for the call of God being effectual or in-effectual? Verily, the real mystery should be the mystery of iniquity in unbelief, that great sin which, with such daring and deadly effect, stands in between the Word of God and its accomplishment. The possibility of such a thing as that God should call, and I refuse, arises from the fact that my will must be free, and cannot possibly be forced. That the will should be such that unbelief is certain until it is renewed by grace indicates such a depth

of corruption and moral evil as reflects the character of
infinite mercy in the provision made for its restoration.
'The LORD hath sworn, and will not repent, Thou art a
priest for ever after the order of Melchizedek.' He promises that the call to salvation shall be as effectual as his call
to priesthood, for 'The LORD shall send the rod of thy
strength out of Zion . . . thy people shall be willing in the
day of thy power.'

4. *The Father's Pledge that the Priesthood Shall be Successful.* The office will be as effectual as the call to it,
triumphant, inviolable, eternal. 'Thou art a priest for
ever.' Observe the force of this pledge as it applies to the
point of danger, the sacrifice and actual death of Jesus,
and guarantees its victorious completion and perfection.
There shall never be a moment in which thou shalt not be a
priest, not even in the dread instant of death on the cross.
In that moment, when all powers and forces shall conspire
to quell and victimize thee, they shall not succeed or
reduce thee to the condition of a mere victim. Thou shalt
never more than then be a priest, for thou shalt offer
thyself in death. No man taketh thy life from thee; thou
shalt lay it down of thyself, and the Father pledges grace
and strength to do it. 'Behold my servant whom I uphold;
mine elect in whom my soul delighteth; I have put my
spirit upon him: he shall bring forth judgment to the
Gentiles.' He through the eternal Spirit shall offer himself
without spot to God. When, by his own priestly action, he
makes his soul an offering for sin, he shall see his seed, he
shall prolong his days, and the pleasure of the Lord shall
prosper in his hand. If Jesus were not a priest on the cross,
then he was vanquished in his conflict with death and hell.
If not a priest, he was a victim in the coarse sense of being
victimized; but no, no! Our Lord, no doubt, became an

atoning victim. He is the Lamb slain, slain from the foundation of the world, and really slain on Calvary, and who is now in the midst of the throne as slain: 'the Lamb of God that taketh away the sin of the world.' But while Justice slew the Lamb, he himself as Priest offered the Lamb. This priest offered no less precious a lamb than himself, and it could not be offered by a less glorious priest than himself.

He was a triumphant priest at the moment that threatened the extinction of his priesthood. Death terminated the priesthood of Aaron. 'Take Aaron thy brother, and Eleazar his son, and bring them up unto mount Hor; and strip Aaron of his garments and put them on Eleazar his son, and Aaron shall be gathered unto his people and shall die there.' 'And they truly were many priests, because they were not suffered to continue by reason of death: but this man, because he continueth ever, hath an unchangeable priesthood.' The oracle proclaimed this, making the Son a priest once for all. It was not in the power of death to extinguish such a priesthood, for it was made after the power of an endless life, to 'destroy him that had the power of death, that is, the devil; and deliver them who through fear of death were all their lifetime subject to bondage.'

Break your bonds in the triumph of your Saviour's death. This is the victory of salvation which faith finds in the cross, victory in death itself. He gave himself as 'an offering and a sacrifice to God for a sweet smelling savour.' Because in spiritual priestly glory he offered himself, in him sinners succeed in offering themselves living sacrifices, holy and acceptable to God. How could a sinner offer himself to God if the Saviour were simply slain, merely a victim, and not a priest? No, this oracle pledges a triumphant offering of himself. 'The LORD hath sworn

and will not repent, Thou art a priest for ever after the
order of Melchizedek.'

5. *The Father's Congratulation.* It is impossible to listen to
the oracle deliberately and reverentially without feeling
this element in it, especially if we have any faith in it and
personal interest in its great occasion, the greatest in the
universe. Who can listen with quiet mind and becoming
adoration when the Lord Jehovah speaks to the Son,
without feeling that here is an utterance of divine delight,
complacency, and joy, such as no voice but its own can
adequately express? 'The LORD hath sworn and will not
repent.' Repent? No, indeed. It repented him that he
made man, but never that the Word was made flesh and
dwelt among us, never that the eternal Son was made a
priest. Repent? No, it evidently implies the positive
thought of delight in assigning this office to the Son of his
love: the highest expression of his divine Fatherly approbation and confidence, for it is a glorious and honourable
office. No doubt death is in the course of it, with its sting
and curse, but there is a joy in it set before him, for which
he does and well may endure the cross. Even in the darkest
hour of his shame and agony he shall be glorious in the
eyes of his God, and wonderful eternal glory shall accrue
from what in it is fitted to repel.

There is everything in it fitted to attract the Son of
God; everything to make him count it a glorious office,
and to count his appointment to it the chiefest love token
of his Father's everlasting delight in him. He glorified
not himself; but he was not unglorified, though not self-
glorified. The Father glorified him when he said, 'Thou
art a priest for ever'; not degraded him, but glorified
him, not when he rewarded him for his services, but
when he appointed him to the office. For it was infinitely

complimentary to the Son of God to be appointed to bear
the pillars of a falling universe, to reconcile all things to
himself, whether they be things in heaven or earth, or
fallen perishing men. Infinitely honouring it was to be the
one exclusive responsible successful agent to make an end
of sin, to wash away the stain from human consciences,
and make them smile in response to the smile of God; to be
head and leader of all worship that God will ever accept in
the universe; to be the medium through whom the moral
universe is secured against recourse to any more sin, death
and curse for ever, through whom the chief of sinners may
be made righteous, sanctified and kept righteous beyond
the risk of ever sinning or falling; to hold back the face of
the throne of judgment and transform it to a throne of
mercy, where power, holiness and grace shall shine, and
where sinners guilty and polluted shall sing, 'To him that
loved us and washed us from our sins in his own blood.' It
is honouring to the Son of God so to purge the heavenly
things themselves with his own blood, that sinful men
may be present among them by faith even now, and find
the most holy place arranged to be a place of safety and a
home, because there we have such an High Priest who is
set on the right hand of the Majesty in the heavens. Is it
not honouring to be called to such an office involving such
services and results? What an occasion for mutual congratulation and delight between the Father and the Son,
an occasion in view of which Jesus said, 'I was daily his
delight, rejoicing always before him.' And may we not
apply to him in such an office the words, 'He will rejoice
over thee with joy; he will rest in his love; he will joy over
thee with singing'? For there is a song in the oath of God.
He singeth while he swears, 'Thou art a priest for ever'.

This divine congratulation is not exhausted towards the
person of the Son. It is extended to every poor and needy

creature who comes to him to put his trust in him for salvation. It is with great cordiality and fulness of joy that God receiveth every repentant and returning sinner through Christ. 'Is Ephraim my dear son? is he a pleasant child? for since I spake against him, I do earnestly remember him still: therefore my bowels are troubled for him; I will surely have mercy upon him, saith the LORD.' I say, it is with great cordiality the Lord receives poor penitent people when they come to him. There is no *scrimpness* in God's forgiveness, as if he stretched a point when he pardoned sin. He pardons with overflowing love, 'For as the heavens are higher than the earth, so are my ways higher than your ways, and my thoughts than your thoughts.' It is nothing more than simple justice to God when the pardoned church replies with like responsive cordiality, 'Who is a God like unto thee, that pardoneth iniquity, and passeth by the transgression of the remnant of his heritage? he retaineth not his anger for ever, because he delighteth in mercy.'

6. *The Father's Testimony.* This is no thought of mine read into the verse, and it is no minute or superfluous distinction, 'For he *testifieth*, Thou art a priest for ever after the order of Melchisedec' (*Heb.* 7:17). He not merely says it, but testifies it, and every word of God is pure. It is not in vain that Scripture assures us that God testifies; not merely teaches, but testifies. The Father assumes the attitude of witness to the priesthood of Jesus. Who but he could be competent to bear witness? Since the priestly work was chiefly one of Christ's soul, none but God could search the heart and testify with adequate knowledge what was going on in the soul of Jesus when priest. The God whose interests are concerned, law magnified, honour solved and vindicated, and glory made great, has, in the

circumstances nothing more to inform the sons of men than this, that Jesus is priest. It is as if he said, 'I can and do bear witness of my own divine knowledge, consciousness, satisfaction and immediate perception of the sweet savour of thy sacrifice, and of the acceptableness of thy intercession. I bear witness from my own sense of the infinite peace made by the blood of thy cross; of that reconciliation made by the body of thy flesh through death, that sole sacrifice for sin. I bear witness of the special complacency I have in thee, warranting so abundantly that great word of love and confidence, "Therefore doth my Father love me, because I lay down my life, that I might take it again." I bear witness that I am a very God of peace and of grace and of all comfort, and that I have become so through this thy glorious priesthood. That thou art indeed a priest for ever, I bear witness by my name, being "The LORD, the LORD God, merciful and gracious, longsuffering, and abundant in goodness and truth", for it is by thy priesthood that my forgiving love finds free expression to the sons of men.'

Speaking from his own immediate knowledge and consciousness as the God of salvation, and from the state of his own feelings and affections to sinful men, who but for Christ's priesthood would have been objects of detestation and wrath, God testifies that 'Jesus is a priest for ever'. And he that hath received this testimony hath set to his seal that God is true. This is the ground of faith: the testimony of God simply received, for faith simply attests the truthfulness of God when he bears witness to the priesthood of Christ. With the Father's testimony, the Holy Ghost joins when he testifies the forgiveness of sins, and consequently the obvious perfection of the sacrifice through which forgiveness is obtained.

If the Father and Spirit should condescend to make

[23]

concurrent testimony to the successful eternal priesthood of Christ, how plentifully testimony may be forthcoming. Bear witness, holy law of God, which by the curse hast slain, and by thy blessing glorified, our heavenly High Priest. Bear witness, thou glorious gospel of the blessed God, by that heavenly balm which thou pourest into wounded consciences, and that sacred peace which thou sheddest abroad in weary souls. Bear witness, ye bright spirits of light, by your joy in the presence of God over every sinner that repenteth. Bear witness, ye ransomed from among men, already arrayed in white robes around the throne, to the priesthood of your Saviour, by the song ye sing in glory. And ye to whom it is given to speak with human lips, will ye not lift the human hand, saying, 'as our soul and body liveth, thou art a priest for ever'? Ye ransomed of the Lord, returned to Zion, join in your witness-bearing, and every soul on earth that has faith as a grain of mustard seed, every soul that believes, trembling, by quiet hearty admiration of him, or, if by nothing else, by longing and mourning after him, bear witness that he is a priest for ever after the order of Melchizedek.

7. *The Meaning of the Oath of God.* It is very little I see of it, but by the help of God's Word let us seek to find out what can possibly be meant by God's swearing, or putting himself on oath. 'An oath for confirmation is . . . an end of all strife. Wherein God, willing more abundantly to shew unto the heirs of promise the immutability of his counsel, confirmed it by an oath.' 'Because he could swear by no greater, he sware by himself.' What is the particular force of the oath? What particular help does it render to faith? Of an honest man we say that his word is as good as his deed. Of Jesus we never read that he put himself on oath. The repeated use of 'Verily, verily, I say unto you'

was the form of speech nearest the oath. Why then should God swear when sustaining the honour and counsels of the Godhead? To see a little of it, what constitutes the last security for all belief? Belief in the Godhead itself. There must be a belief in the Godhead itself before belief in Christ. The inevitable necessity of God's existence is the last security. It is not an optional thing to God to exist or not. God cannot but exist. This is the final distinction between God and all creatures. Creatures are so weak and deficient in being that it was possible once they might never be at all, and except for God's will they never would have been. About God that never could have been possible. He is too glorious a being for it to be possible that he might never have been. He is so glorious that he could not but be, and be the glorious, unchangeable and everlasting God that he is.

Do you say, 'Oh! that my salvation rested on a ground like that. I would rest secure then, if it were the case that in the nature of things I could not but be safe'? Ay, but in the nature of things you cannot have that security. Your salvation cannot be an inevitable necessity like the existence of the Godhead. For one reason, you never could be grateful for it in such a case. A creature without gratitude is not a saved but a lost creature. Your salvation must depend on the will of God, and *cannot* spring inevitably without God's will from his nature, as some, by perversion of the truth that 'God is love' say, and sing 'Jesus loves me' as if Jesus could not help loving them. Your salvation must be at the disposal of the divine will, of free sovereign grace. More, it must be from free acceptance on your own part, as well as free giving on God's part, dependent in a sense on your will – your will renewed by divine grace, according to the Father's promise to the Priest of Zion, 'Thy people shall be willing in the day of thy power.' But it must be by *your* will, in order, by the grace of the divine Spirit, to secure *your* willing, confiding acceptance of Christ in his priesthood, and his salvation thereby. To charm you to a confidence as great as if (and more grateful far than if) God's own being necessitated your salvation, God appeals to his own being in proof that his will in all that concerns your redemption is immutable, and, that all may know it who hear the word of truth and Christ therein, he says to the Son, 'Thou art a priest for ever'. These are the terms, 'As I live, saith the LORD.' An appeal is made to the life of God, the necessary, immutable, infinite fulness of life in the Godhead; and not as of necessity, but of sovereign, good, loving pleasure, he pledges the life of God to the priesthood of Christ, and to the reliableness of the promise of salvation through him.

Not of necessity then, but of sovereign free grace and love, for which eternal thanks be to his name, he places the life of the Godhead to the life of the Son's priesthood. Lifting his hand to heaven, he gives us to know that he would not count it worth while being God if he could not say, 'Look unto me, and be ye saved.' He swears to the glorious perpetuity of the priesthood through which salvation comes, and gives his oath to those who trust in his Word, 'that by two immutable things, in which it was impossible for God to lie, we might have a strong consolation, who have fled for refuge to lay hold upon the hope set before us.' This truth causes the faith of his people to root at last in the everlasting life of God himself, and the eternal life through which Christ is constituted a priest. From that great epoch it becomes true, that 'as the Father hath life in himself, so hath he given to the Son to have life in himself.' And he is able to say, 'As the living Father hath sent me, and I live by the Father: so he that eateth me, even he shall live by me.' Thus, by free grace, a security is attained as strong as of necessity, and not with the iron coldness and hardness of necessity, but so as love shall still be lord of all. Such help the oath affords in bringing it to pass that it is by faith, that it might be by grace, that the promise might be sure to all the seed.

One word as to the date of this oracle. It has no date, strictly speaking; it dates with the covenant, the everlasting covenant, and transcends time, and liveth for ever, like the priesthood. You have heard that with God there is no tomorrow. To that add that with God there is no yesterday. The fact that God is involves that he was and that he is to come. 'He that cometh to God must believe that he is.' I say that this oracle transcends time and lives for ever. Hence it may be conceived of as repeating itself at every new era in the epoch of redemption: when he brings the firstbegotten into the world at the incarnation, at the baptism, the cross, the empty grave and the glorious ascension of Christ. It may be heard consecrating every movement of the High Priest with its awful stability, sacredness and reliableness. Always, also, when a poor sinner touches the hem of his garment, and opens his heart to him, the voice from the excellent glory may be heard saying that the Lord swears that, in the experience and sacred shrine of that believer's soul, Christ is priest for ever. When the gospel is preached it repeats itself, and when the sacraments are dispensed. When it was said to us this morning, 'Go ye up to the house of God', we were to be present at the enthronement of this glorious priest at his table; and the voice may there be heard, 'Thou art a priest for ever.' May we be enabled to say, 'Blessed priest, we will not see thee sworn in and glorified without hastening to present our claim.' 'Purge me with hyssop, and I shall be clean; wash me, and I shall be whiter than snow . . . Create in me a clean heart, O God; and renew a right spirit within me.' 'Bring my soul out of prison, that I may praise thy name: the righteous shall compass me about; for thou shalt deal bountifully with me.' Bring me to 'the banqueting house'. 'Why art thou cast down, O my soul? and why art thou disquieted within me? hope thou in God: for I shall yet praise him, who is the health of my countenance, and my God.'

[28]

❦ 3 ❦

Confession and Forgiveness

*'I said, I will confess my transgressions unto the LORD;
and thou forgavest the iniquity of my sin'* (Psa. *32:5*).

The point so strikingly brought out in these words is
the connection – the sure and immediate connection –
between the confession of sin and its forgiveness. This
connection is doctrinally asserted in the memorable
declaration, 'If we confess our sins, God is faithful and just
to forgive us our sins, and to cleanse us from all unrighteousness.' It is affectingly exemplified in the parable
of the prodigal's repentance, for no sooner had he poured
into his father's bosom his ingenuous and unreserved
acknowledgement of his iniquity, 'Father, I have sinned
against heaven, and before thee, and am no more worthy
to be called thy son', than the father immediately, in full
and unreserved forgiveness, said to his servants, 'Bring
forth the best robe, and put it on him.' The belief of this
connection was evidently the great encouraging consideration that sustained the hope of David's smitten heart in
Psalm 51, 'Wash me throughly from mine iniquity and
cleanse me from my sin. *For* I acknowledge my transgressions: and my sin is ever before me.' And in looking
back on his deep exercise of spirit, as recorded in the
remarkable and instructive Psalm before us, there was
nothing that stood out to his view more prominent or

[29]

memorable than just that sure and immediate connection between his confession of sin and the forgiveness which the Lord in his grace had so promptly and distinctly given him to experience. 'I said, I will confess my transgressions unto the LORD; and thou forgavest the iniquity of my sin.'

The circumstances were eminently favourable for giving him unmistakable experience of this truth, that true confession entails a sure and instant and perfect pardon. His sufferings were so intense and the source and cause of them so obvious that it was impossible he could be mistaken either as to the epoch or the process of his relief. He was enduring unwonted agony under conviction of sin and the divine displeasure. The hand of God was pressing him sore. It was heavy upon him. It was so without intermission: 'all the day long', 'day and night'. He had no breathing time from his distress. This incessant mental anguish was extorting from him bitter sighs and groans: 'my roaring all the day long'. It was preying on his body and draining all his health: 'My bones waxed old through my roaring . . . my moisture is turned into the drought of summer.' How could he fail to mark distinctly the epoch of his transition from suffering so intense to a relief so delightful as to change sighs like these into the beatific song: 'Blessed is he whose transgression is forgiven, whose sin is covered. Blessed is the man unto whom the LORD imputeth not iniquity, and in whose spirit there is no guile'? Equally impossible was it for him to avoid seeing that this blessed emancipation was directly allied with a well-defined change in his own dealings with God. While the divine displeasure was resting on him and the divine hand pressing him sore he was not ignorant of the reason. He did not need to pray, 'Lord, shew me where-fore thou contendest with me.' His sin had found him out.

His sin was ever before him. On any other supposition there is no meaning in his admission that at this time he was 'keeping silence' towards God. 'When I kept silence, my bones waxed old through my roaring all the day long.' He had that on his mind and conscience concerning which he could have spoken out had he been willing. But he preferred to keep silence.

Though in all things else we may suppose him to have been upright and true, this one matter of reserve between him and his God entirely secluded him from the divine fellowship, and cut him off from all his spiritual comforts. He had wronged his God by the iniquity for which his God was now making inquisition. He was not prepared to admit that he had done so, and the necessary and immediate result was a manifest and complete suspension of his communion with God. Was it any wonder that, being truly a man of God, with God's law written in his heart, living and working and testifying against him there, he could find no rest in his spirit? All his enjoyments were embittered to him. His pent-up bosom burned with a hidden fire. However, he determined to try a more excellent way. He would give his sense of sin full scope and play. He would open up to God his inmost soul. He would rend his heart. He would frankly own his offence, and own that God was entitled to be offended. He would ingenuously confess that he had wronged him. He would defend and excuse himself no more. He would sue for mere mercy, for generous and gracious pardon. And when he did so his success was immediate and complete. 'I acknowledged my sin unto thee, and mine iniquity have I not hid. I said, I will confess my transgressions unto the LORD; and thou forgavest the iniquity of my sin.' Entering at once into the joy of a perfect deliverance, how could he fail to see that the only barrier which had blocked up his path to pardon and peace was the refusal to confess his sin which he had so long and sullenly maintained, or fail to see that his contrite and complete confession introduced him, by the grace of God, into the blessed experience of an immediate and complete forgiveness?

It is this precious lesson of his own most clear and unmistakable experience which he records in the text: his experience of the intimate and immediate connection between confession and forgiveness. 'I said, I will confess my transgressions unto the LORD; and thou forgavest the iniquity of my sin.' I confessed and he forgave. Immediately and fully he forgave. He did not propose delay. He did not hold out a possibility, a probability, a prospect of forgiveness. He did not promise to take my case into his favourable consideration. He did not propose to take me on probation. But without condition and without delay, without holding back or reserve, at once he fully forgave the iniquity of my sin.

Now this unfailing and immediate connection between forgiveness and confession will become manifest if we can show, in the first place, that confession is necessary to forgiveness, and, secondly, that nothing more is required. Further, we shall see that confession is necessary because forgiveness is dispensed through a propitiation, and that confession is sufficient for the self-same reason. The illustration of these two positions will serve also to bring out incidentally, but perhaps all the more clearly, what true confession implies.

1. In the first place, then, *confession is indispensably necessary* because forgiveness is bestowed only through a propitiation. 'We have redemption through his blood, the forgiveness of sins.' He 'washed us from our sins in his own blood.' 'Be it known unto you therefore, men and

brethren, that through this man' who was slain on the cross and now raised from the dead 'is preached unto you the forgiveness of sins: and by him all that believe are justified from all things, from which ye could not be justified by the law of Moses.' 'Justified freely by his grace through the redemption that is in Christ Jesus: whom God hath set forth to be a propitiation through faith in his blood.' 'Much more then, being now justified by his blood, we shall be saved from wrath through him.'

i. *Sin is the transgression of the law.* Without bringing sin to the light of the law, it is impossible to have any correct views of its nature or any clear conviction of its heinousness. Now the law of God is the expression of his holy nature and the assertion of his righteous authority. The substance of what the law requires bears the impress of his own character, being holy and just and good, and the form of command in which its requirements are uttered – 'Thou shalt . . . thou shalt not . . . thou shalt not eat of it' – embody his sovereign and authoritative claims. Sin therefore is a reflection on and a disparagement of the holy nature of God, a rejection of his authority, a rebellion, a revolt, a mutiny against his sovereign sway. Unless this reflection against the nature of God, this rejection of the authority of God, this rebellion, is to be suffered to succeed, the law must be armed with a sanction or penalty against the breaker of it. To plead that there should be no penalty for sin, is just to plead that the law should be abrogated and set aside, that the sinner should be allowed to say, 'God's holy nature shall be no rule to me. God's authority shall impose no obligation on me.' And this penalty, clearly so indispensable, must be as absolute and unconditional, as extensive, as the precept whose authority it sanctions. If the precept demands the whole man – all his heart and soul and mind and strength, wholly and for ever – then the penalty must demand also the whole man, devoting him wholly and for ever a curse unto God. The precept and the penalty are the alternative arms of the balance of the sanctuary, the balance of the universe, and they must be absolutely equal if that balance is not to be false. So truly equivalent or alternative are these two things – the law's precept and the law's penalty – that every plea that would exempt from the one would exempt from the other also. If the precept is not binding on me, my contrariety to it cannot make me liable to the penalty. Every attempt on the sinner's part to justify himself from liability to the penalty proceeds on the basis that, at least in the circumstances, he was free from the obligation of the precept. When Adam would ward off the sentence of death on the ground that the woman gave unto him, and she on the ground that the serpent beguiled her, the obvious meaning is that, in these circumstances, they could not rightfully have been bound to obey, that these trying circumstances limited the obligation or weakened the binding force of the divine command. Manifestly this was what they expected God to grant or admit if they expected their plea to be accepted and held good.

Now this is what God in no circumstance will grant. The authority of his law is absolute and unconditional. It is not to be set aside by any circumstances, actual or conceivable. It claims to be above all circumstances, to rule and govern in all circumstances. It is sovereign, supreme and perfect. While circumstances change, it is unchangeable. While circumstances are limited, it is unlimited, encompassing them all, and applicable to them all. It does not command us to love God with all our heart in particular circumstances. But, absolutely and unconditionally, it commands us to love God with all our heart.

This absolute and unconditional authority is not arbitrary, for its justification is in the infinitely love-worthy nature of God.

It is this absolute and unconditional authority of God's law which provokes the enmity of the carnal mind. Were *our* nature, as *God's* nature is, holy and just and good, we would have no quarrel with his law, however absolutely its authority were asserted. Acquiescing in the substance or matter of the divine law as it expresses the holy nature of God, we would acquiesce in its imperative form as expressing his absolute, unlimited authority also. Beholding the glory of God as holy, just and good and beholding this glory, as in a glass, in his perfect law, requiring only what is holy, just and good and forbidding only what is impure, unrighteous and hurtful, we would see no limit to the authority with which it should enforce its demands. But having sinned, having become unholy, unrighteous, evil, we regard that absolute authority as our sworn foe. The carnal mind resents it. For the most part our enmity to it is shown by our tacitly and coolly setting it aside, virtually denying it altogether. But when our conscience is aroused and our sin begins to find us out, when we are compelled to face our guilt and danger and seek some refuge from threatened wrath, we act precisely as our fallen parents did, we seek to limit and erase the authority of God's law. We set up the plea of circumstances, temptations and difficulties and make these a shield against the condemnation that we have incurred. We quarrel with the righteousness of the sentence of death as the wages of sin. We entrench ourselves in some position from which we hold it unreasonable, unmerciful and cruel for the law of God to dislodge us. We would make our own conditions with God. We would bring his law down to compromise with our ability. We would extort concessions that shall limit its absolute sovereignty, maintaining that, all things considered, we are not justly liable to everlasting destruction, to the doom of an absolute, eternal curse.

And were God to yield to us, were he to exempt us from the penalty of his law on consideration of any circumstances whatever, what were this but to say that in these circumstances its authority was not binding, that its authority therefore was not absolute, but limited by circumstances, imperfect, conditional, liable to be set aside in favour of more powerful, more inflexible, more influential, more important powers? Yes, to remit sin without a propitiation is to remit really not our sin but our duty. To abrogate the penalty is to declare the precept not binding. It is to bring down the law from the lofty seat from which, with all-embracing application, it rules the universe and all its circumstances and events, to leave the universe without a bond of perfectness.

ii. But *God dispenses pardon through the propitiation of the cross*, and thereby maintains the absolute, the truly unconditional authority of his holy law. Purposing to pardon a people whom no man can number, he resolves to deal again on the same principle of federal headship on which he has dealt with mankind already. He finds a second man, the Lord from heaven. He appoints his own Son to be our last Adam, Emmanuel – God manifest in the flesh – and appoints that, as by one man's disobedience many were made sinners, so by the obedience of one shall many be made righteous. He substitutes him in our place, and in love and joy he consents to be our Substitute. He is made under the law. He is made sin for us. He is made a curse for us. The penalty takes effect on him in all its fulness. He puts away sin by the sacrifice of himself.

He puts away sin by satisfying divine justice, and in doing so he magnifies the law and makes it honourable. Behold how he justifies the law as holy, just and good, loving God with all his heart, even when, though holy, harmless, undefiled and separate from sinners, he is visited with his wrath and curse due to his people's sins, loving men, even when persecuted by them unto death, and nailed to the shameful tree, the object of their hatred and abhorrence. Behold how he justifies its penalty as righteous: 'Lo, I come to do thy will.' 'I have a baptism to be baptized with; and how am I straitened till it be accomplished!' And behold, above all, the glory put on the unfettered sovereignty of that law, its utterly absolute and unconditional authority. For had it been possible that any limit could be set to its authority, any circumstances owned as capable of suspending its dominion or putting a check on its demands, would not this have come to light when Emmanuel stood before God to mediate for the guilty and to save them? Might not the circumstance of his Godhead have done it? Might not the Father's infinite unchanging love to him as his only begotten and eternal Son have done it? Might not his bloody agony have done it, and his holy cry of woe unfathomable, 'O my Father, if it be possible, let this cup pass from me'?

And if neither the holiness, nor Godhead, nor Sonship, nor searchless agony of the Son, if none of these most awe-inspiring circumstances shall limit the authority, the absolute authority, of God's holy law, shall that sovereign law bend before the circumstance and plea that 'the woman gave unto me', 'the serpent beguiled me', the duty was difficult, the temptations strong? Shall the plea of Christ's Godhead and Sonship and holiness and bloody agony have no force, but the sovereign law rises unmoved, transcendent over them all, and shall our miserable

If Christ's giving of thiself be not sufficient how can anything we can do be good enough — Christ paid the penalty

The law is satisfied

excuses and defences really defend and excuse us? Shall they transcend that law, and transcend these supposed pleas and actual facts which, in the death of the Lord of glory, that law itself transcends? Oh, what shame – what light of refutation – the cross of Christ casts on all our efforts to evade the absolute authority of God's law and justify ourselves against its condemnation!

By that cross is preached unto us the forgiveness of sins, free and unconditional and immediate, without money and without price. 'Ho, every one that thirsteth, come ye to the waters', and 'him that cometh to me I will in no wise cast out.' 'Though your sins be as scarlet, they shall be as white as snow', and 'whosoever will, let him take the water of life freely.' The grace of God in forgiveness is as free and unfettered in its sovereignty, as absolute, unlimited and unconditional in its proposal, as his law is absolute in its authority. It shall compass and quell all circumstances adverse to your salvation, as truly as, and in like manner as, God's holy law compasses all circumstances of your sin and quells all the pleas you found upon them. Untrammelled by any circumstances, unhampered by any conditions, it offers free and immediate, full and irreversible, forgiveness to every hearer of the gospel; and whosoever will, let him come. Even the confession of sin of which we speak as absolutely indispensable would be utterly misunderstood if it were regarded as setting any limit, qualification or condition on the free forgiveness which is proclaimed through the cross of Christ.

iii. But if you really are willing, if you truly come and do receive this forgiveness, if you actually embrace it, intelligently acquiescing in it, without which it is impossible it can be embraced, *you embrace it for what it is in God's account – what it really is in itself – pardon through propitiation*, pardon through the remission of sin. You embrace it as no mere exemption from wrath, no mere being let off from danger, no hushing up of your iniquity. You embrace it as exemption from liability to wrath because the Lamb of God has been liable and has answered your liability in your place. You do not embrace it with your eyes shut to the propitiation of Calvary. You embrace a shadow and a lie if you do. 'Look unto me, and be ye saved.' 'Him that cometh to me I will in no wise cast out.' You look to Christ, you come to Christ, specifically as made sin for you, as made a curse for you. You embrace him specifically as your Substitute, as guilty, condemned, crucified and dead. And what can this imply, if not that you are guilty, condemned and liable righteously to death? Were he merely a conqueror of your foes, foes who, without your fault or crime, had brought you to the brink of ruin, you might embrace his deliverance without anything so humiliating as the admission of guilt, the admission that you were righteously ruined and lost already. Were he merely in a general sense your friend, a friend so generous that in some sense for your good he even loved you unto death, you might accept his friendly aid, without necessarily owning before God that you were worthy of his everlasting wrath. But if, specifically and exactly, Christ was made sin for you, and has obtained forgiveness for you by the shedding of his blood as a ransom for sin, and you in this light freely receive him as God freely makes him over to you, your reception of him is the most practical and overwhelming acknowledgement you can make that your life was righteously forfeited to God's righteous law. And now you seal the justice of the sentence by believing on the blood that cancels it.

You cannot receive the forgiveness as one thing, while God offers it as wholly another. God will not trifle with you, using words in a double sense. Nor in the very nature of things can you have any success in attempting it. You cannot have forgiveness as that to which upon the whole you feel entitled, that which, in the circumstances, you think it would be harsh and unrighteousness to withhold. You cannot have forgiveness on this understanding, while God offers it on the understanding that your sin deserved his wrath and curse, and that even his own Son's Godhead and holiness and value in his sight could not exempt him, standing in your place, from having to bear that wrath and curse instead of you. Christ, by the sacrifice of his death, puts away *sin*. You, while defending and excusing yourself on any plea of circumstances from the sentence of death, are labouring to put away the *law*. By the sacrifice of Christ, God offers you remission of sin. By self-justification, on any plea of circumstances, you are seeking remission of your duty and permission for your sin. Can a covenant of peace and reconciliation between you and your offended Lawgiver be sealed on a misunderstanding so fatal and complete?

No! But if one died for all, then were all dead. If no plea of circumstances could shelter him, none can shelter us. Our mouth is shut. Our condemnation is just. And in entering into Christ our refuge, in consenting that Christ be held as made sin for us, we do so with the unconditional and unreserved acknowledgement, 'Against thee, thee only, have I sinned, and done this evil in thy sight: that thou mightest be justified when thou speakest, and be clear when thou judgest.' I acknowledge my transgression, my iniquity, my unrighteousness, my inexcusableness. My ill-desert I do not deny nor hide. It is ever before me. 'Wash me throughly from mine iniquity, and cleanse me from my sin. For I acknowledge my transgressions: and my sin is ever before me.' 'I said, I will confess my transgressions unto the LORD; and thou forgavest the iniquity of my sin.'

Thus necessary is confession unto forgiveness; and that because forgiveness is by the blood of Jesus.

We may pause here for a moment to notice what, in this light, true confession is so manifestly shown to be.

True confession is *taking guilt to ourselves before God*. It is the unreserved acknowledgement of the heinousness of sin, and our consequent, inexcusable ill-desert, our righteous liability to the wrath of God. It springs from an insight into the justice, holiness and goodness of God's law as expressing the holiness of God's nature, and from an acquiescence in the absolute authority of that law as asserting God's rightful and inalienable claims.

True confession of any sin *carries with it the confession of all sin*. For the same insight into the holiness of the law and the same acquiescence in the absolute supremacy of the law which is needful to our confessing any sin as sin gives us insight into the sinful element that is in every sin. To confess any sin simply because we see it to be contrary to God's nature and opposed to God's authority implies the confession of every thing in which the same contrariety and opposition appears. The axe is laid to the root of the tree. The want of universality here impeaches and disproves our sincerity.

True confession *implies resolution of amendment*. For I cannot see sin to be so heinous as to justify God in assigning everlasting death as its wages and at the same time willingly or knowingly continue in it.

Such confession, in its very nature unreserved, universal, reformative, is essentially involved in a believing application to the blood of Jesus and is the fruit of the Spirit's regenerating grace. It is the living action of the law written on the heart. Such confession is necessary if the sovereignty and absolute authority of the divine law is to be upheld, as it is upheld by the cross of Calvary.

2. But secondly, such *confession is sufficient*. It is absolutely necessary but nothing more is necessary. For, with a view to forgiveness through the blood of Jesus, what more than confession can be supposed requisite? 'For thou desirest not sacrifice; else would I give it: thou delightest not in burnt offering. The sacrifices of God are a broken spirit: a broken and a contrite heart, O God, thou wilt not despise.' What room, indeed, can there be for sacrifices, satisfactions, penances, probationary delay, good behaviour or good works? How can such requirements, or any others that can be conceived, intervene between confession and forgiveness, when forgiveness is bestowed in the sovereign grace and tender love and precious blood of the Everlasting Covenant?

i. In the first place, *by accounting confession insufficient, the absolute sovereignty of divine grace is violated,* as much as the absolute sovereignty of divine law is violated by accounting confession unnecessary. Self-defence, self-justification on the plea of circumstances, erects these circumstances above the divine law, employs them to circumscribe and paralyse its action. But the demand for more than self-condemnation, the tarrying for any satisfactions or good works or probationary trials, similarly erects circumstances above the freedom of divine grace. It circumscribes and paralyses its action till these circumstances take effect. It hampers the power and limits the reign of the sovereign grace of God, bringing it down from its absolute supremacy. It shortens the divine hand so that it cannot save till first these satisfactions have been brought, these probationary trials safely passed.

ii. And secondly, *the demand for something more than confession casts a reflection on the tender mercy and saving love of God.* For what could it argue but a deficiency of love in God, if, with the penitent at his feet, defenceless, self-surrendered, ingenuously owning his iniquity, the Lord should tarry for a single moment ere he forgave, and still make new demands, and speak of still- unfulfilled conditions, or propose delay and probation and good works, before he would consent to withdraw the condemnation and the burden of his wrath? What but some personal revenge, some grudgings of dislike to us, some pleasure in our wretchedness and woe, could possibly account for such a style of dealing with us? The carnal mind is ever ready, it is true, thus to conceive of God, so much so that God has found it necessary to swear by his great name, saying, 'As I live, saith the Lord GOD, I have no pleasure in the death of the wicked.'

It is not because he finds any satisfaction in our misery that he does not, without any sacrifice or ransom, at once emancipate us all from the terrors of his wrath. It is because, with all his fatherly love and all his yearning longings for our salvation and our happiness, the absolute authority of his blessed law makes our happiness, our escape from woe, impossible so long as our guiltiness remains unpurged, unacknowledged and unconfessed. It is from no want of desire for our salvation, no want of love to our souls. 'God commendeth his love toward us, in that, while we were yet sinners, Christ died for us.' He so loved as to give his only begotten Son that we might not perish. And, divine justice being satisfied in the great propitiation, how absolute and immediate, how tender and overflowing with love, must that reception be which the contrite and confessed offender will meet with. 'When he was yet a great way off, his Father saw him, and had compassion, and ran, and fell on his neck.' 'Is Ephraim my dear son? is he a pleasant child? for since I spake against him, I do earnestly remember him still: therefore my bowels are troubled for him; I will surely have mercy upon him, saith the LORD.' 'Ho, every one that thirsteth, come ye to the waters, and he that hath no money . . . come, buy wine and milk without money and without price.' 'Behold, now is the accepted time; behold, now is the day of salvation.'

iii. For consider, thirdly, how *any other supposition must disparage and reflect on the perfection of the great atonement.* If Jesus exclaimed, 'It is finished', and by his one offering for ever perfected them that are sanctified, what more can be necessary to a perfect forgiveness than the sincere confession of sin? This glorious offering in all its preciousness and all its perfection is freely offered to you in the gospel. Not to you as contrite and confessing sin, but freely to you as a sinner of whatever magnitude or dye, this sacrifice is offered. Moved by the good Spirit, you freely receive it. You receive Christ and him crucified. You receive him by faith, since God gives him to you by his Word, and you cannot in such a case conceive of any other mode of receiving him than by faith. And, counting the Word of the Lord good and sure and true, you cease to find any difficulty in receiving by faith that sacrifice, that crucified Saviour, whom, by his true Word, the Lord makes freely yours. You receive him because, convicted, burdened, weary with sin, you long for a place of repentance and confession. A refuge in Christ is altogether what you need. A union with Christ, made sin for you, suits all your wants. You can ingenuously now, in him, take home the charge of guilt to your conscience, without evasion and without reserve. You can, without excuse, without vain defence, take guilt now to yourself, for now, being one with Christ for this very end and precisely to this effect, one with him who was made sin for you, your taking guilt to yourself is the very way to take it and lay it upon him with whom you are, in the eye of God's law, altogether one.

Apart from *him*, the ingenuous confession of iniquity, the taking of guilt unreservedly to yourself, was to place yourself beneath the terrible, pitiless and righteous wrath of heaven. Apart from him, you braced yourself up with all possible guile, all manner of evasive pleas, struggling as a matter of life or death, eternal life or death, with the sovereign righteous law of heaven, and maintaining that struggle at whatever cost of inward fire consuming you. But in Christ the sin-bearer – made sin for you – you are emancipated. You are enlarged to abandon the unequal struggle. For you see no meaning in this blessed sacrifice, this Lamb of God, this High Priest of your profession, no reason why God has given him unto you, save that standing now before God with new-born truth in the inward parts you may spontaneously and safely acknowledge your iniquity. You may take home to yourself all the guilt of your transgression, because underlying all this transaction you are one with a sin-bearer on whom now you lay all your sin by taking all its guilt to yourself. You condemn yourself. You take guilt to yourself. But your union with him who in his death is your perfect sacrifice secures that in the very act of thus taking guilt to yourself your condemnation vanishes immediately. You are crucified with Christ, nevertheless you live. You were worthy of death, but the death is now passed, and you stand in him who is the Resurrection and the Life. You stand in him in whom, as your sacrifice and living priest, the Father is for ever well pleased. You stand in him in the

CHRIST FOR US

light of the Father's countenance wherewith he hath blessed your sin-bearer for ever. You stand in the covenant and realm of redeeming love. And as you do so, does not your soul burn within you with another fire, a holy glow of truth and love, a genial warmth of loving grief and gratitude as you look on him whom you have pierced? But do you not know in all your heart and in all your soul that nothing more was needed to your full forgiveness than the true confession of your sin? Can you not bear witness with the psalmist, the Spirit bearing witness with your spirit, 'I said, I will confess my transgressions unto the LORD; and thou forgavest the iniquity of my sin'?

And if it be so, if you have found the necessity and sufficiency of confessing your sin unto the Lord, let your whole life and walk with God be one prolonged and continual confession. 'Pray without ceasing', is the singular command of an apostle. But if confession be a part of prayer, does not the believer confess without ceasing when, having once rent his heart unto the Lord, he keeps it open and sincere before him, cherishing a contrite sense of sin, and having, in singleness of mind, no secret, no reserve, from his God? How, otherwise, can he habitually enjoy the peace with God which Christ hath made for him by the blood of his cross? Or what else is meant by the declaration of John – standing side-by-side as it does with the promise, 'If we confess our sins, God is faithful and just to forgive us our sins' – 'If we walk in the light, as he is in the light, we have fellowship one with another, and the blood of Jesus Christ his Son cleanseth us from all sin'? And how can the believer, walking with God in such continual confession, fail to find continual, unhindered entrance into all the treasure of comforting, upholding, sanctifying grace which this Psalm goes on to celebrate? 'For this shall every one that is godly pray unto thee in a time when thou mayest be found: surely in the floods of great waters they shall not come nigh unto him. Thou art my hiding place; thou shalt preserve me from trouble; thou shalt compass me about with songs of deliverance . . . I will instruct thee and teach thee in the way which thou shalt go: I will guide thee with mine eye . . . Be glad in the LORD, and rejoice, ye righteous: and shout for joy, all ye that are upright in heart.'

Thus blessed is he whose transgression is forgiven, whose sin is covered. Thus blessed is the man to whom the LORD imputeth not iniquity and in whose spirit there is no guile. And thou, O Lord, wilt not forsake the work of thine own hands; thou wilt perfect that which concerneth him. Thou wilt maintain that man's integrity. Thou wilt set him before thy face for ever.

❧ 4 ❧

Crucified with Christ

'Knowing this, that our old man is crucified with Christ, that the body of sin might be destroyed, that henceforth we should not serve sin' (Rom. 6:6).

The two great evils which perplex the believer are the guilt of sin and the power of sin – its guilt, defiling his conscience and subjecting him to the anger of God; its power, corrupting and enslaving his heart and preventing him from serving the living God. His relief from both these evils is by the cross of Christ. From the *guilt* of sin the cross of Christ delivers him, for while in sin there is an efficacy to awaken the wrath of God and to disturb the conscience, making it like the troubled sea which cannot rest, there is in the blood of the cross a still greater efficacy to propitiate or pacify God and to purge the conscience from dead works. But from the *power* of sin also the cross of Christ delivers the believer, for it is the source or channel of an efficacy greater than the strength of our depravity, invincible though that depravity be under our own management. And this superior efficacy checks the triumph, overthrows the dominion and breaks the bondage of sin, so that the believer is set free to be the servant of righteousness and of God.

It is to this last service which the cross of Christ renders to the believer that our attention is called by the text; and no one who is anxiously concerned for the ordering of his state and heart and duty towards God can fail to take a lively interest in the subject. May we be blessed in the consideration of it.

Let us then, in the first place, observe in these words a certain doctrine or fact stated concerning the believer. 'Our old man is crucified with Christ.'

In the second place, let us observe the two-fold design and effect stated, first, that the body of sin might be destroyed, and second, that henceforth we should not serve sin.

Thirdly, we shall make a practical application.

1. In the first place, then, let us consider the fact or doctrine here asserted concerning the believer: 'Our old man is crucified with Christ.'

To open the way to the understanding of this truth, let us consider the following things in their order.

i. Observe then in the first place that the Scriptures in explaining the scheme of redemption make frequent use of expressions of this general form: 'Christ for us'. 'He was made sin for us.' 'He was made a curse for us.' 'He gave himself for us.' 'He gave himself a ransom for many.' He is set forth manifestly crucified for us. He died for us. He appeareth in the presence of God for us. These, and many other similar expressions, are grounded on the fact that, according to the counsels of the everlasting covenant, Jesus was by the Father appointed, and of his own free and joyful will became, our Surety, our Representative. The scheme of redemption is founded on a marvellous exchange of places between Christ and his people, he taking theirs, they being translated into his. He became their federal Head. He became Christ for them.

ii. Observe in the second place that the Scriptures, in asserting our actual participation in this redemption, make frequent use of expressions of this other general form: 'We with Christ.' 'We are crucified with Christ.' 'We are dead with him.' 'We are buried with him.' 'We are quickened together with him.' 'We are raised up together with him.' 'We are risen with Christ.' 'We are made to sit with him in heavenly places.' In fact every expression of the form 'Christ for us' may be regarded as having its corresponding relative expression, 'We with him'. Now the truth of these expressions is grounded on our actual union to Christ by the Spirit. For he that is joined to the Lord is one spirit; or he that is of one spirit with the Lord, he that hath received the Spirit of Christ, is joined unto him. And being so joined or united with him, in all that he did and became and suffered for us we have communion with him. Let us simply be united to him then. If he lived for us, we now live with him, for as he was, so are we in the world. If he was tempted for us, we are now tempted with him: 'Ye are they which have continued with me in my temptations.' If he watched for us, we watch with him: 'Could ye not watch with me?' If he died and rose and appeared in the presence of God for us, we die and rise and appear in the presence of God with him, passing safely with him through the executed and exhausted curse of God, through the subdued and rifled kingdom of death, onwards unto the gates of righteousness and up even to the Father's throne of grace. All this is with Christ, having access by faith with him into the grace wherein we stand, and rejoice in hope of the glory of God, when we shall depart and be literally with him, which is far better.

iii. Observe, thirdly, that in this manifold communion with Christ the first and leading element is communion with him in his death, in his cross. And the reason is that it was by his death that he obtained for us that promise and gift of the Spirit whereby we are united to him and made a new creature in him, called unto his communion or fellowship. Christ was born for us in the manger, but that does not secure the Spirit for us, though it was a glorious step thereto. For us he was baptized in Jordan. For us he was tempted in the wilderness and triumphed in his temptations. For us he lived and laboured and sorrowed and watched and prayed. For us he agonized in Gethsemane, was apprehended as a malefactor, was led away captive and bound, was stricken and smitten and afflicted and, as a sheep before her shearers is dumb, so he opened not his mouth. And in all this, if the Spirit once come forth and unite us to him, we have communion with him in the merit and spirit of the whole. But if his interposition for us go no further, the door of the Spirit's forthcoming from Christ to us and from the Father through Christ is still locked. It is the cross, the perfect expiation of the cross, that opens that door, for, 'Christ hath redeemed us from the curse of the law, being made a curse for us: for it is written, Cursed is every one that hangeth on a tree: that the blessing of Abraham might come on the Gentiles through Jesus Christ; that we might receive the promise of the Spirit through faith.' For it is through Jesus Christ and him crucified that the Holy Ghost is shed on us abundantly. The cross is the pathway, the channel, by which the Spirit comes. The cross is the reason why he comes. It is the holy justification of a holy God in sending forth the Spirit to a miserable sinner. See to it that by faith you own this same reason as your reason for expecting the Spirit. And as by faith you look along by the cross of Christ to your Father's throne, doubt not but there is coming forth unto you abundantly the Spirit of the Son, whereby we cry, Abba Father.

But if it be directly and immediately for and by the cross
that the Spirit of Christ cometh to you, then the immediate and first and central communion that you have with
Christ is in his cross: ye are crucified with Christ. The
cross is yours. His perfect propitiatory sacrifice in all its
merit is yours. You are sanctified, cleansed, dedicated
unto God, offered up and acceptable unto him by the
offering of the body of Christ once for all. This is your
fundamental privilege as a believer. On this foundation all
your other privileges rest. From this centre all your other
privileges flow forth. 'Know ye not, that so many of us as
were baptized into Jesus Christ were baptized into his
death?'

iv. Observe, however, in the fourth place that there is a
difference between our being crucified with Christ and
our old man being crucified with him. They both take
effect in the same moment, the moment of our being
quickened by the Spirit and united to Christ. By that
union, and in that instant of it, it becomes true that we are
crucified with Christ, and that our old man is crucified
with him. Yet are these two distinct things. And the
difference may perhaps be seen in their different effects.
The old man is crucified with Christ that he may be
destroyed. We are crucified with Christ, not that we may
be destroyed, but that we may escape destruction, that we
may have life. I am crucified with Christ: nevertheless I
live. In the one case there is a crucifixion and a destruction, in the other a crucifixion and a life. And this
crucifixion and life are simultaneous, not first the one and
then the other, but both together, not the life succeeding
the crucifixion when it is over and gone, but accompany-
ing the crucifixion from the first. For Paul says not, 'I have
been crucified with Christ, and now I live', but, 'I am

[52]

crucified with Christ: nevertheless I live.' He does not make one of them a past event, and the other present. Neither does he say, 'I am crucified with Christ, and henceforth I shall live.' He makes them both present and simultaneous. While the crucifixion is going on, the life is going on too. The crucifixion does not quench the life. The life lives in the crucifixion. The crucifixion indeed does not quench, but sustains, the life. This mystery was seen in Christ himself, this simultaneous crucifixion and life, the death in the heart of which life was living. Even when crucified, nevertheless he lived. How indeed could this be true of his members if it were not true of the living Head himself? Even when he died in his human nature, he was living. He was always the Living One, yea, the Life, the very Life; and never more gloriously so than in his death-destroying death.

The Father sent eternal life to us in his Son, and his Son's perfect sacrifice in death surely did not suppress or extinguish the Life himself. He who is a Priest after the power of an endless life was triumphantly living when he offered himself to God in his death upon the cross, a sacrifice of a sweet-smelling savour. He was triumphantly living, and triumphing over death. God, infinite, eternal, unchangeable, in human nature on the cross, was surely a living person when in that glorious perfect sacrifice he gave his life a ransom for many. Pre-eminently could Jesus say – not merely, after his resurrection, 'I have been crucified: nevertheless now I live' – but in the moment of dying he could say, 'I am crucified: nevertheless I live.' Life was not abolished, but broke forth triumphant and abundant in his death. It was the Living One who was crucified for us, living in the favour of God which is life even in the moment, yea, especially in the moment, of his death.

'Therefore doth my Father love me, because I lay down my life, that I might take it again.' And his undiminished life, yea, the fountain of life, flowed over in his death for them. Here is the perfection and specific glory of his death as a sacrifice for our sins – a perfection that could be found only in the God-man, Emmanuel. And, save for this, our Redeemer's crucifixion would have been his destruction, his and ours, his the prelude and seal of ours. But our Redeemer is the Living One, eternal and unchangeable in his Godhead, the beloved of the Father, also dwelling personally in holy humanity, and never destitute of the Father's favour which is life. Accordingly, when crucified, nevertheless he was living.

Let his people simply have union and communion with him, and they can say, 'I am crucified with Christ: nevertheless I live'. There is an apparent contradiction in this case, as there is in his, the contradiction of a death and a life which are both true together. But the reconciliation in both cases is the same: union and communion with Christ makes the two cases into one. Nay, the explanation is given by the apostle, 'I am crucified with Christ: nevertheless I live; yet not I, *but Christ liveth in me.*' Christ crucified, nevertheless living, lives in us, and this communion with him in his curse-exhausting death, and in his life of uninterrupted boundless favour with the Father, we have *by faith*. For, 'the life which I now live in the flesh I live by the faith of the Son of God, who loved me, and gave himself for me.' Thus it is when we are crucified with Christ. We share with Christ both in his crucifixion and his life.

It is otherwise with our old man. Our old man is affected by Christ's death only. We and our old man are not identical. Our old man is that principle of sin, of enmity to God, of depravity, of flesh, of carnal-

mindedness, in which our whole nature is enslaved and
imprisoned until we are regenerated by the life giving
Spirit of Jesus. It denotes that original corruption of our
nature whereby we are utterly indisposed, disabled and
made opposite to all good and wholly inclined to all evil. It
is not indeed called the old man in the case of the
unregenerate, just because in their case the principle of sin
reigns unbroken, having the whole field, the whole man,
to itself and beneath its sway and bondage. It must be
displaced from the throne and succeeded by a new man
before it can be in the position to be rightly called the old
man, precisely as in the days before Christ, the Scriptures
then possessed by the church could not be called the Old
Testament, according to the simple argument of Paul that
it is only when he saith a new covenant, or introduces a
new covenant, that he makes the first old. So when the
Holy Spirit in regeneration introduces into the soul the
new man, he makes the first old. When he implants the
vital principle of grace, uniting the soul to Christ and
making it a new creation in Christ, then the depravity that
still remains, strong and powerful and perplexing though
it may be, is less powerful than the Almighty Spirit of
Christ who abides in his grace and faithfulness for ever.
And the believer's personality and character and destiny
are all now in accordance with the new man created in the
image of God.

Oh, how joyfully will the believer acquiesce in this
himself! Made willing in the day of Messiah's power,
renewed in the spirit of his mind, seeing the beauty of
holiness, the sweet moral glory of the character of God in
the face of Jesus Christ, in whose image the new man is
created; seeing also the adroitness of sin, and alarmed by
the old man's fertility in the abominable thing, as an ever-
flowing, overflowing fountain of sin: how gladly does he

renounce, disown, put off, the old man! How joyously does he identify himself with or put on the new! What holy relief his upright spirit finds in liberty to say, in the conscious struggle with sin, and as a counterpoise to the pain of not succeeding in that struggle as his holy will desires, 'Now if I do that I would not, it is no more I that do it, but sin that dwelleth in me.' I and my old man are distinct, yea, opposite. I consent to all God's law as holy, just and good. In my old man there dwelleth no good thing. I retreat into my new man. I am at home there. I put off the old man. It is not I, but sin. Thus thorough is the distinction between us who believe and our old man.

Let us remember that Christ was crucified for us, not as a new man, not as believers, but as sinners. Nay, he was made sin for us. He represented us as in the old man, not yet made old by the creation of the new. He bore in his own body on the tree not only our sins of action, of word, of thought, but the iniquity of our whole principle of natural, original corruption. He personated us under the unbroken dominion of our depravity. He stood for us as we stood before God in the old man, not yet made old but reigning invincible. 'What the law could not do, in that it was weak through the flesh, God sending his own Son, in the likeness of sinful flesh, and *for sin*' – personating sin, made sin, representing sin, representing the body of sin, representing the old man in all his original, unbroken power – 'condemned sin in the flesh' – condemned the body of sin, the principle of sin, our old man. Our old man was condemned, our old man was crucified, when Christ was crucified. This alone exhausts what was necessary if Christ was exactly and wholly to exchange places with us. Christ was crucified for us as sinners – sinners wholly enslaved to sin – dead in trespasses and sins. He was crucified for us, for our sin, our sin not in the branches only, but in the root. Not in sin's procedure only, but its principle, not in its streams only, but in its fountain. For our old man, that ever-fertile root of sin, that ever-active principle of sin, that ever-flowing fountain of sin, for this, in our place, was Jesus crucified. For our old man did Jesus bear the curse, the condemnation, the crucifixion. Then was sin condemned in the flesh. Then was our old man, in point of law, crucified with Christ. Let this point of law be personally realised in us in point of fact through our engaging by the Spirit into Jesus in vital faith, and then the assertion of the text becomes the spiritual fact of our experience: 'Our old man is crucified with Christ.'

2. But now, what are the divine purposes and the effects of our old man being thus crucified with Christ? They are two-fold, namely, first, the ultimate effect, and secondly, an immediate effect.

i. First, the ultimate effect. Our old man is crucified with Christ *that the body of sin may be destroyed*. The effect of this crucifixion ultimately will be the destruction, the extinction, the annihilation of sin, of the old man, with all his members and means and instruments of evil, of the body of sin: 'that the body of sin might be destroyed'.

Every creature of God that has sinned must be offered up in sacrifice, become a victim, a devoted thing to God. And this is true both in the lost and in the saved. The former become a sacrifice, a victim, in their own persons. The latter are offered up a sacrifice to God in and with Christ in his propitiatory sacrifice on the cross. The finally impenitent and unbelieving die in their sins. It is one of Christ's most terrible denunciations: 'If ye believe not that I am he, ye shall die in your sins.' Keeping his own personal, original position and character as a sinner –

keeping apart from Christ and rejecting Christ's Spirit –
the impenitent sinner dies with sin, with the body of sin,
with the old man, not in his case made old but reigning in
all his power, with sin or the old man inextricably bound
up and identified with his character and person and
standing before God. And the curse due for his sin, for sin
in its procedure, for sin in its reigning principle, becomes
the sinner's own eternal inheritance. This is the sinner's
terrible destruction – the choice also which he himself has
made, for he has refused to have his sin destroyed. And
now it cannot be, for the destruction of sin is of the
blessing of Christ and the working of his Spirit. But the
lost soul is barred from all blessing. He is lost beneath the
curse. It is he himself who is destroyed by the curse of a
dishonoured and unsatisfied law, forsaking him to the
eternal tyranny of sin.

But the believer also is offered up in sacrifice to God. In
and with Christ, he is so offered up. Remember, that great
'Christ for us' has also its 'we with him'. Hence, if Christ
were offered for us, we are offered with him. Unto this end
indeed did Christ offer himself for us unto God, a sacrifice
of a sweet-smelling savour, that we might be offered with
him. 'For their sakes I sanctify myself', I consecrate,
dedicate, or offer up myself, 'that they also might be
sanctified', that they may be separated, set apart or offered
up also. Moreover he that sanctified and they that are
sanctified are all of one. Hence we are sanctified and
offered up to God through the offering of the body of
Christ once for all. But it was on account of our sin, our old
man in his invincible dominion, that Christ was offered
up. The curse due on account of our old man is wholly
borne and exhausted by Jesus in his death, and the
positive favour and blessing cometh upon us also for
Christ's righteousness' sake. The fruit of that blessing is

that our old man is doomed unto annihilation, every element of destruction passes away from us, and the body of sin is set apart for destruction. For in the cross of Christ there is the curse and the blessing both, and there is both a salvation and a destruction. United to Christ, our curse is his and is all borne away by him, his blessing is ours and abideth. But united to Christ we are disjoined from the old man. We put off the old man when we put on Christ Jesus the Lord. And, separated in legal standing from the old man by being legally one with Christ, the Righteous One, and separated as to distinguishing character from the old man by being imbued with the Spirit of holiness, the salvation accrues to us and the destruction to our old man.

And when our old man is crucified with Christ – brought under the influence and power of that ever-marvellous cross of Christ – shall there not be found power in the cross sufficient ultimately to abolish the whole body of sin? Is it not the very purpose of the cross to accomplish this? Did not the eternal Son of God give himself for us that he might redeem us from all iniquity? Hath he not loved the church and given himself for it, that he might sanctify and cleanse it with the washing of water by the word, that he might present it to himself a glorious church, not having spot or wrinkle or any such thing; but that it should be holy and without blemish, the body of sin all gone for ever? Is not the accomplishment of this blessed issue the very end for which Christ's soul was in travail, and which, when he seeth, he shall see of the travail of his soul and be satisfied? Is not this the very purchase which he made by his cross? Its achievement is a work of power and grace on and in his church and each member. And, being such, it is committed to the hands of the Holy Spirit. And was not the Spirit the sovereign, free, unhindered, Almighty Spirit obtained by Jesus for us through his cross, that we through the Spirit might mortify the deeds of the body and might crucify the flesh with its affections and lusts, and that the Spirit might abolish for ever in us the principle and presence of sin? And shall anything be too hard for the Spirit of the Lord? It is the purpose, and the purchase, and, through the Spirit, the power of the cross to accomplish this. By the cross of Christ, then, our old man shall ultimately be altogether abolished. 'O wretched man that I am! who shall deliver me from the body of this death? I thank God through Jesus Christ our Lord.' 'Knowing this, that our old man is crucified with him, that the body of sin might be destroyed' – that it may wither and waste and pine away, and finally vanish for ever.

This wasting, however, is progressive. This extinction is prospective.

ii. Consider therefore the present, the current effect of our old man being crucified with Christ. For there is an immediate and present, as well as a prospective and ultimate, consequence. Our old man is crucified with Christ that the body of sin may ultimately be destroyed, and *that even in the meantime, and henceforth, we should not serve sin.* The immediate design and issue of this arrangement is that you may refuse to serve sin, that you may, on good warrant and with good effect, refuse to serve sin.

Observe that sin, the powerful principle of our depravity, is here represented as a lord, a tyrant-master, a king. 'Sin hath reigned.' So long as you are out of Christ, so long as you are unregenerate, you are the willing servant and slave of this king. You are in his kingdom, the kingdom of sin, and you love to have it so. You commit your interests to this mighty lord, this grand monarch, and, by your own will, sin reigns over you. Under the government of this king you conduct your life. To him you appeal for relief from your own inward native insufficiency. To him you carry the complaining cry of conscious self-dissatisfaction, 'Who will show me any good?' To his hands you commit your happiness. And sin ministers to your gratifications, your pleasure, the pleasures of sin. But this reigning monarch will not give the protection of his kingdom, such as it is, or other privileges, such as they are, the pleasures that are for a season, without founding a claim upon his doing so. He acquires a claim upon his subject, and he is an exacting lord. He is a hard and austere taskmaster. He lays on us an exacting tax or wage: 'The wages of sin is death.' Sin exacts death, and he urges and makes good his claim by the bond of the broken covenant, 'The soul that sinneth, it shall die.' Nor is there any help for it: 'What fruit had ye then in those things whereof ye are now ashamed? for the end of those things is death.' The end of them! The issue in which they terminate, the goal to which they tend, and to which they carry you, is death. Till that goal be reached, till that terrible tax be paid, even to the uttermost farthing, till you come to the very end of those things, which is death, sin stands over you a remorseless lord and tyrant, still reigning, for sin reigns and will reign unto death, maintaining all its lordly tyrant-power unbroken, and all your efforts cannot break it. You have no righteous claim to be free. You have no effective power at your disposal, either from within or from without, to free yourself. You must move on, no help for it, on to the end which is death.

But believe on the Lord Jesus Christ. Be united to him by the pleading, striving Spirit. Be one with Christ. Bring in by faith the intervention of the death of Christ. Let the

Spirit shut you up to Christ, and to him expressly as crucified. Be ye crucified with him. And let your old man be crucified with him. Then sin's wages, sin's righteous tax upon you, are paid. They are paid in Christ, in the cross of Christ. The goal to which sin, the tyrant, and you, sin's slave, were travelling onwards, inextricably bound together and identified with one another, as with one interest and kingdom and destiny, that goal is reached. You have got to the end of those things, which is death, and the exaction of sin on you is righteously broken and gone. God in his gracious estimation distinguishes now, and separates, between you and sin. He cheers and stimulates you to assert and make good the separation. The righteous curse is no more on you, sealing you to destruction. It is wholly gone in Christ, who hath redeemed you from the curse of the law, being made a curse for you. And destruction now hangs not over you, for you have passed safely and unharmed in Christ through the curse into the land of light and blessing, into a large and wealthy place, into the favour of God which is life, and his loving kindness which is better than life. Destruction hangs not over you, but over the body of sin, not over you who have put on Christ, the Blessed, the Accepted the Beloved, but over the old man whom you have disowned and put off. And now in the merit of your Redeemer's cross you have the right and warrant, in the believing fellowship and strength of your Redeemer's Spirit, obtained for you by his cross, to break with this tyrant wholly and for ever, refusing all subjection henceforth, that henceforth you should not serve sin, and should not be obedient to its dictates and instigations, should not minister to or serve its desires.

Such is the tenor of the apostle's argument. His whole reasoning in the latter half of the previous chapter

(Romans 5) proceeds from the fact of Christ being the last Adam, the federal Head and Representative of his people, in whom all his people served and suffered and died and live again, even as in Adam all sinned and died. At the close of that chapter he had said, 'Sin hath reigned unto death.' By Christ's vicarious death sin has got all its claim. This tyrant has received all his demands. And he adds the glorious contrasting statement that grace reigns 'through righteousness unto eternal life by Jesus Christ our Lord'. Then he takes up and prosecutes the enquiry, Shall we go on to sin because grace reigns, or so that grace may abound? And he sharply sets aside this vicious notion on the ground that we are dead to sin. How shall we that are dead to sin live any longer therein? Yes, one might reply, if sin's claim even unto death is all fulfilled, and sin's rights and power are thus gone, and I am dead to sin, then indeed I may not, ought not, cannot live any longer therein. But when did this death occur? How has this claim been all fulfilled, and the constituting bond been paid? When did I and sin reach together that goal where, as by a resistless spell, my tyrant's power was made empty and his right of captivity over me abolished? Tell me that, show me when and how I am dead unto sin.

And the apostle is ready with his reply. He falls back on the vicariousness of Christ's death, and the communion therein which faith secures. Do you not know, he says, that so many of us as were baptized and engrafted into Christ were baptized into his death? By the Spirit on his part, by lively faith on yours, you have been engrafted into Christ, and are become one with him. But with what view, to what end, with what direct and immediate design were you so engrafted into him? What had the Spirit immediately in view, nay what had ye yourselves in view, in this union with Jesus? Loaded with the guilt of sin, the curse of God, the sentence of death, what was it that you saw in Christ that made him in your estimation so precious that you longed to be united to him, shut up in him, hidden in him, found in him, dealt with by the Holy One of Israel as in him – his Beloved? Was it not exactly his death, his vicarious, cursed death in the room and stead of sinners, was it not exactly his cross that set him forth in your esteem as the very Saviour you needed and desired? And was it not with an explicit and express reaching forth of your desire after the appropriation of this death, after communion with him in his death, after the imputation of his death to you, that you ventured at his own gracious and constraining call to flee unto Jesus and hide yourself in him and him crucified? And now, therefore, engrafted into his death, his very death is yours. Continue to appropriate and to improve it as your own, on the sole and all-sufficient warrant of God's word of promise and command, maintained by faith, that this death of Christ is yours. It is death, perfect and complete. It is finished. Appropriate it as your own, in all its extent and perfection, if you appropriate it at all. What indeed can induce or move you to make it yours by faith, if its absolute perfection does not? And unto all this perfection and completeness of death – a death which Jesus dieth no more, in no repetition, in no degree of it any more, for death hath no more dominion over him – to all this extent and perfection of his vicarious death for you, reckon yourselves dead indeed unto sin in and with your Substitute, in and with Jesus Christ your Lord. And as for other lords that have had dominion over you, affections and lusts, the vice-regents of sin, let not them reign for their great leader, that old lord that once reigned over you. See you not that he hath already reigned unto the utmost of all his claim – reigned unto death, that perfect death which is the final issue and outgoing, the goal and end of his dominion? It will be with clear and perfect right therefore, with true appreciation of an accomplished fact, when you now refuse to let him reign any longer. 'Let not sin therefore reign in your mortal body, that ye should obey it in the lusts thereof.' And though he come with the aspect of a roaring lion, he must crouch and quail at your refusal.

But there is more in this arrangement. The death which has broken up your identification with sin has passed on you, passed safely, unharmingly, unhurtingly, on you in Christ. 'Ye are dead, and your life is hid with Christ in God.' You are crucified with Christ, nevertheless you live. But not only has death passed on you unharmingly, death has passed also on your old man, and passed on him destroyingly. In the cross there is life for you. In the cross there is destruction for him. He is not crucified with a counteracting life, a counteracting and triumphing and hidden and eternal life, underneath all, as you are. He is crucified and nothing more, crucified to linger and waste and perish. The death brought in between him and you, unto your separation, acts both on you and on him. But how differently! On you it acts to quicken and to make alive, on him to mortify and slay.

3. In the energy, then, of that almighty death of Christ, which is deadly only to your old man and life from the dead to you, in the energy of such a separating power, reacting between you and your old man and creating a repulsion on both sides, break off, I pray you, vigorously and with joy from your tyrant. Draw near to your new Lord in the singleness and gladness of your heart. In the manliness and the joy of your new found holy liberty, exclaim, 'O Lord, truly I am thy servant; I am thy servant, and the son of thine handmaid: thou hast loosed my

bonds.' I am not the servant any more of him who is now nailed to that tree to perish there, crucified to be destroyed, but of him who was once nailed to that tree, not to perish there, but to triumph as the Prince of Life, the Living One. Though he was crucified, nevertheless he lived; and, behold, he is alive for evermore. With him, therefore, being crucified, I nevertheless live, and, behold, I also am alive for evermore; yet not I, but Christ liveth in me, after the power of a life that is endless, and the security of a life that is hid in God.

ᕽ 5 ᕽ

The Mediator's Reward

'Father . . . glorify thy Son' (John 17:1).
'Thou lovest righteousness, and hatest wickedness: there-
fore God, thy God, hath anointed thee with the oil of
gladness above thy fellows' (Psa. 45:7).

The first of these passages is a prayer, and the second is
the answer to it, given forth prophetically and by
anticipation many ages before the prayer itself was uttered. This gives a practical demonstration of that full and
joyful, that liberal and instant manner in which the Father
has rewarded the Mediator, celebrated in Psalm 21: 'For
thou preventest him with the blessings of goodness.' That
is, 'Thou anticipatest him, crowning him immediately
and spontaneously, almost before he can present his
claim, with the rewards of his complete obedience.' The
topic brought before us by these verses is the Mediator's
reward, consisting in the glory and gladness communicated to him by the Father, and no subject could be found
more worthy of investigation.

Before entering, however, on the elements of Christ's
mediatorial glory, one or two preliminary remarks should
be made. And, first, it is very evident from the content and
language of both the verses that this prayer is made by
Jesus, and answered to him, not in any private character
or capacity as an individual, but specifically as Mediator,

as the surety of that better covenant established on better promises, for the fulfilment of some of which he now pleads. From the passage in the gospel it is very evident that it is Jesus as Mediator who prays that he may be glorified, for the whole prayer is well known as Christ's intercessory prayer, and it is as the surety of the covenant and in virtue of the blood of the covenant that Jesus enters within the veil, into the holiest of all.

The same thing is equally obvious from the answer, and that in three respects: First, he is evidently addressed as Emmanuel, as one of the brethren, when it is promised that he shall be honoured and made glad above his fellows. He is thus addressed as made of a woman. Second, he is addressed as made under the law and is approved of as having magnified the law and made it honourable. 'Thou lovest righteousness and hatest wickedness.' And still more emphatically, thirdly, he is addressed as in covenant with God, and he can be so only as in covenant for others, only as surety of the perpetual covenant of grace. For the Father says to Jesus, 'God, thy God, hath anointed thee.' He here claims a peculiar interest in Jesus and accords unto Jesus a peculiar interest in himself, for this is the very form of expressing a covenant interest and relation, as you may see in almost every reference to the covenant of grace. These almost always conclude thus: 'I will be their God and they shall be my people' or 'I will be a Father to them.' God always makes himself over in covenant: 'I will be *thy* God.' He gives communication of himself as the very object to be accomplished in the covenant and, as in making a covenant with Abraham, in a secondary sense, he said, 'I am thy shield, and thy exceeding great reward', so in making the same covenant, primarily with the seed promised, even with Jesus, the surety of the one and only covenant profitable to sinners, the Father makes use of the same form. He says, 'I am thy God', and Jesus acknowledges the same relation, now newly instituted, saying 'I delight to do thy will, O my God.'

Thus Jesus becomes the Father's in a new sense, the Father's filial servant, and obedient Son, and the Father becomes Christ's in a new sense, even his God, his all-sufficient strength, his everlasting portion. These things are valuable and important as indicating to us the certain truth that this prayer and its answer entirely relate to the surety of the new covenant. Whatever truths we may be enabled to bring forth from them must strongly bind our consciences to honour the Mediator by humble and joyful faith in his ability and glory. This subject may well entice and encourage you to ask the way to Zion and set your faces thitherward, joining yourselves to the Lord in the ever-blessed covenant. You may well see how perpetual and glorious this covenant is from the unfailing and ineffable glory of him who is its surety.

Observe, secondly, that there is here a decided connection of merit between Christ's obedience and reward. 'Thou lovest righteousness, and hatest wickedness: *therefore* God, thy God, hath anointed thee with the oil of gladness.' As far as Jesus himself was concerned, this was essentially a covenant of works. To him it was clearly the old arrangement, 'Do this and live.' And indeed, life can be given on no other condition. There must be righteousness rendered before there can be life bestowed. The grace of this covenant in its aspect toward sinners does not consist in God's bestowing forgiveness without a satisfaction, or his favour without a previous righteousness, but in providing the satisfaction and righteousness both, and in giving sinners an interest therein, not in consideration of any work of theirs, but by free imputation. Thus it is by faith that it may be by grace. But to Jesus the reward is not of grace but of merit. He receives his equivalent. He enters on the possession of the covenanted, stipulated reward. Because he hath poured out his soul unto death, therefore will I divide him a portion with the great, and he shall divide the spoil with the strong. He became obedient to death, even the death of the cross, wherefore God also hath highly exalted him. He endured the cross for the joy that was set before him. This also is a valuable truth showing in a very strong light the stability of the covenant, inasmuch as the justice and righteousness of God are enlisted on the side of the promises, and thus the covenant is ordered in all things and sure.

And, thirdly, we cannot omit pointing out the solemn light in which the subject sets the necessity of prayer. The infidel thought sometimes occurs to us: 'What need for prayer, or what good can issue from it? If God has promised blessings they will be given whether they are asked or not, and if it is not his design to bestow them, then no importunity on our part can change his design.' Now the ordinary and simple answer to this is God's own declaration: 'I will yet for this be enquired of by the house of Israel, to do it for them' (*Ezek.* 36:37). This is said after the most absolute and unconditional promises of the new heart and all consequent grace flowing through the new covenant. Thus while God gives unconditional promises in Christ, he, as it were, promises unconditionally to himself that the promises shall first be asked in earnest prayer; and between these two things there is really no contradiction. At all events the very same thing is found holding true in the history of the Mediator. No promises could have been given more distinctly than those made to our Lord Jesus Christ, and, provided he fulfilled the terms by which he bound himself, nothing could be more certain than that all the stipulated rewards should be his. 'I shall give thee the heathen for thine inheritance, and the uttermost parts of the earth for thy possession.' Still we know that Jesus had to ask this. 'Ask of me, and I shall give thee the heathen for thine inheritance.' Though the promise is unconditional, still Jesus has to convert it into a prayer: 'Father . . . glorify thy Son.' Therefore we refer to these two verses, and this lesson so clearly learned from them, any one who may say that, because an absolute and unconditional promise has been given, prayer for that blessing is superfluous, inasmuch as it will be bestowed whether we pray or not. Christ's practice was very different, for all promises made to him by his Father are presented in the altered form of prayers and pleaded by the Son that they should be fulfilled. If this was so when Jesus actually merited these promises and stood on the footing of God's obedient and righteous servant claiming the promised exaltation and reward, how much more is prayer necessary with us, when we have no merit to plead, no righteousness of ours to present.

There is yet a fourth remark suggested by a comparison of these two verses. You will observe that in the prayer Jesus simply asks that his Father should now glorify him. The answer promises, 'I have anointed thee', that is, publicly honoured, consecrated or glorified thee. 'I have gloriously acknowledged thee before all angels as my Son, as my King on my holy hill of Zion. I have announced thee to the universe as my first-born, higher than the kings of the earth.' This is clearly implied in the anointing. And as when Solomon was anointed all the people shouted, 'God save the king', so every knee shall bow and every tongue confess that Jesus is Lord, and herein is he glorified when crowned king of Zion. But while his prayer is thus fully answered, you will observe that it is more than answered. This simple anointing answers all that Jesus asked, namely the reception of all glory, that he may be clothed with glory and with majesty, so that by eternal exhibition of his grace and beauty and power all may love and admire and adore. But there is more than a simple anointing given, there is more bestowed than an exhibition of his glory. There is promised an anointing with the oil of gladness, a communication of internal joy and delight. Thus Jehovah the Father more than answers the prayer of his Son. He puts upon his head a crown of purest gold; honour and majesty are laid upon him. But in addition to this, God hath made him most blessed forever. He hath made him exceeding glad. Thus as king Solomon was not crowned with any cold or barren honour, but with joy and rejoicing, so this greater one than Solomon finds the day on which he is crowned a day of the gladness of his heart. His glory is accompanied with joy and his gladness is a joy that is full of glory. Thus does the Lord still prevent or anticipate him with the blessing of goodness exceeding and preceding his requests. And Jesus, like all his people, finds a covenant God and Father to be able to do exceeding abundantly above all that he can ask.

With these preliminary remarks we come now to enquire into the nature and elements of the glory which Jesus has received as Mediator of the Covenant of Redemption. From what we have already said you will see that this enquiry is by no means accomplished by an enumeration of all the perfections and glories attributed to the Godhead. All these belong to Jesus from everlasting and they were his at the very moment of his humiliation and abasement. Of these he never could be denuded. Consequently, it is not here that we are to find the elements of the glory which these verses allude to. We are enquiring after a glory which has been communicated to Jesus, a glory which he might have entirely lacked and still been God, a glory, therefore distinct from his essential divinity, which never could be communicated because it was his everlastingly, without the possibility of change or of diminution. It was for the purpose of bringing this distinctly into view that I showed that Jesus speaks and is by the Father recognised as speaking in the character of the Messiah, the Mediator, Emmanuel, the Surety of the covenant. It is, therefore, his Messianic, or Mediatorial or covenant glory which we have here to investigate, and may he who takes of the things of Christ and shows them to the soul give us much humility, reverence, wisdom and faith in speaking and hearing on this sacred theme.

The covenant glory of the Redeemer is that which, by his obedience unto death, he has received from the Father, and the bright effulgence of this glory rests indivisibly upon his whole person as Emmanuel. The elements of this glory may be considered with respect to Christ's humanity, Christ's deity and Christ's whole person. Now, however, we shall consider only the glory communicated to Christ's humanity.

1. The whole human nature of the Redeemer consisting of soul and body has by the rewarding grace of the Father been rendered immortal and eternally infallible. This is the first element of the Saviour's glory and is necessarily presupposed in all others. And that this element is a real gift of God is obvious if you consider that the humanity of Jesus is but a creature and must like all other creatures partake of that defect or want of self-sufficiency which is the special mark of distinction between everything created and the Creator. No creature can be self-sufficient, for to be self-sufficient is to have the cause of existence, and therefore the cause of continuance, in one's self, which can be affirmed of none but the Creator only. Hence no

creature can be immortal except by the will and power and gift of the Creator. Adam had no claim on God to continue life to him for one moment, and the benevolence of the covenant of works appears in this, that, in return for a service which Adam was bound to render in any event, God freely obliged himself to give his creature immortality. The human nature of the second Adam is in itself as destitute of self-sufficiency as that of the holy first Adam. Its sufficiency is of God, and because Jesus has fulfilled the conditions which Adam failed to fulfil he has gained, with other blessings, this for himself, that his human nature shall be immortal and shall not see death. Thus Jesus dieth no more and the glory of immortality is a necessary element of his great reward. But besides immortality his human nature has obtained also an everlasting infallibility. This also, if possessed at all, must be a blessing communicated. For just as no creature is self-sufficient or adequate for its own preservation in being, so no creature is infallible or adequate to its own preservation in rectitude. Thus, in this sense of inherent, essential, self-derived attributes there is none good but God. And this statement, made by Jesus to the young man, was most appropriate, for Jesus, while possessed of Godhead, himself very God, saw that this young man recognized nothing but his humanity which, like every other creature, possessed no essential infallible quality of moral rectitude. Nothing but grace can preserve any creature from falling, and from its very nature grace is a thing which God is not bound to bestow. Therefore holy angels have fallen and holy man hath fallen too from their high original and created estate. Had Adam fulfilled the terms of the covenant under which he had been placed he would have merited confirming grace which would have rendered him infallibly righteous and blessed along with all his posterity.

What the first Adam failed to do the second Adam accomplished, and therefore does he merit and obtain for his human nature those communications of confirming grace in virtue of which the glorified humanity of Jesus shall never fall from righteousness, but it shall ever be true of his human nature, 'thou hast loved righteousness and hated wickedness.' It is quite true that we do very commonly contemplate this truth as a very certain truth – that the human soul and body of Jesus will ever abide in the love and practice of all holiness, but we do not sufficiently attend to the cause of this. We look upon it as a matter of fact, but we look upon it improperly as a matter of course. It is not so. There is nothing in the human nature of Jesus in itself considered to keep it from falling. In this world it was created holy by an exercise of the power of the Holy Ghost – and preserved holy by the same Spirit given to him without measure – and, having finished the work given him to do, he is rewarded in part by an everlasting, unfailing infallibility conferred upon him by the Father. Conferred, I say, for I beg to remind you again that this infallibility is no matter of course, any more than the immortality. Both are communicated, and each forms a part of that glory which Jesus has gained as Mediator. The possession of immortality and infallibility by the human nature of Emmanuel is a portion of his reward, and could not have been communicated unless Jesus had fulfilled all righteousness.

Indeed, unless Jesus had stood to all his stipulated promises in the covenant, neither of them could have been his. Immortality could not have been his, for his resurrection is a proof of the completeness of his work. And infallibility could not have been his, for such a failure or withdrawal would of itself have been an exhibition of fallibility. Jesus, however, having accomplished all that the Father had given him to do, was raised from the dead, being quickened of the Spirit. His body was not left to see corruption nor his soul left in the state of the dead, but as God's Holy One, now infallibly holy by his Father's rich grace, he was received as he who was dead but is alive again and dieth no more. Not that his human nature has in itself any essential property corresponding to these things, but only because in Christ's communicated glory this forms part, namely, that his human nature should be anointed with undying strength and grace sufficient to give holiness infallible. 'He asked life of thee, and thou gavest it him, even length of days for ever and ever' – natural immortality – 'and through the mercy of the most High he shall not be moved' – a promise of a spiritual and moral infallibility through grace.

2. A second element in the glory of the Mediator with respect to his humanity is that his human nature is advanced to the everlasting and ever-blessed enjoyment of God as its portion and inheritance. It is this ineffable fruition of God that is always understood by the expression, 'the light of God's countenance'. It is this that the saints of God pray for when they beseech God to lift up upon them the light of his countenance, even the felt possession of God's favour and the enjoyment of him as their supreme good. Now it is important to observe that this is the very expression used to express at least a portion of the glory and joy of the resurrected and ascended Saviour. 'Thou hast made him most blessed for ever: thou hast made him exceeding glad with thy countenance,' evidently implying that the human nature of Jesus was admitted to the immediate favour and full fruition of the living God. This is what his people enjoy. Their gladness, no doubt, is of an inferior degree. Still it is in degree that it

differs, not in the kind and nature of the joy. All believers say, This God is my God for ever and ever. Even the man Christ Jesus can say nothing more and his joy is not of a distinct or higher nature, however much more intense it may be in degree. 'In thy presence is fulness of joy,' says David, 'at thy right hand there are pleasures for evermore.' And while this was the genuine expression of the Psalmist's joy in God as his God, the very words are by a New Testament commentator put into the mouth of our risen Saviour, so exactly does the experience of Jesus and all believers correspond when they celebrate God as their own God in covenant. That the man Christ Jesus shares in this manner with his people in the full fruition of God as his and their common portion is evident from the text where a joy above that of his fellows is promised but where it is clearly implied that it shall be of the same nature. It is not, 'I will anoint thee with an oil of gladness distinct from thy fellows', but 'with the oil of gladness *above* thy fellows.' The same thing is still more evident from the very wonderful passage in Romans 8:17 where the children of the covenant are said to inherit God, being heirs of God and co-heirs or joint-heirs with Christ. The full and immediate enjoyment thus derived by direct drawing from the grace and sufficiency of the Godhead exceeds what created heart can declare. Eye hath not seen and ear hath not heard what he hath prepared for them that love him. And surely, since these things belong to the man Christ Jesus in the highest degree, his fruition of the Father must be altogether ineffable – his portion as the firstborn of every creature must be very glorious beyond all conception.

Now, this is clearly a portion of his mediatorial honour and happiness. It is the joy of the relation in covenant which now subsists between his human nature and God as his God and Father. Here we find a disclosure of the meaning of the lovely expression, 'the God and Father of our Lord Jesus Christ', as implying something more than the relation between the first and second Persons of the Godhead. It is a covenant relation, not of itself necessary to the Godhead of either, but a relation entered into for the greater display of divine glory and the exercise of grace to the guilty and the ill-deserving. 'My mercy will I keep for him for evermore, and my covenant shall stand fast with him.' 'He shall cry unto me, Thou art my father, my God and the rock of my salvation. Also I will make him my firstborn, higher than the kings of the earth.'

3. A third element in the glory which, in reward for his obedience unto death, has been communicated to the human nature of the Mediator, consists in this – that it has been exalted above all created excellence and dignity. Because of his obedience unto death God hath highly exalted the man Christ Jesus and given him a name that is above every name. He hath made him higher than the kings of the earth, and higher than all principalities and powers and thrones and dominions and might and excellency, that in all things he might have the pre-eminence. This a glory which the human nature of the Lamb of God derives from its hypostatical union with the divine nature of the Son, and it is a high degree of dignity, altogether beyond our comprehension. The humanity of Jesus is not deified or in any way mingled with or lost in his divinity: it is and must ever remain a creature still. But while sustained in a state of glorified natural immortality and ineffable moral perfection and infallibility by the rich and immeasurable grace of the Father and gift of the Holy Ghost, and dignified still farther by its direct union with the deity in the person of the Son, its glory above all

created beings must be transcendent and to us inconceivable. Even though all those thrones and dominions which surround Emmanuel in ranks rising upon ranks in glory and in beauty unspeakable and numbers without number – I say, even though heaven's wide temple with all the dazzling glory of her angelic throng were disclosed to us and we were thus in sweet vision lifted far aloft in the scale of creature excellence even to the seraphim or the archangel richest in the flood of grace and glory among all heaven's holy ones – still we would be but slightly aided in our views of a glorified Emmanuel, for, far above every name that is named and every throne that is set in heaven, sits the glorified body of the divine Redeemer, the highest and nearest seraphim veiling their faces with their wings, and the posts of heaven's gates moving and sounding even with the unbroken silence of his glory.

Still, this also is a communicated glory – not essential to his Godhead – bestowed upon his humanity. It is his humanity which is the subject of this honour and it is a portion of what Jesus prayed for when he said, 'Father . . . glorify thy Son', and a portion of what the Father promised when he said 'I have anointed thee with the oil of gladness above thy fellows.'

How full of material for unbounded hope to the believer is this glory of the humanity of Jesus! If we believe on this glorified Emmanuel, then behold our very brother, flesh of our flesh, bone of our bone, exalted to the highest created glory. This is our nature which has the highest seat in heaven. This is he who, because the children were partakers of flesh and blood, himself also likewise took part of the same, and now, having offered a full sacrifice for sin, he has carried humanity within the veil, even to the holiest of all, to the very throne of God, where he sits infinitely exalted above all creatures. And now he that sanctifieth and they that are sanctified are all of one, so that his people shall not stand in the outer court but have a way opened up through all the seraphic hosts of heaven till they come even to his throne, the centre of the glories of the universe, where they shall forever dwell nearest to Emmanuel's person, because dear to his heart as the purchase of his agony and pain.

4. There is yet another large revenue of glory accruing to the humanity of Jesus from the fact that Emmanuel is constituted the representative of Godhead to all the universe. The glory of Emmanuel in this respect is a double one. Firstly, the unchangeable and essential glory of divinity is thus once more fully exhibited. This is not properly an increase of glory to Jesus because he possessed all this before: it is merely an increment given to his declarative glory. But secondly (and this is the chief thing to be considered), it is a distinct increase of glory to Emmanuel that his human nature should be elected as the medium through which a fuller and sweeter expression should be given to that light of God which in itself is invisible from its very splendour, inaccessible and full of glory. It is very great glory to the humanity of Jesus that all the treasures of Godhead, even of divine grace and glory and wisdom and knowledge, of light and of love, should have been deposited in him to dwell in him bodily – and that this indwelling of all divine perfection should have been accomplished in such fulness and with such wisdom as that he who seeth Jesus hath thereby seen the Father. The Word has been made flesh and dwelt among us and we have beheld his glory, the glory as of the only begotten of the Father, full of grace and truth. We behold now the light of the glory of God in the face of Jesus Christ, who is the brightness of the Father's glory and the express image

of his person. The mystery of this is utterly unfathomable. There is even in the material creation a something divine, there is even in mute natures a quiet throb or pulse that tells of a sort of divine life or a high original divine fiat. And still more are these in the soul of man. Even though the image has been shattered into fragments, there are yet some remnant traces of a likeness to the great and all-creating God. And to rise higher yet, in the soul renewed and regenerated there is an evidence of a present God in his beauty and in his glory, for there is a life hid with Christ in God. But these, as emanations of the Creator's grace and beauty, are but drops communicated. In Jesus there is the full image, the express likeness of the living God. His humanity gives utterance or expression or exhibition to the fulness of the Godhead, and, while the Godhead is glorified by such a declaration, the human nature is greatly glorified in being employed and fitted for an end so worthy of God to accomplish, and so beneficial to his creature to behold. And when, by thus glorifying the human nature of Jesus with an honourable function and dignity so unspeakable, the Father is himself glorified, we behold the full meaning of Jesus' words, 'Father . . . glorify thy Son, that thy Son also may glorify thee.'

Other parts of Emmanuel's glory have not been considered. But even here we may see how fully warranted the children of God are to entertain the most unbounded hopes of future and unspeakable joy. There is nothing in Jesus' glory in which his people shall not partake: and if we be questioned this day concerning our hope of the gospel, how well would it be for all of us if we were able to say – and there is no reason or cause why we should not say it except our God-dishonouring unbelief – 'Whatever glory Emmanuel has in possession, that is mine in prospect, for he is but the first-fruits, the wave offering, the already glorified pledge, the firstborn of all his elect and called and justified creatures, the first begotten of the dead.' If these things are so, if these hopes are well grounded in a full and changeless promise, and if such hopes are ours, how ought we to live above the world. The world should sink into nothing before the energy of a faith which should altogether displace it by its power of bringing forward the things that are unseen and eternal.

And to those who are seeking the way to Zion, desirous of joining themselves to the Lord in a perpetual covenant, how inspiring and encouraging to know that the Surety of that covenant, who is bone of our bone, and not ashamed to call us brethren, is, in our own nature, so highly honoured of him who is the only legitimate source of all glory in the universe. Let your thoughts dwell much upon the covenant glory of Emmanuel and this may, in the hands of him who reveals Jesus and takes of the things that are his and shows them to the soul, be the means of drawing forth all your affection to him as the Chiefest among ten thousand and the altogether lovely One. And, before you are aware, the citadel of that cruelly hard and unbelieving heart, which you mourn over as still shut against the Saviour, may be found easily and sweetly to surrender at the Saviour's call, so that he shall come in and sup with you and you with him.

∽ 6 ∽

Perfected For Ever

'For by one offering he hath perfected for ever them that are sanctified' (Heb. 10:14).

We have here a certain effect attributed to the offering or sacrifice of Christ, and the parties specified to whom that effect accrues. The parties said to reap the benefit of Christ's one offering are those that are sanctified and the benefit they reap is that, by his one offering, Christ hath for ever perfected them.

1. The parties spoken of: *'them that are sanctified'*. To sanctify, in the language or usage of the Epistle to the Hebrews, has a somewhat special meaning. It points, not so much to that inward change of heart and nature which grace accomplishes in changing the soul from the predominance and pollution of sin, and which usually presents itself to our minds when we speak of sanctification, as to the original idea of separation or dedication to God. In this sense, what is sanctified is what is set apart especially to God, what he now appropriates and claims as his, which it is henceforth not merely sin but the special sin of sacrilege to alienate from him. Those that are sanctified are those that are set apart from the world and consecrated to God. They were originally implicated in the world's sinful estate and the world's curse and doom. They were

partakers of the world's guilt and misery and woe. They formed part and parcel of that world – that whole world which lies in the wicked one. But they have been selected and effectually set apart from that guilt-doomed world. They have been placed on another footing, on another platform. Their brotherhood with the world has been broken and, being translated out of it, they have received a new and distinct and separate standing. They have heard and obeyed the call, 'Come out from among them, and be ye separate.'

And it is unto God that they have been separated. They have become an offering unto God in righteousness, a kind of first fruits from among his creatures, laid upon his altar, and accepted there by him as his pleasant, chosen portion. 'Know that the LORD hath set apart him that is godly for himself.'

This separation from the world to God has been transacted in virtue of the sacrifice of Christ. In the tenth verse of this chapter we read the words, 'By the which will we are sanctified through the offering of the body of Jesus Christ once for all.' And to this agree the words of our Lord in his intercessory prayer, 'For their sakes I sanctify myself, that they also might be sanctified.' Mark here a proof of what we have said is the meaning in this connection of the word 'to sanctify'. As applied to Christ's people it must have the same sense as applied to Christ himself. 'I sanctify myself, that they also might be sanctified.' But assuredly he needed no inward purification of his heart from sin. He sanctified himself when in his death he separated himself from the world and consecrated himself to God. For in his love and condescension he had implicated himself with this evil world. As our substitute and legal advocate he had put himself in our place. He found us lying in the world, that world that lieth in the wicked one. And taking our sin upon himself – and taking up thereby our place and standing before God – he found himself bound up in responsibility, in position, in experience, in destiny with this evil world, from which he could save his people only by separating them. And he could separate them from the world only by first joining himself to them, and to that world in which they lay. He was made of a woman, made under the law. He was numbered with the transgressors.

He had therefore to separate himself again. He had to effect his escape. He had to do so, as legally personating those whom he came to save, to separate and set them apart to God. And he had to do so in a lawful way, not in any way that might offer itself, but in a way that the divine law might sanction, honour and reward. This separation he effected by his death on the cross. The bond of the divine curse assigned to Christ the very same position and standing in God's sight which belonged to the world. The sentence of divine law bound up the surety with the client. Unexpiated sin resting on Christ implicated him in all the world's condemnation and doom. He could separate himself righteously and effectually from the world only by expiating the sin that bound him up with it. He could consecrate or dedicate himself to God only in death – the death which is the wages of sin. But when he had fully satisfied divine justice and given himself to God, a sacrifice of a sweet-smelling savour, the bond that bound him with the guilty world was snapped asunder and his position and standing as the substitute of sinners became a very different one from that of the world of sinners themselves. He had effected a safe landing on another platform and in another kingdom and *there* he was accepted with infinite pleasure as consecrated unto God. He 'sanctified himself', that is, he effectually and really separated himself from that world with whose place he had really implicated and conjoined himself. He effectually and acceptably consecrated himself unto the Father.

And he did this that the same might be effected in his people. 'I sanctify myself, that they also might be sanctified.' For he did so in their cause, in their service; nay, in their room and name and person. It was solely in their cause, in their name, that he was ever bound up with the world and needed to separate himself from it. The whole design and effect, therefore, of sanctifying or separating himself is that they also might be separated and sanctified. In all this, he acted as their legal representative. It was in reality the sanctification of his clients which he effected when he sanctified himself. Faith in him identifies the soul with him. Faith, therefore, is the victory which overcomes the world, and passes over from its condemnation and death to the kingdom of life and liberty. It was the will of God that he should sanctify himself as his people's representative. By this will, therefore, 'we are sanctified through the offering of the body of Jesus Christ once for all.'

Concerning this separation of the believer from the world, observe two things: Firstly, it is complete; and secondly, it is final.

i. *It is complete,* as complete in the believer's case, as in Christ's case, for it is Christ's separation which the believer shares. Hence, in describing their separation from the world Christ not only parallels it but identifies it with his own: 'They are not of the world, even as I am not of the world.' His home and rightful dwelling is in another and a very different sphere. He wrought out his right and title to it by his one offering, his obedience unto death. He entered into it at his ascension. Truly, he is not of the world. He is in the holy place in the glory of his Father. But he is there as representative and forerunner of all who believe. His home is theirs. 'I go to prepare a place for you. And if I go . . . I will come again, and receive you unto myself; that where I am, there ye may be also.' In the meantime, they are not of the world any more than he is. They are 'raised up together' with him, in point of title, in point of prospect and in point of present sympathy, and made to 'sit together in heavenly places in Christ Jesus'.

ii. *This separation is final.* It is 'the offering of the body of Jesus Christ once for all' which has effected this separation, and it has effected it once for all. For as he cannot die again – 'In that he died, he died unto sin once' – so that separation from the world which his death effects is conclusive and irreversible. He can no more be 'made under the law'. He can no more be 'numbered with the transgressors'. He can no more be implicated and identified with the world in its criminality and condemnation. Never can he fall from that mediatorial glory to which, out of the world's sin and curse, he cleared his victorious path. Nor can they who are united to him! They are separated and set apart with God for ever; sanctified 'once for all'. Their living head, 'after he had offered one sacrifice for sin for ever, sat down on the right hand of God.' And when, by faith, they take hold on him and, with him, emerge from the world's position and the world's doom into the light and liberty of the city of God, it is a conclusive escape which is theirs. They pass with Christ into 'a kingdom which cannot be moved'. 'They shall never perish, neither shall any man pluck them out of my hand.' They are sanctified unto the Father; they are his; and 'My Father . . . is greater than all; and no man is able to pluck them out of my Father's hand.' Are you not separated from the world? Are you still implicated and identified with it? There is another kingdom, another realm in which you may meet with God in peace and in fellowship of love. It is no dream land, no fairy land or enchanted ground, though blessings manifold and endless may make it so. It is very real, though unseen. It is real *because* it is unseen, for the things that are seen are transient, but the things that are unseen are eternal. Pass over at once to it and to all its privileges! Between you and that land, that home of righteousness and peace, there is nothing but the sacrifice, the offering of Christ. Pass over, by the way of the death of Christ, and at once you are separated from the world; at once you escape from its present condemnation and its coming ruin. That one offering is an open gate. It is a bridge that spans the yawning gulf. And as fleet as an electric message through Atlantic depths from shore to shore is faith's power to carry the believing soul from the land of condemnation into the home of salvation and liberty and peace.

Have you so believed on Jesus? Have you dealt with his cross, not as if it were a furnace of fire separating you from the kingdom of God, a wall of fire from which you shrink affrighted, but as an open door brought to you by the free gospel of the Lord? And have you passed over to the land of righteousness by believing acquiescence? Then maintain your separate standing! Do not let go the fruit of that one offering whereby you are once for all sanctified. If it has any virtue at all to you, it places you on a thoroughly different footing from the world and sets you apart unto the Lord. It consecrates you to him, with his infinite approbation and acceptance. Assert your position! Take it up boldly! Demonstrate it! Stand fast in it! 'There is therefore now no condemnation to them which are in Christ Jesus.' I say again, abide in your own spiritual land, your own now-natural spiritual land. Claim it as your own. Cherish a holy patriotism for the kingdom of God, which is righteousness and peace and joy in the Holy Ghost. Oh, for more of this heavenly patriotism among believers. Lives there a Christian man with heart so dead, who never to himself hath said, This is mine own, my native land – the home of righteousness and eternal peace? Cling only to that one offering and you cannot too valiantly refuse to fall beneath the power of the world's god – you cannot too gladsomely triumph in your escape from the world's ruin and sin.

So much for the parties spoken of in the text: 'those that are sanctified'. They are separated from the world and consecrated to God. They are so in all the sweetness and virtue and holiness and worth of the blood of Jesus.

2. And being so, there is another service which Jesus by his one offering is here said to have rendered to them, namely he has *perfected them for ever.*

Now to understand the import of this privilege let it be observed that it is a privilege which the sacrifices of the Mosaic economy could not confer. In Hebrews 7:19 it is expressly said that 'the law made nothing perfect, but the bringing in of a better hope did; by the which we draw nigh unto God.' From this it also follows that to be 'made perfect' has at least a very intimate connection with having the right and the power to 'draw near unto God'. The want of perfection by the law is contrasted by the apostle with the liberty of drawing near to God which we have by the gospel. Such liberty is manifestly, therefore, at least a part of the perfection which was continually desired under the earlier dispensation. We read that the tabernacle was 'a figure for the time then present, in which were offered both gifts and sacrifices, that could not make him that did the service perfect, as pertaining to the conscience' (*Heb.* 9:9). The perfection in question, therefore, has reference to the conscience. It is a perfect state of conscience that the apostle has in view. And he goes on to explain it more fully. For in opposition to that earthly tabernacle and the sacrifices in *it* which could not give perfection of conscience, he sets forth the tabernacle or temple of Christ's body, and the atonement of his own blood which he offered in the temple of his flesh. 'Christ being come an high priest of good things to come, by a greater and more perfect tabernacle, not made with hands, that is to say, not of this building; neither by the blood of goats and calves, but by his *own* blood he entered in once into the holy place, having obtained eternal redemption for us' (verse 11). It is this tabernacle and this sacrifice, namely the body and the blood of the Son of God, which is set forth in contrast with the Jewish temple and offerings, and the contrast turns on their respective ability or inability to make perfect as pertaining to the conscience. And what that implies is explained when he goes on to claim for the true sacrifice the property or powers which he celebrates in the next verse: 'For if the blood of bulls and of goats, and the ashes of an heifer sprinkling the unclean, sanctifieth to the purifying of the flesh: how much more shall the blood of Christ, who through the eternal Spirit offered himself without spot to God, purge your conscience from dead works to serve the living God?' (13-14). So that, comparing these verses, we learn that to be 'perfect' has reference to the conscience; and to be 'made perfect as pertaining to the conscience' is to have the conscience purged from dead works so as to have liberty, enlargement, right and power to draw near to God and serve him.

The import of this privilege is plain also from the tenor

of the argument in the tenth chapter. In the first verse the frequency of the legal sacrifices is given as a proof that they could not perfect the worshippers. 'For the law having a shadow of good things to come, and not the very image of the things, can never with those sacrifices which they offered year by year continually, make the comers there-unto perfect.' He then argues that the perfection of the worshippers would have been inconsistent with the reiteration of the sacrifices. 'For then', that is, if they had succeeded in perfecting the worshippers, 'would they not have ceased to be offered? because that the worshippers once purged should have had no more conscience of sins.' To be perfected, therefore, is to be purged so completely and conclusively as to have no more conscience of sins, and to be cleansed in spirit from the weakening fear and shrinking shame which conscious guilt engenders. That cannot be effected by a sacrifice which needs to be repeated, since 'in those sacrifices there is a remembrance again made of sins every year.' And no wonder, for these sins have not really been taken away. 'It is not possible that the blood of bulls and of goats should take away sins.' Therefore an awakened conscience, seeing sins not taken away, refuses to part with its sense of condemnation, and its guilty fear makes remembrance still of its deserts. It feels its own filthiness and is filled with dread and shame towards God. It is unable to draw near to him in peace and is disqualified from serving him with honour, with truth, with enlargement or with the hope of acceptance. By his one offering Christ has for ever secured for his people freedom from dread, guilt, fear and shame, and given them liberty and joy in approaching him in worship and service. 'By (his) one offering he hath perfected for ever them that are sanctified.'

What is there, then, in Christ's offering his sacrifice on

the cross that renders it an instrument fit and adequate for thus perfecting the conscience of the believing sinner? There are at least three elements: i. Voluntariness, ii. Divinity, and iii. Oneness.

i. There is *voluntariness* in this one offering.

Christ offered himself. 'When he cometh into the world, he saith, Sacrifice and offering thou wouldest not, but a body hast thou prepared me . . . Then said I, Lo, I come (in the volume of the book it is written of me,) to do thy will, O God' (*Heb*. 10:7). 'The good shepherd giveth his life for the sheep . . . No man taketh it from me, but I lay it down of myself' (*John* 10:11, 18). There is voluntariness in this sacrifice. The victim is also the priest, active in presenting himself to God in death. He offers himself, being voluntarily 'obedient unto death', and so becomes marvellously able to make his people perfect as pertaining to the conscience. See how this comes to the rescue when the conscience is truly alive to sin. Suppose I am in that condition and have not attained to the blessed state of having no more conscience of sin. On the contrary, I *have* conscience of sin – a true conviction in my conscience of the inexcusable unrighteousness and the consequent ill-desert of sin. In this case, I feel that God is just in judging and clear in condemning. I am not merely alarmed at the prospect of approaching danger, but the Holy Ghost has riveted in my conscience – much against my struggling evil heart – an irresistible conviction that God is holy and righteous in passing a sentence of death upon me, in declaring me liable to his wrath and curse. I see that 'the law is holy . . . but I am carnal sold under sin.' I see that the law, in its precept, is unobjectionably righteous, and that I, voluntarily, without a murmur, with my whole heart and soul, ought to obey all that its precepts appoint. But I see more than that, if it is the Holy Ghost who is giving me true and holy conscience of sin. I see that the law, in its curse, is as unobjectionably righteous, and that my duty to God requires me to own and acquiesce in the righteousness of that curse, proving my conviction and acquiescence by going forward voluntarily and without a murmur with my whole heart and will to suffer it. For if it be righteous, I am bound to own its righteousness. I am bound to take part with God against myself in his righteous treatment of me, a sinner, when he denounces his righteous curse upon me. Indeed, my rebellion continues unabated till I thus acquiesce, and, without one reclaiming grudge against the Most High, place myself wholly by my own act in his hands. I am bound to surrender myself voluntarily into the hands of his offended justice. If I cannot find the liberty and means of doing *that*, my conscience never can be perfected; it never can find scope and play for its truest office.

Oh! but who shall surrender himself voluntarily into the wrath of God? Who shall obediently go forward to dwell with everlasting burnings? Let me consider the gospel tidings of a substitute. I have to go forward voluntarily towards an offended and angry God, to a judge armed with his almighty malediction to meet my approach. But if I am not adequately convinced of sin, if repentance has never visited my heart, if I need to be dragged into his presence, I cannot go willingly in a day of his power. There can, therefore, be no suitableness in a substitute who does not go voluntarily. He cannot meet my case unless he goes as I should go, with me, before me, instead of me, of his own proper will – spontaneously, freely, because his heart and good pleasure are in it. My conscience urges me forward unto God. It calls upon and commands me willingly to return unto him, angry though he be. A sacrifice is proffered to me which by faith I may carry with me when I return. I ask – my conscience asks – is this a voluntary sacrifice? I must in my return to God identify myself with this sacrifice. The presentation of this sacrifice to God originally and my return to God with it in the hand of faith must thoroughly blend together. But *that* they cannot do unless there is voluntariness alike in both. My return to God, my voluntary placing of myself in God's hand, angry and offended though he be, must meet and blend into the surety's presentation of himself at the divine tribunal to bear for me the anger I have merited. But it cannot blend into one with an enforced, unintelligent, unspontaneous offer like those of calves and heifers in the older dispensation. I must return to God willingly, obediently, if my enmity, my rebellion, my alienation is ever to terminate. Saith my surety, 'Lo! I come, to do thy will, O God.' Voluntarily I go with thee, before thee, in thy room; and thou voluntarily in my fellowship. 'I lay down my life of myself.' And thus there is room for our being identified. It needs only voluntariness, willingness in thee: Whosoever will, let him come. This voluntariness of the death of Christ meets a great essential demand of conscience. I am to be identified with my surety in my return to God. But if he does not go forward voluntarily to appease the wrath of God by bearing the curse which I am bound voluntarily myself to go forward and endure my identification with such an unwilling substitute would suppress at least one righteous dictate and demand of my conscience. Consequently it could not 'make me perfect as pertaining to the conscience.' But in Christ I find a willing substitute. I find one who acquiesces in the righteousness of the curse; who voluntarily subjects himself to it in my room; and who, going voluntarily forward to meet all its terrors, solicits me, now, voluntarily, to go with him, while he shields me from all the wrath, bearing my guilt and cleansing my conscience. He procures for me pardon and peace, enabling me to meet not an angry but a reconciled God and making me for ever perfect as pertaining to the conscience, to serve the living and true God.

ii. There is *divinity* in this one offering, and that meets another longing of the trembling and guilty conscience, looking out for perfection.

Let us say, I have conscience of sin as against God, the Holy One, and the great desire of my heart is how I may be truly rid of it and have perfect peace with God. But how can I measure the evil of my iniquity, seeing I cannot measure the greatness of that Being against whom it is committed, and how then shall I measure the sacrifice that shall suffice for putting away my immeasurable sin? It is as committed against God that my sin assumes its aspect of exceeding sinfulness. But who can by searching find out God, who can find out the Almighty unto perfection? He covereth himself with light as with a garment. The seraphim veil their faces with their wings in his presence, and cry, 'Holy, Holy, Holy is the LORD of Hosts, the whole earth is full of his glory . . . Then said I, Woe is me! for I am undone; because I am a man of unclean lips . . . for mine eyes have seen the King, the LORD of hosts' (*Isa.* 6:3–5). And what filled the holy prophet with such trembling and amazement, with such sensitive and appalling conscience of sin? It was a deep impression of the awful majesty and glory of his God. Like Job, he had heard of him by the hearing of the ear, but now his eye seeth him; wherefore he abhors himself and repents in dust and ashes. And if God is so endlessly full of glory, and sin against him proportionately heinous and hell-deserving, how shall my conscience ever find a sacrifice great enough to expiate so great an evil, or great enough to reconcile so great a Lord? I am lost in my attempt to fathom the ill-deservingness of sin because I am lost in the attempt to appreciate the excellence and glory of him against whom I have sinned. Equally, I am lost in the attempt to answer the enquiry, 'Wherewithal shall I come before the LORD?' or to tell the measure of excellence and value which a sacrifice adequate to the case must possess. Show me any limit to its worth and preciousness, and I cannot enter into peace because the illimitable glory and perfection of God stamp upon my sin against him a further brand of wickedness than all the power and preciousness of any finite or measurable atonement can erase. The more my conscience is enlightened, and the more it adores God for his unsearchable glory, the more resolutely it rejects any sacrifice whose worth I can, or ever could, fathom or exhaust. If the God against whom I have sinned is boundless and infinite in his glory; if his consequent claim upon me to love and serve him is equally unlimited and absolute; then, in my refusal thus to love and serve him, there is an amount of ill-desert equally unbounded, because it must be measured just by the glory and worthiness of him whom I have disobeyed. So an adequate sacrifice must be one unmeasured in its value – one whose worth and efficacy no creature can fathom and eternity itself can never wholly disclose. 'Against thee, thee only, have I sinned.' What bleeding lamb upon thine altar shall truly put away my sin?

But let the sacrifice be divine, then just as deity gives unsearchable depth of ill-desert to sin, so unsearchable depth of well-deserving merit is given to the sacrifice. Let Godhead put on our flesh. Let God be found manifest in the flesh, in the form of a servant, and be obedient unto death, even the death of the cross. Let this be the priceless, the immeasurable sacrifice for sin, awaking the songs of angels and the echoes of all eternity to say 'Worthy is the Lamb that was slain.' Let my conscience of sin, immeasurable in its evil and its evil desert because it is against the glory and the rights of unsearchable Godhead, be confronted with a sacrifice immeasurable in its worth to the same unsearchable Godhead and the case is then truly met, the exact craving is wholly satisfied. The bed is not shorter than that a man can stretch himself upon it, the covering is not narrower than that a man can wrap himself in it. There is nothing left for the most sensitive, acute, enlightened conscience to desire. I take home such a sacrifice to my heart as answering all the extent of my case as I know it now, or can ever know it. I feel that however my conviction of sin may increase, as I see more and more into the greatness of the infinite God whom I have offended, so my confidence in the sacrifice must equally increase, for it is the sacrifice of the same God manifest in the flesh. I see in it a divine, illimitable, all-sufficiency; and I own that by the sacrifice of God manifest in the flesh I am made perfect 'as pertaining to the conscience.' By his one offering he hath perfected for ever them that are sanctified.

iii. The *oneness* of this offering has also to be considered. 'By *one* offering he hath perfected for ever them that are sanctified', even by 'the offering of the body of Jesus Christ once for all.' For Christ to offer himself oftentimes, yea a second time, were to confess a failure in his first offering and to acknowledge his intention of attempting now to remedy that failure, and achieve the end at last. It is a sacrilegious imagination, put forth, alas, only too glaringly in the popish doctrine of the mass. Christ's offering was one, and once. By the eternal Spirit he offered himself and so the efficacy was not transient but eternal. It was not transient, needing the act to be renewed, but eternal, leaving the act to be one, and once. As the fulness of the Godhead dwelt in him bodily, so when he offered himself the act was not partial but complete. Therefore, 'this man, after he had offered one sacrifice for sins for ever sat down on the right hand of God.' Yet the oneness of his priestly offering stands connected with priestly reward and glory now. The slain Lamb is of himself alone sufficient for all the ends of God's glory in the magnifying of his law and meeting all its demands and is now enthroned amidst the praises of the universe and the glory of his Father. His sacrifice, set in the central and most august place of glory in the universe, is seen to be a divine, heavenly, eternal thing. It was so even on earth when it was offered amidst earth's manifest characteristics of weakness, vanity and transience, yet not partaking of them. Even on earth it was a heavenly thing; even in human nature it was divine; even in time and in the instant of its offering, it was eternal. But it seemed earthly; it seemed human merely; it seemed temporal and transient. But away from earth's narrow limitations, and away from time's transience, now it is exalted as divine to heaven and to heaven's eternal throne. Manifestly now the one offering of Christ is heavenly, divine, eternal; and more than one such offering, offered once, there cannot be. As well might there be more Godheads than one; more true eternities than one. Its eternity, its divinity, its heavenliness, are all bound up with its oneness. He offered himself. He was the sacrifice; but he is heavenly, divine, eternal; heavenly, yet offered on earth; divine, yet in the human nature; eternal, yet transacted in time. All this is now disclosed in the enthronement of the Lamb that was slain and the oneness of his offering stands blended with it all.

By the oneness, therefore, of this offering – and the heavenly, divine, eternal perfection therein implied – he has perfected for ever them that are sanctified. It is irrevocable peace with God which he has thus established, eternal redemption he has thus procured. One everlasting covenant he hath thus sealed and made sure: an all-embracing pardon, an unchangeable acceptance, an inviolable adoption. By this one sacrifice he perfects you now; instates you in perfect friendship with God in perfect acceptance, perfect pardon, perfect peace. Whatever conscience of sin you now have, he perfectly and at once removes it the instant you believe on him.

But he not only perfects you now, he perfects you for ever. Though sin rises again and comes into the conscience as before, as it will do through your remaining corruption and infirmity, still, no new foundation has to be laid for your fresh forgiveness and your stable, steadfast peace. Christ by his one offering has perfected you for ever. His one offering subsists as a continual burnt offering, heavenly, divine, eternal – especially eternal, be it borne in mind – originally contemplating your case as an immortal being and a denizen of eternity, and effectually, once for all, rectifying it for ever. The sin that dwelleth in you still, and makes you in yourself guilty again and still a sinner, does not make void the sacrifice of Christ. The sacrifice of Christ makes *it* void. The one offering has perfect, perpetual power. And what is that power? It is the power of making your perpetual unworthiness because of sin void perpetually. For it is as if, while sin continually rises, the blood of Jesus Christ is on it continually to put it continually away. If in its oneness it were not present continually it would need repetition, and therefore must contain inefficacy. But it is one, perfect, eternal, all-sufficient. 'There is therefore now no condemnation to them which are in Christ Jesus.' 'Stand fast therefore in the liberty wherewith Christ hath made us free.' 'By one offering he hath perfected for ever them that are sanctified.'

Oh! how little we know of those just reasons, in all their glory, which prompt the blest doxology, 'Unto him that loved us, and washed us from our sins in his own blood, and hath made us kings and priests unto God and his Father; to him be glory and dominion for ever and ever. Amen.'

7

Free Indeed

'If the Son therefore shall make you free, ye shall be free indeed' (John 8:36).

Jesus had just charged his hearers by implication with being in a state of bondage, for he had prescribed to them a method by which they might attain to liberty. 'If ye continue in my word, then are ye my disciples indeed; and ye shall know the truth, and the truth shall make you free.' The parties thus addressed at once felt the accusation which such language involved, and, their pride being stung by it, replied with mingled haughtiness and asperity, 'We be Abraham's seed, and were never in bondage to any man: how sayest thou, Ye shall be made free?' In answer to this challenge to prove or point out their bondage, Jesus leads them from civil and political slavery to think of that which is moral and spiritual, and sets forth his own glorious prerogative to give deliverance from the bondage of sin. 'Verily, verily I say unto you, Whosoever committeth sin is the servant of sin. And the servant abideth not in the house for ever: but the Son abideth ever. If the Son therefore shall make you free, ye shall be free indeed.' Now it will tend to open up to us the meaning of our text if we consider, in the first place, the bondage from which Jesus delivers his people; and in the second place, the scheme of the procedure or work of the Son in

making them free, and, in so doing, the certainty, excellence and perfection of the liberty thus acquired as indicated in the emphasis of the expression, 'If the Son
therefore shall make you free, ye shall be free indeed.'

1. We are to consider the position from which Christ
vindicates and redeems his people. And the immediate
context supplies us with a description of this bondage. He
that 'committeth sin is the servant of sin. And the servant
abideth not in the house for ever.' These two things are
true of him that committeth sin: first, that he thereby
becomes the servant of sin, and second, that he becomes
liable to expulsion.

i. He that committeth sin is the servant of sin: he falls into
the service of sin and the bondage of corruption. And this
is true not only of those who more openly wear the livery
of Satan but of all whom the Son hath not made free. It is
not merely some of the more debasing sins which by use
and wont render him who lives in them their wretched
slave so that he strives in vain to break his fetters. Very
unmistakably indeed in such cases is the truth evidenced;
but it is one of universal application, and is this: that all
guilt entails bondage as its direct inevitable heritage. It is
impossible to step from the realm of innocence into that of
sin and then return at pleasure. He who crosses the
straight line of perfect righteousness and enters by one
hair's breadth into the domain of iniquity forfeits his
freedom thereby and sin becomes his master. He did not
mean this. He did not bargain for it. He meant merely to
make sin his servant, so that sin should minister to his
gratification. He meant to remain the master and to serve
himself of sin so far as he desired to do so, and beyond this
all should remain as before. But he is not the master and

sin his servant, but the reverse. He becomes the slave and sin the tyrant. 'Of whom a man is overcome, of the same is he brought in bondage.'

Why is this? Why is he enslaved from the moment of the entrance of sin? Rather, how could it be otherwise? Act as he may, now that he has sinned, how can he avoid continuing in sin, in the miserable bondage of corruption? Does he try to act as if nothing had happened? What! Offend the Almighty and think nothing of it? What power sin must have got, to hurry and drive him to such reckless violence. Or does he feel that the offence has to be accounted for, and does he listen to the only account that God will make of it – 'Cursed is everyone that continueth not in all things which are written in the book of the law to do them'? Does he find God the Righteous One cursing him for his transgression: giving him no hope, no mitigation of his doom? And can he love a God that curses him? Can he serve an angry God? Can he seek the presence and do the will of an omnipotent being, who professedly has nothing in store for him but avenging retribution? In what state must he be who has such a view of God? Must not the feelings which such a view of God begets be those of dread, dislike or rebellion? Must not sin have fixed its throne and reign in the heart of him who sees nothing for him in God but wrath and condemnation? That heart is enslaved to sin. The committing of sin leaves no alternative but prolonged, eternal bondage to sin, save as liberty is proclaimed by a Redeemer. The committing of sin, if it leaves the offender untroubled for his offence, proves him to be the besotted slave of sin already. If it fills him with terror, it fills him thereby with distrust, dislike of God. In entertaining such feelings towards his Maker he is seen in this also to be the slave of the evil to which he has yielded. Let the poor sinner act as he may, struggle or resolve as he may, he is a struggling or a willing captive, but in any case a captive. He may make terms with his tyrant to be free from sin in some forms, but to be free from sin in every form he seeks in vain. He is sold under sin. 'Know ye not, that to whom ye yield yourselves servants to obey, his servants ye are to whom ye obey; whether of sin unto death, or of obedience unto right-eousness?' To escape again into liberty is beyond the sinner's power. To fall back again upon the guileless love of innocence, the true supreme love to God, without which *all* is sin, to go forth into the light of true and honest and devoted love which is the kingdom of light – he that hath once committed sin cannot do this.

He is detained a prisoner in the evil kingdom whose territory he has entered. He may seem to have great free range within that kingdom, but he is confined to it. He can never leave it again until a stronger than he give him freedom. The curse of God's law forbids it, and beats him back if he would struggle to be free. Sin shall have dominion over him because he is under the law. And then as he realises this he comes to give up the struggle. Why should he continue it? It is of no use. His efforts are all made void. He comes to consent even to his bondage. He saith, 'There is no hope: no; for I have loved strangers, and after them will I go.' Could he only get rid of the guilt, he might shake off the power also of sin. But he is obnoxious to his Maker's wrath, he cannot see his face in peace; there is no cheering voice speaking to his inmost heart to kindle there the hope of deliverance; he is forsaken and alone in all that pertains to sin and the fruit of sin. There is absolutely none to help him. The Lord is angry and condemns. His own conscience condemns and terrifies and weakens him, and always does so more, the more it understands his true position. The law can give him no help in that it is weak through the flesh and only shuts him up under sin. He is punished for his sin by being made the slave of sin. 'Whosoever committeth sin is the servant of sin.'

ii. But a second feature of the state from which Jesus emancipates the sinner is a constant liability to be cast out and expelled for ever. And this follows from his being a servant. 'The servant abideth not in the house for ever.' He has no right, no title to the privileges of the house. Ishmael may dwell for a time in Abraham's family. Sinners may dwell for a time in the visible church, spared in pure patience, in mere longsuffering, but the curse is suspended over them still. They can plead no claim upon the Father – no title to a place among the children – and therefore they have no permanent abode in the family. Ah! If the Son has not made you free, you hold your present reprieves and temporary benefits by the most precarious and dangerous of tenures. You have, in fact, no tenure and no title at all. The servant abideth not for ever. The first messenger that comes may bring the message of expulsion. 'Cast out the bondwoman and her son: for the son of the bondwoman shall not be heir with the son of the freewoman.' The next visit the Father makes to his children may bring with it your instant warning to leave. The next special blessing designed for the household may require, before it can be carried into effect, that you should quit, be cast out. If your continuance should stand in the way of their benefit, blessing or enlargement, the children shall not be sacrificed so that the slave may retain what was never his. And so, if the Son hath never made you free, you may have to leave at a moment's warning. At midnight the cry may arise 'Behold, the bridegroom cometh', and the servant of sin shall be cast out into outer darkness. When he thinks for a moment that his abode is permanent and to be presumed upon, this may especially provoke the heavenly voice, 'Thou fool, this night thy soul shall be required of thee.' Or the least word or act whereby the slave may stumble one of the least of the children may awake the demand which Sarah made on behalf of Isaac, 'Cast out the bondwoman and her son.'

How bitterly this aggravates the bondage and infuses more deeply the poison of a servile spirit. The sinner often feels it in its plainest form in the fear of death. Through fear of death he is all his lifetime subject to bondage. A spirit of bondage unto fear takes possession of him when he thinks of his latter end. In every disease that threatens or every pain that seizes him he dreads a messenger come to cast him out. When he thinks of death he remembers that the servant abideth not in the house forever, for he has no plea, no title, no advocate. In one moment he may be cast out where there is weeping and wailing and gnashing of teeth. And, if not made free, the time will come when he must be cast out. He may be tolerated for a time but he cannot be forever. The tares may be left to grow among the wheat, lest in being prematurely torn up the wheat should be torn up also. The Father leaves the servant for a time among the sons, consulting for their good, their safety; but consulting for their good may require the casting out of the servant without a moment's delay, and will at last demand it. For what saith the Scripture? 'Cast out the bondwoman and her son.' Here then is the position from which Christ brings emancipation to his people. They are by nature in bondage to sin and by law exposed to instantaneous expulsion. Whether or not they are awake and alive to the misery of their condition, they are alike in a state of pitiable ruin. If they see and understand and feel their state, they struggle with

a giant too mighty for them. They must serve sin in some
form. In every act they do they are serving sin, serving sin
alone. Even when they seek to do that which is righteous,
their nature has an unholy dread of God and makes a
servile, selfish, insulting effort to buy a title to dwell
forever with the children in the house. Their righteousness is sin. They are in all things the servants of sin.
And their abode is terribly precarious; insecure as the life
of the moth, insecure as the vapour that appeareth for a
little time, and then vanisheth away.

2. Let us try to set forth the outlines of the scheme or
procedure whereby the Son makes servants free, at the
same time speaking of the excellence of the liberty which
Jesus thus communicates.

i. Jesus lays the foundation of his work of giving liberty in
redeeming from the curse. The curse is the real cause of
bondage and must be removed if freedom is to be restored.
It is in virtue of the curse that Satan possesses his usurped
dominion over the sinner. It is the curse which brings man
into bondage to corruption. It is the sore and unremovable
curse which fills his spirit with bitterness, or hurries him
to seek in earthly pleasure and its oblivion temporary
release from fear, or pours deceit into his heart and leads
him to try a thousand wiles whereby to break its force or
evade its application to himself. For if God's curse is lying
on you, then with the sole exception of the ever-glorious
scheme whereby the Son can make you free, there is no
way of dealing honestly and honourably with it but by
consenting to endure it. It is righteous. It is true. It is
strong in its truth and justice. Take any other view of it,
deal any otherwise with it and you are entangled in the
devil's lie concerning it, and falsehood evermore is

slavery. See the man who has committed himself to what is false. He is hurried on to add another lie to cloak the first. Again and again this wretched policy drags him deeper and deeper into falsehood. To keep consistency among his various lies racks his ingenuity and stifles all his moral sense, and the scheme of deceit which he has fabricated makes its very author its slave. Even so, admit the lie of Satan, deny the awfulness and horror and certainty of God's curse, become indifferent and unconcerned, and you are entangled in a web of falsehood that spreads through all your thoughts of God and sin and eternity. Or take Satan's lie concerning this curse in some other form, consider it arbitrary, cruel and unjust, and you are the victim of the malice and malignity which such a thought infuses into all your feelings. Or feel its greatness and admit its justice but attempt the schemes and devices which the sinner's ingenuity suggests for evading the curse: every one of these is another lie, enslaving and entangling the soul; filling it with more and more deceit; cherishing the servile, shrinking spirit which the conscious use of guileful expediency begets.

In every form whatever in which you do other than acknowledge the infinite rectitude of God in lodging his curse upon you, you sink into deeper bondage, which the conscience rivets, testifying, as it must ever do when at all enlightened, that your schemes are dishonourable towards God, that your spirit is insincere with the all-searching One; that you have no care for the glory of your Maker, and that your object is to make him lay aside his justice and induce him to break his word. Ah! There is no one that is under the curse but either lies down in his bondage, accepting it without a struggle, or maintains a warfare with that bondage in vain.

The foundation of Christ's emancipating work consists

in this, that he frees the struggling sinner from having to deal with that curse at all. 'Christ hath redeemed us from the curse of the law, being made a curse for us.' He was 'made under the law, to redeem them that were under the law.' He bears the curse himself. He reckons with and satisfies the sentence of condemnation which sin has merited. He stands forth as the Substitute of his people, to admit the justice, to bear the vengeance, to exhaust the woe of that curse with which in vain they struggled. He emancipates them at once from the temptation and necessity of every false and guileful thought or purpose or desire in reference to the curse. They need no more seek to be under the power and bondage of darkness, hiding themselves from God and hiding the truth of their case and prospects from themselves. They need no more be under the bondage of a servile spirit, seeking to purchase their discharge from the sentence which divine justice has pronounced. They need no more be under the bondage of that terror which arises from seeing in God nothing but an austere man and a hard task-master. They need be under no bondage to any lie which Satan may suggest. The circumstances which suggested that he might welcome or relieve them are altogether changed; and a foundation is laid for complete emancipation for the miserable bond slave of sin.

To this, however, must be added, though time forbids us to dwell upon it, the positive obedience which Christ rendered to the law. By an actual righteousness, as well as remission of sin, he brings in, on his people's behalf, an everlasting right or title to a permanent abode in the house. Thus, bearing the curse, he makes way for liberating the servant of sin; and, fulfilling the law, he makes way for bestowing a secure and pleadable tenure in the everlasting house of God.

ii. The twofold foundation being thus laid for emancipating the captive, proclamation is made of the new constitution or arrangement which this work of the Son has
introduced. The glorious gospel is set forth as the revelation of this liberty which Christ hath purchased, as
making free offer and tender to the servant of sin of the
redemption or emancipation which the Son of the Highest
has effected. The gospel call is a call to this liberty. 'Ye are
called unto liberty,' says the apostle. For this reason it is
designated the joyful sound, with allusion to the sounding
of the silver trumpet when the year of jubilee arrived. And
as surely as the echo of the jubilee trumpet carried the glad
announcement over all the land that the captives might
immediately go free, so surely does the gospel invitation
announce immediate deliverance to the captive and the
opening of the prison to them that are bound.

Its effectiveness in doing this consists in its being
presented in the form of a promise, absolutely and in every
respect free, unlimited by any reservation, unimpeded by
any condition whatsoever. Yes, the power of the promise
to make you free lies in the fact that it is free itself. A free
promise makes the children of that promise free. Ishmael
was not of promise. He was of Hagar, the bondwoman.
Isaac was the child of promise, the son of the lawful wife.
And these things are an allegory. For these are the two
covenants, the one from Mount Sinai which gendereth to
bondage, which is Hagar. The children begotten under
that covenant are in bondage as Hagar was. But the
covenant from Mount Calvary is a covenant of redemption, of emancipation, and answereth to Sarah whose child
was by the promise of God, the promise that was absolute,
mighty, self-fulfilling. He that was of the bondwoman was
born after the flesh, but he of the free woman was by
promise. Therefore was he free himself, the free-born son

who abode securely in the house. 'Now', says the apostle addressing the believer, 'we, brethren, as Isaac was, are the children of the promise . . . Stand fast therefore in the liberty wherewith Christ hath made us free.' The free promise is the instrument of bestowing freedom. Without merit and without purchase price, it gives interest in that new arrangement by which the curse is exhausted and done away in Christ. Calling for no worth and no work to entitle to this interest but gratuitously giving it to the condemned, it frees the soul from every slavish fear, from every servile device, from every lie of Satan, from every guileful thought, from every mental reservation, from all that is not frank and free and as in the light before the Lord. Yes, the promise of forgiveness and righteousness in Christ the accepted Substitute, when seen, known and embraced as the free sure word of God's unfettered grace, liberates the son from all bondage and brings the poor sinner whom it fills with joy into the light and liberty of the children of God.

But how shall it be seen in its freeness and fulness of grace? Who shall give the sinner's heart the power to understand and appreciate the truth which maketh free? How shall we know the things that are freely given us of God? The answer to this completes the scheme of Christ's work in bestowing liberty on the servant of sin. 'Where the Spirit of the Lord is, there is liberty.' We are actually liberated by the renewing of the Holy Ghost which is shed on us abundantly through Jesus Christ our Saviour, that, being justified by his grace, we should be made heirs according to the hope of eternal life. 'For ye have not received the spirit of bondage again to fear,' says the apostle, 'but the Spirit of adoption, whereby we cry, Abba, Father.' 'God hath not given us the spirit of fear; but of power, and of love, and of a sound mind.' It is he

who is the immediate agent in giving the liberty wherewith Christ makes his people free.

He comes as a convincing Spirit, certifying the slave of
his bondage, causing him to feel it and to long and look out
for deliverance. He enlightens him in the knowledge of
Christ as the Saviour of the lost; the Redeemer of the
bound. He renews his heart to receive the testimony of the
gospel in its free invitation to forgiveness and full sure
promise of justifying grace. And, accomplishing by the
promise the bestowment of blessing of which it testifies,
he makes a people willing in the day of his power, gives
liberty to the will that was perverted and bound by sin
before, and conveys the blessedness of those who know
the joyful sound. They are enabled by the blood and the
Word and the Spirit of Christ to go forth from the pit of
darkness and the pit of corruption. Observe, brethren,
how Jesus does all his work on the souls of his people by
his Word and Spirit. It is the Son that makes them free,
yet we read in a prior verse, 'Ye shall know the truth, and
the truth shall make you free.' Again this emancipation is
attributed neither to the Son, nor to his truth or Word or
promise, but to his Spirit. 'Where the Spirit of the Lord is,
there is liberty.' Now all this just implies that the Son is
the Author of this liberty, that the Spirit is his
Ambassador in the church giving the actual possession of
this glorious privilege, and that the truth is the instrument, the letters patent of emancipation, by means of
which the free Spirit of Jesus operates his glorious com-
mission. Christ the Author, the Spirit the Agent, the truth
the means, this is the scheme of spiritual liberty. And all
three, the Son, the Spirit and the proclamation of the
Word are all beautifully combined in one announcement
which Jesus himself has made, 'The Spirit of the Lord is
upon me, because he hath anointed me to preach the

gospel to the poor; he hath sent me to heal the brokenhearted, to preach deliverance to the captives . . . to set at liberty them that are bruised.'

∾ 8 ∾

Precept, Promise, and Prayer: An Illustration of the Harmony between Divine Sovereignty and Human Agency

'Make you a new heart and a new spirit' (Ezek. *18.31*).
'A new heart also will I give you, and a new spirit will I put within you' (Ezek. 36:26).
'Create in me a clean heart, O God; and renew a right spirit within me' (Psa. 51:10).

It is proposed in the following discourse to enquire into the relations which subsist among these three verses, with the view of exhibiting the helplessness and responsibility of man in connection with the sovereignty and grace of God in the matter of the new heart (and indeed in salvation generally); if by the blessing of the Divine Spirit, we may lead you to despair of man, with whom 'this is impossible', and with mingled anxiety and hopefulness to have recourse to him with whom 'all things are possible' (*Matt.* 19:26) – 'even God, who quickeneth the dead, and calleth those things which be not as though they were' (*Rom.* 4:17).

That these texts are closely related to each other must be obvious even on the most cursory examination. The same expressions occur in each of them, and they all clearly point to one and the same subject of momentous interest.

Further attention, however, will show that, while the subject is the same in *all*, it is presented in a different light in *each*. In all, the one unvaried topic of regeneration is placed before us; but in passing from one to another the point of view from which we look upon it is changed. In the first, it is presented to us embodied in a command, 'Make you a new heart and a new spirit.' In the second, it is embodied in an offer, 'A new heart also will I give you, and a new spirit will I put within you.' In the third, it is embodied in a supplication, 'Create in me a clean heart, O God; and renew a right spirit within me.' The first comes from God the Lawgiver; the second comes from God the Redeemer; the third comes from man the suppliant. The first is the loud and authoritative voice of Majesty; the second is the still small voice of Mercy; the third is the humble, earnest voice of Entreaty. In the first, God presents his authority and demands his right; in the second, God presents his mercy, and makes offer of his gift; in the third, man presents to God his own offer again, and pleads for its fulfilment. The first is an utterance from the throne of justice; the second is an utterance from the throne of grace; the third is an utterance from its footstool. The first is a precept; the second is a promise; the third is a prayer.

A true veneration for the Word of the living God will at once deliver us from the sin and folly of looking on this as a random combination, the product of mere chance, and will dispose us to behold in it an exhibition of divine wisdom, and the result of a divine arrangement, fraught, we may well believe, with much practical instruction, and calculated to give comprehensive and satisfactory views of certain vital truths 'once delivered to the saints'. It is not with the materials of a curious speculation, savouring more of ingenuity than utility, that we are furnished in these verses, and in the threefold light which they cast upon the self-same subject. On the contrary, they are replete with principles which pervade the Word of God, and the life of God in the soul – principles which are the only real key to the harmony of divine truth, written both in Scripture and 'in fleshy tables of the heart'. And it may deepen this impression on our minds if we consider that the three verses chosen as the subject of illustration are not the only three in Holy Scripture so related to each other, but an instance only of a general rule – a specimen merely of a very frequent arrangement. It might be shown by a large enumeration of cases that every duty incumbent upon us, as the sinful creatures of the Most High, may be regarded in the same threefold aspect: *first*, as enjoined in a command to performance; *secondly*, as involved in a proffer of help; and *thirdly*, as acknowledged in a supplication for help. Let the following suffice.

Is it our duty to seek a knowledge of God – an acquaintance with his name, his character, his nature? Assuredly, for 'this is life eternal' (*John* 17:3), and thus only shall we 'be at peace'. Then the command is, 'Acquaint now thyself with him' (*Job* 22:21); the promise is, 'I will give them a heart to know me' (*Jer.* 24:7); and the appropriate prayer is that of the Psalmist, 'Give me understanding according to thy word' (*Psa.* 119:169). If following his example, 'thou criest after knowledge, and liftest up thy voice for understanding . . . then shalt thou understand the fear of the LORD, and find the knowledge of God' (*Prov.* 2:3, 5). Again, the duty of saving faith, so often neglected *in the character of a duty*, is presented to us in Scripture under the same threefold aspect. It is matter of precept, 'This is his commandment, that we should believe on the name of his Son Jesus Christ' (*1 John* 3:23); it is matter of promise also, 'By grace are ye saved through faith; and that not of yourselves, it is the gift of God' (*Eph.* 2:8); the gift of God, promised 'in the behalf of Christ', and bestowed in answer to the intercession of the priest, now upon his throne – 'I have prayed for thee, that thy faith fail not' (*Phil.* 1:29; *Luke* 22:32); and it is matter of daily supplication with all saints, 'Lord, I believe; help thou mine unbelief' (*Mark* 9:24). Another very interesting illustration of this principle, and one in which we do not need to bring the texts from different portions of the Word, is found in the sixth chapter of the Gospel of John, where Jesus is speaking of himself as the true manna, the bread of life which cometh down from heaven. In the midst of this discourse, he lays the following injunction on his disciples, Labour 'for that meat which endureth unto everlasting life' (verse 27) – an injunction which he immediately follows up with the precious corresponding promise, 'which the Son of man shall give unto you'; and, rightly exercised under the teaching of their Lord, the apostles hasten to offer up to him the appropriate prayer, 'Lord, evermore give us this bread' (verse 34). And not to multiply further instances, let it be borne in mind that not even the duty of prayer itself is exempt from this principle of triple relation. We have a commandment to 'pray without ceasing' (*1 Thess.* 5:17); but we have a promise too, 'Likewise the Spirit also helpeth our infirmities: for we know not what we should pray for as we ought: but the Spirit itself', even 'the Spirit of grace and supplications', 'maketh intercession for us with groanings which cannot be uttered' (*Rom.* 8:26; *Zech.* 12:10); and the special prayer applicable in these circumstances we learn from the example of the apostles, 'Lord, teach us to pray' (*Luke* 11:1).

In short, the Word of God is full of this important and beautiful arrangement. You will always find a promise adapted to the precept, and a prayer grounded on and appropriate to them both.

Our intention, then, is to lead you to contemplate somewhat of the wisdom of God in this arrangement, to enquire into the practical spiritual purposes which it subserves, in the hands of the Divine Spirit, in awakening the soul and leading it to God, making good that paradox of grace which engrafts the most joyous hopefulness upon the convicted sinner's abject helplessness – the gracious Creator's strength being perfected in the guilty creature's weakness. In other words, let us examine the divine economy of precept, promise and prayer, when brought powerfully into contact with the anxious and enquiring soul.

1. And, *first*, as to the Precept. What place does it hold in this arrangement? What is its office? What good practical purposes does it serve?

'Make you a new heart and a new spirit.' At first sight this command may appear to be worse than useless. Does it not enjoin a thorough impossibility? The practical and the possible seem to be utterly put to flight. 'Can the Ethiopian change his skin, or the leopard his spots?' (*Jer.* 13:23). 'Who can bring a clean thing out of an unclean? Not one' (*Job* 14:4). 'In me (that is, in my flesh) dwelleth no good thing' (*Rom.* 7:18). But surely the power to make a new heart and a new spirit is a good thing – one of the best of things, the most wonderful, the most glorious, the most holy. It belongs not to me. I am 'dead in trespasses and sins' (*Eph.* 2:1). I have as little power to make a new heart as I had to create my living soul at first. My present heart can be of no use to me in this matter, for it is 'deceitful above all things, and desperately wicked.' I cannot even 'know it' (*Jer.* 17:9). The law of God can be of no use to me, for it cannot accomplish this holy achievement, in that it is 'weak through the flesh' (*Rom.* 8:3), my fleshly heart being enmity against it, not subject to it, neither indeed can it be (*Rom.* 8:7). The assistance of my neighbour can avail me nothing, for he cannot redeem himself, and as little can he 'by any means redeem his brother . . . For the redemption of their soul is precious, and it ceaseth for ever' (*Psa.* 49:7-8). And, oh! surely this command is but a mockery of my helplessness? Is not this a cruel triumphing over my inability? What tendency can this have to remove the evil? Surely there is no step taken here to give a practical movement to my helpless soul.

Yes, there is. Your very meditations prove it. For

i. This command has evidently *made you conscious of your helplessness*, and I call that a practical movement, a very practical movement – an invaluable result – and the indispensable prerequisite to all others. Would your thoughts ever have been directed towards your helplessness at all, but for such commands as this? Would you ever have imagined your heart so wicked, so carnal, so polluted, so abominable as it is? Would you ever have imagined it such that it cannot be mended or improved at all, but must be altogether removed and replaced, but for this injunction, 'Make you a *new* heart'? Would you ever have imagined that you had wandered so far from God, but for the loud voice in the distance behind you crying, 'Return, return'? Would you ever have known how thoroughly your soul is paralysed in spiritual death but for the command, 'Arise from the dead'? (*Eph.* 5:14). Would you ever have known how completely your senses are all sealed in spiritual sleep but for the authoritative voice of God? And even that, as you can testify, is only like a dying echo, through your dream, crying, 'Awake, awake, thou that sleepest.' Say not that the precept is useless. If you have been aroused to earnest thought at all, the precept has already done you good service. If your meditations on this impracticable commandment – this 'hard saying' – are at all honest and heartfelt, they are abundant testimony to the practical worth and working of the precept on your soul. It has led you to think of your helplessness. You have one invaluable lesson already. Follow on, for 'to those that have shall be given.' 'Thank God and take courage.' For,

ii. This is not all that the precept can do for you. It will not only lead you to think of your weakness and helplessness, but it will tend to *show you how complete and thorough your impotency is, and to deepen the sense of this upon your soul.* For it will not do to have merely some vague and general idea of your inability; you must have a deep and pervading spiritual conviction of this truth. It must not be a matter of hearsay, but of actual experiment and experience. I can conceive a sick man confined to his couch, murmuring and fretting over the injunction of his physician which prevents him from rising and walking through his chamber. He feels that he is indeed weak, but he knows not how much disease has debilitated his shattered frame. He thinks it a hard restriction to be deprived of the liberty of trying his strength. If nothing else will convince him, let him get the proof of experience. Let permission be given him to walk across his chamber, and as in the attempt he falls helpless into the arms of the friendly physician whose wisdom he doubted and whose advice he despised, he will at last acknowledge how thoroughly his strength has been prostrated. This is not to be supposed an accurate illustration in all points, for the natural man does not possess even those wretched remnants of strength which the case imagined involves. Paralysis and

[120]

even death itself are the favourite images of Scripture. Yet what I wish you to observe is that in the sinner's spiritual experience the command 'Make you a new heart' holds a place and serves a purpose exactly similar to the permission given to the sick man to try the measure of his bodily powers. You may have some dim notions of your helplessness. But bring it to the test of experiment. This precept gives you the opportunity, nay, lays you under the obligation to do so. Go and try to make yourself a new heart. Labour to regenerate your own soul. 'Whatsoever thy hand findeth to do, do it with thy might.' And then tell your success. Break off every old habit, if you can. Give up every outward act of sin. Mortify the deeds of the body. But have you changed your heart? Have you given it new dispositions, new desires, new delights? In short, after labour the most painstaking, the most strenuous, the most unintermitting, have you succeeded in yielding obedience to this commandment? Have you 'made you a new heart and a new spirit'? No. But you have proved experimentally that it is wholly beyond your power. By the precept you have been taught experimentally what you but dimly surmised before, even your thorough, unmitigated, and hopeless helplessness. You had heard of that helplessness 'by the hearing of the ear'; but now your whole soul feeleth it. You have now a far more deep and pervading and pressing conviction of this humbling truth; for the spiritual precept, and your efforts to obey it, have proved to you conclusively, because experimentally, that you are wholly 'carnal, sold under sin' (*Rom.* 7:14). Is not this another practical movement? 'I had not known sin, but by the law' (*Rom.* 7:7). I had not felt my helplessness but by the precept.

iii. But the precept can do you more service. It can originate another and perhaps a still more important practical movement. It may have already taught you how thoroughly helpless you are by nature. But that is not enough. Besides evoking the testimony of experience and consciousness, the precept *has power to touch the springs of conscience*; and without this it would indeed be utterly ineffective.

Let me commend the truth to your conscience in the sight of God, who searcheth the heart. With what *moral* feelings do you regard this thorough helplessness? Is it not the case that you regard it, or are at least continually tempted to regard it, more in the light of a melancholy misfortune which makes you very much to be pitied than as a heinous crime which makes you very much to be condemned? Is it not the case that you look upon yourselves chiefly as sufferers in this matter, and scarcely, if at all, as malefactors? Do you not think that your case calls more for sympathy than for blame – that you should rather be soothed than threatened? We remind you that this is very often the cast and current of your meditations. Because you cannot obey this command, you therefore imagine you are not responsible for disobeying it – because you are thoroughly helpless, therefore you imagine you are as excusable. And thus the deceitful heart, ever tender to its own sores and plausible in its own defence, contrives to shake itself clear of the irksome feeling of obligation to keep the impracticable commandment. In such circumstances it is strange with what wretched sophistry conscience will submit to be baffled and silenced and with what contradictory excuses its remonstrances are put away; so much so, that out of his own mouth the sinner may be condemned. 'If we were only in more favourable circumstances, we might and would obey this precept; but as matters stand, with the whole head sick and the whole heart faint, with nothing in us but "wounds, and bruises, and putrifying sores", surely we cannot be expected to come up to the high standard which this commandment sets before us.' Now, in giving vent to such meditations as these (and it is to be feared they are not uncommon) do you really consider what you say? *If you were in more favourable circumstances, you would obey this precept.* What do you mean by *more favourable circumstances?* Your circumstances, spiritually considered, must be such that you have within you either the old heart or the new. No possible condition can be imagined between these two; and what, therefore, does this promise, so potent in silencing the conscience, ending all debate, and putting all anxiety to flight, what does it amount to but simply this, that if you had the new heart already, you would then 'make you a new heart and a new spirit' – you would do the work after it had been fully accomplished? Truly, if by such a proffer conscience were momentarily silenced, the deceitful heart ought in its turn to be thoroughly ashamed; and if these are its wretched delusions, it is surely high time it were for ever got rid of and replaced.

Do you still suggest that your helplessness sets you free from blame and responsibility? If you have any reverence for the Word of God, the precept ought at once to cure you of such perverse imaginings. For here you have the Lawgiver himself giving forth his deliverance on your case, and his utterance is in the form of a *command*. It is not an utterance of pity, or of sympathy, or of lamentation, over your prostrate impotency. The Lord does not say, at least *here* he does not say, 'Oh, that you were able to make you a new heart and a new spirit'. On the other hand, this is an utterance of authority. It is an unhesitating and peremptory injunction from the God who rules in righteousness. You may have begun perversely to imagine that your helplessness had removed you from under his authority and beyond the limits of his government. But it is not so. He is still the God with whom you have to do; with whom you have to do, not as sufferers merely, but as subjects still; and, in testimony thereof, listen to the voice of his *commandment*, 'Make you a new heart and a new spirit.' He comes to deal with you, not as *sufferers* whose *disease may* issue in death as its *result*, but as *rebels* whose *crime must* issue in death as its *doom*. He comes to tell you that you have not got beyond his dominions – that still he is your lawgiver and your judge. Could he be a judge at all, if rebellion carried you beyond his right and his power of judging? Could he be a lawgiver at all, if entitled to legislate only for the righteous? Nay; 'the law is not made for a righteous man', but for exactly such as you, 'for the lawless' (*1 Tim.* 1:9), for all those who, like you, are seeking freedom from the obligation of this very law, which commands you to 'make a new heart and a new spirit'. Surely, then, it is miserable affectation for a guilty sinner to sorrow over his helplessness as a misfortune, and then to think that all that can be expected of him is discharged, and he is responsible for nothing more. Let him learn rather to tremble over this helplessness as a crime, the very fountain-head and cause of all crimes.

Is this demand said to be unreasonable? This might be pleaded if there could be two opinions as to the source of our inability to obey, but not if it springs from our perverse and irrepressible and willing habit of doing evil – not if we are incapable of making a new heart because our natural hearts have not only shown symptoms of enmity to God but are very enmity itself. Is it possible for any one to affirm that the very depth of our iniquity and the uniformity of our criminal habits must set us free from the charge of all crime? Is it possible that the consciences of men can be so perverted and debauched? No: not so long as they are found 'the mean while accusing or else excusing one another' (*Rom.* 2:15). Suppose it possible for some man, some monster in human form, to acquire the habit of murder, so that he could not refrain from assassinating every victim that crossed his path – that by habit, and a monstrous love for blood, he had become utterly incapable of obeying the commandment, 'Thou shalt not kill' – would any one tell me that this man's inability to obey excused him from the penalty of disobeying? Would not the doom of death be sealed upon this human fiend, amidst the loud execrations of outraged humanity? And is the case any different, or less urgent, when the just and righteous King of Glory sits in judgment? Shall his high and righteous bar be degraded by the admission of a plea which would be scouted as insane at a human tribunal? Shall the very strength of the grasp which the law has over the rebellious heart be pleaded as a reason why the lawgiver should abdicate his throne, and denude himself of all his claims? Nay, verily: not to obey is itself a crime – not to be able to obey is a second, riveting and fastening the first as with iron. Rather it is a habit of crime plunging the soul in a sea of guilt.

Thus, then, the office of the precept is most vital and important. It first of all informs the sinner that all is not well, and points to the seat of the disease. Then it leads him experimentally to a knowledge of his miserable condition, his thorough helplessness and inability to save himself. And lastly, it presses on his conscience a deep feeling of his responsibility and criminality. Thus he learns much of himself, and he learns much of the God with whom he has to do. He is taught to feel his own weakness and worthlessness. He is taught, also, God's authority and power. He is led to see his thorough subjection to the heavenly Majesty, and his no less thorough incapacity to do the duties of a subject. You may have been 'alive without the law once', but when the precept comes in spiritual power, sin revives and you die (*Rom.* 7:9). You die to all pride, and peace, and hope. You learn two solemn truths, which, when taken together, give you no rest till they mercifully shut you up to the only remedy. You know your helplessness; but you cannot sit down contented, for you know also your obligation and responsibility. You know your obligation; but you do not become legalists, for you know also your helplessness. You feel that you cannot obey; but this does not set all at rest, because you feel that you must obey. You feel that you must obey; but neither does this settle all, for you also feel that you cannot. It is 'as if a man did flee from a lion, and a bear met him' (*Amos* 5:19). 'Fear, and the pit, and the snare, are upon thee, O inhabitant of the earth. And it shall come to pass, that he that fleeth from the noise of the fear shall fall into the pit, and he that cometh up out of the midst of the pit shall be taken in the snare' (*Isa.* 24:17, 18). In neither can you remain. You struggle from the pit of helplessness, because you feel you are bound over to obedience. You avoid the snare of legalism, because you know you cannot render the obedience required. Oh! what a source of unspeakable spiritual agony is there here! And so must it still remain, while the 'inhabitant of the earth' looks not beyond the earth for deliverance. But look up, and lift up the head, O wearied sinner, look away from thyself; long enough has that poor self of thine agonized thee – truly thou wilt find no help there. Look up 'unto the hills, from whence cometh thy help'; and then, baffled with thy weak and helpless attempts to 'make thee a new heart and a new spirit', and prostrated, too, with the thought that it must be done, turn now from the terrible precept and listen, 'Be still and know that he is God.' Thus saith the Lord, 'A new heart also will I give thee, and a new spirit will I put within thee.'

2. We come, then, to the consideration of the Promise.

i. And, *in the first place*, it is obvious that the *wisdom* of God is wonderfully exhibited in bringing in the promise at this precise point. If it had come sooner, the soul would not have been prepared to receive it. If it had come later, the soul would have been already given over to hopeless despair. The promise cannot go before the precept, for then the soul would not feel the need of it, and consequently its value would not be appreciated; and the promise cannot come after the prayer, for then prayer would have no foundation on which to ground her supplication. But the Lord, who knoweth the spirits which he hath made, and who 'needed not that any should testify of man: for he knew what was in man' (*John* 2:25), sees the end of a spiritual conflict from the beginning, and all the parts thereof in their order; and he comes in with his separate dealings at the proper time, and at the proper point. Thus, when the precept has done the preparatory work in righteous authority, the promise begins to reign on the throne of meekness and of mercy. The precept, like affliction, may not have seemed joyous, but rather grievous; nevertheless it hath wrought the humbling 'fruit of righteousness', preparatory to the gifts of mercy, in 'them which are (rightly) exercised thereby' (*Heb.* 12:11).

The reign of the precept, if we look not beyond it – if we regard it as an end – may have been a reign of terror. Viewed, however, as a means, as the prerequisite merely

to the 'better things to be revealed', it has indeed been the
reign of grace begun, although the grace as yet has been
concealed. But now 'the better things themselves' are
brought to us by the promise. If the precept could have
brought these things, 'if that first covenant had', in this
respect, 'been faultless, then should no place have been
sought for the second', no room for the promise. But
because the precept has a tantalizing 'shadow' only 'of the
good things to come, and not the very image of these
things', because it can never 'make the comers thereunto
perfect' – because 'the law can make nothing perfect' –
therefore 'there is verily a disannulling of the commandment going before, for the weakness and unprofit-
ableness thereof', to make way for 'the bringing in of a
better hope' – 'he taketh away the first that he may
establish the second'; and what the precept 'cannot do, in
that it is weak through the flesh, God' through his own
Son can do, by the 'promise, which in him is yea and
Amen' (*Heb.* 7:18–19; 8:6–13; 10:1–9; *Rom.* 8:3). Is the
precept then useless? No, by no means. Is it then against
the promises of God? God forbid; for if there had
been a precept 'given which could have given life, verily
righteousness' and a new heart 'should have been by'
that precept. 'Wherefore then serveth the' precept? 'It
was added because of transgressions', and nature's
helplessness, 'till the seed should come to whom the
promise was made.' And its indispensable and blessed,
though painful, work is this that it 'hath concluded all
under sin' and helplessness, and proved this in their own
experience and to their own consciences, 'that the promise
by faith of Jesus Christ might be given to them that
believe. But before' the promise 'came we were kept
under the' precept, 'shut up unto the' promise 'which
should afterwards be revealed. Wherefore the' precept

'was our schoolmaster, to bring us to' the promise and to him who is 'the surety of a covenant established upon better promises', 'that we might be justified by faith' (*Gal.* 3:19–24).

Thus there is the economy of a Mosaic dispensation, carried on preparatory to that of a Christian dispensation, in God's dealings with every regenerated soul, as truly and really as in the history of the collective church. This preparation in the church was not more necessary than it is in the individual heart; and just as there was a divine wisdom seen in emancipating the church from the 'tutors and governors' at 'the time appointed of the Father', when 'he sent forth his Son', so there is a 'fulness of the time' in the history of every believing sinner when God sends forth the promised Spirit of his Son into the heart, as faithfully as he sent forth his Son into the world, emancipating the despairing soul as fully in the one case from the grievous bondage of the precept, as he freed his people in the other from those beggarly elements, and from that 'yoke of bondage which neither they nor their fathers were able to bear'. In the days of Moses, the church was not ready for the simplicity, the liberty, the manliness, and the spirituality of the Christian dispensation. And so, at the opening of the soul's spiritual discipline, by reason of its childish ignorance and wayward pride, God introduces first a dispensation of precept; and when this has accomplished the work whereunto he sent it, at the proper point and time, he brings in his dispensation of promise. 'This also cometh forth from the LORD of hosts, which is wonderful in counsel, and excellent in working.'

ii. How is the *grace* of God adored by the fainting soul when, after the conflict with the precept, the promise comes brightly into view. The *wisdom* of God is seen in the promise, coming in at the very time when it was needed. But the grace of God is glorified in bringing in the very gift which was needed. 'Make thee a new heart and a new spirit', says the precept. 'Ah,' replies the sinner, 'that is not in my power. I am carnal, sold under sin, "dead in trespasses and sins". I cannot frame my heart otherwise than it hath been formed by iniquity. I am as an unclean thing, and all my righteousnesses are as filthy rags. I do fade as a leaf, and my iniquities, like the wind, have taken me away (*Isa.* 64:6). A deceived heart hath turned me aside, that I cannot deliver my soul' (*Isa.* 44:20). In this helpless state is it a partial promise that is given? Is it a greater earnestness to try the work ourselves, that God offers to communicate? Does he promise to help us out with the laborious achievement, if we will arise and put our hand to the work ourselves? Does he engage to fill up or supplement our deficiencies? Does he offer to overlook our failures, if only our attempt shall be sincere? Oh no! These may be the doctrines of a wretched Arminianism. These may be the desires of a half-humbled soul. But they are not the promises of God. These would be boons of little value; they would tend to no practical result, no saving issue. There would indeed be mockery in promises like these; for the very condition on which such offers are supposed to be made never could be realised in us till the whole work were done. But the very thing that we cannot make for ourselves, God promises unconditionally to bestow, freely to bestow, without condition, without money, and without price. The precept, having done its painful work, seems, as it were, to be recalled, and, while the form is annulled but the whole substance retained, it once more returns in the form and the language of peace and hope and joy. Like the same law given to Moses a second time, not amidst thunderings and lightnings and darkness, and tempest, but amidst light and peace and favour, all God's goodness passing by before his servant, sheltered now in the cleft of the rock; so here, the preceptive form, which caused the tempest and the terror in the soul, being all done away, the very same substance, in all its integrity, is restored, but now beaming in the light and lustre of a free and a gracious promise, 'A new heart will I give unto you, a new spirit will I put within you'. It is the very thing required, without restriction and without abatement, offered freely and without condition, without money and without price.

iii. But the *grace* of God is still more wonderfully glorified by the consideration, that, while this is the very thing which we need, and which God offers to bestow upon us, it is also the very thing which we are bound to render unto him. And here again the good fruits of the precept as the forerunner of the promise come clearly into view. The precept teaches that we need this, for it teaches us experimentally our want and our helplessness. But when it teaches our responsibility, our obligation to make us a new heart and a right spirit, our crime and our guilt in not doing so, then we see, not the depth of wretchedness and misery merely, but the essence of rebellion in our inability. Oh! when the responsibility is really felt, as well as the helplessness, how does the manifold grace of God grow before the view of the admiring soul! If I feel that I would be better if I had a new heart, and, at the same time, feel my utter incapacity to make me a new heart and a right spirit, how gracious is the great God to come and offer me the very thing I need – the very thing that I cannot do without! But when, besides this, I feel my deep and unchangeable responsibility to make this new heart which yet I cannot make – when I feel my criminality in delaying every moment to do it, and my criminality in being unable to do it at all, either now or at any future time, oh! how shall I speak then of that grace which pities both my weakness and my guilt, and delivers me most fully from the death-bringing consequences of both? It is much when he looks upon me in my *low* estate, but it is more when he looks upon me in my *lost* estate. It is great grace when he, 'in due time', pities me as a weak and helpless sufferer, 'yet without strength' (*Rom.* 5:6); but it is greater far when he pities me as a daring rebel, a sinner, an enemy (verses 8–10). Grace abounded when, sympathizingly, he gave me that new heart which I was unable to make; but grace much more abounded when, forgivingly, he gave me that new heart which I was bound to make, and was guilty for my inability to make. 'Bless the LORD, O my soul . . . who *healeth* all thy *diseases*' as well as *'forgiveth* all thine *iniquities'* (*Psa.* 103:2–3).

iv. And now the *sovereignty* of divine grace can be obscured or concealed no longer. This also the believer is taught to feel and to acknowledge by reason of his previous discipline under the precept. In learning his obligation and responsibility, he at the same time necessarily learned the majesty and kingly authority of God. We have seen that the precept teaches not only the soul's utter helplessness, but also the soul's entire subjection to the righteous justice of the lawgiver. We are made to feel completely in God's power. We are exposed to his righteous anger, and incapable of effecting our deliverance from threatened wrath. The Lord maintains his right to command, though we have lost our power to obey. Whatever impotency we are groaning under, he is seen to reign as king. He has the destinies of all souls at his own free, unchallenged disposal. He is the Sovereign God:

righteous in forsaking all if he will – righteous in pouring out wrath unto the uttermost. What an overpowering dignity is seen in his sovereign majesty, his uncontrollable right and power! How exalted above all created excellence! How full of uncreated, all-governing glory – a glory terrible indeed, if no grace is mingled with it! But if this high Sovereign shall give his gracious promise, then how resplendent is his *sovereign* grace! If he who is the God of all majesty, and excellency, and dignity, and sovereign glory – if he who ruleth among the armies above and the inhabitants of this earth below, free and uncontrolled in all his ways, and in all his purposes – if he who is the sovereign disposer of ten thousand times ten thousand angels, and who is sovereign over *me*, as his precept and commandment do fully prove – if he who as such a sovereign hath the fullest right to execute on me wrath even to the uttermost – if he shall single out and distinguish me from among the mass of helpless, dying, daring rebels, and, glorying in his words, shall cry in my astonished and delighted ear, 'I, even I, am he that blotteth out thy transgressions for mine own sake', and, as 'I am that I am', 'a new heart will I give unto thee, and a new spirit will I put within thee' – oh! how shall my grateful but too straitened soul ever realise, or comprehend with all saints this mystery of sovereign grace, all made mine in the free and gracious promise of a sovereign God! Wondrous and adorable sovereignty of my God! I quarrel with it no more – I hail it with rejoicing. The Lord is my Sovereign; 'the Lord is our Lawgiver; the Lord is our King'; as such 'he will save us' (*Isa.* 33:22). None can deny his right. Who shall condemn when the Sovereign God hath justified (*Rom.* 8:33)? None can resist his power. Who shall stay his hand from working? Who shall say unto him what doest thou? How powerful, how

authoritative is the grace of this holy Judge – the
Sovereign King of Zion!

Behold then, O my soul, how God, by giving thee his
precept first prepares thee for his promise – opens thine
eyes to behold his wisdom, enables thee to see his grace,
his multitude of tender mercies, begets in thee a deep
sense of his righteous authority, which, when the promise
comes, is transferred with all its sovereign majesty to that
redeeming love which then excels in glory and shines forth
in dignity and splendour. Thus the creature is abased and
the sovereign God is exalted, and no flesh can glory in his
presence. Thus there is glory to God in the highest, and
grace to men. The grace is compassed with sovereign
glory, and the glory is full of sovereign grace. 'O Lord, we
beseech thee, shew us thy glory!' Fulfil to us thy gracious
promise! 'Create in me a clean heart, O God, and renew a
right spirit within me.'

3. We have already made use of the Prayer. Indeed we are
brought almost insensibly to the third and last link of this
beautiful chain – the last line of this threefold cord.

And now the office which prayer performs in this divine
and spiritual economy will be obvious to all. It ap-
propriately comes last because it is grounded on and takes
its warrant from the promise, pleading fulfilment that
thereby the object of the precept may be gained. The
prayer, when offered, grows out of the promise; the
prayer, when answered, satisfies the precept. The precept
teaches man that he is helpless; the promise tells him there
is help; the prayer secures the help. The precept teaches
man that he is responsible and guilty; the promise tells
him there is forgiveness; the prayer obtains the pardon.
The precept teaches man God's authority; the promise
tells of God's grace; the prayer tries and tests God's

sufficiency. The precept teaches man his dependence; the promise declares dependence in God to be well placed; the prayer puts dependence in God accordingly. The precept teaches man humility; the promise gives man hope; the prayer shows man's trust. The precept gives scope for God's righteous justice; the promise gives scope for God's faithfulness; the prayer gives scope for man's faith. In all cases, the prayer is necessary to complete the cycle; and, if the precept and the promise do but graciously exercise the soul, the prayer will and cannot but follow. He who listens to the precept and feels his need, his helplessness, his responsibility, his crime, and then listens to the promise, counting him faithful who hath promised, 'who also will do it', that man will and must have recourse to the prayer. He is shut up to prayer by every principle in his nature, by his sin and misery, by reason and conscience, by fear and hope. He must pray. He cannot help it. He is carried captive to prayer by a blessed necessity, a willing and therefore victorious and joyful necessity.

To the prayerless, therefore, there is here very clear and simple ground for self-examination and self-condemnation. Dear brethren, matters must stand thus with you; you have received aright neither the precept nor the promise of your God; for they always bring the prayer along with them. No man can put asunder what God hath joined; and therefore if you are living in the habitual neglect of earnest prayer, it must be because you have listened proudly to the precept, faithlessly to the promise. You are quarrelling with the precept, and denying your helplessness; and herein you falsify the Word of God, your own experience, and the experience of all the saints and the spirits of just men made perfect. Or you are denying your responsibility and God's authority, casting his cords away from you and saying, 'Who is the LORD, that I should obey his voice?' Or you are quarrelling with the promise; either condemning his wisdom by counting his promise worthless, or condemning his faithfulness by insinuating that his truth will fail. One or other of these fearful alternatives you must choose, if you are not habitually plying the throne of grace with prayer; and perhaps the guilt of all these crimes together is cleaving to your consciences. Oh, how unprovoked and how God-provoking must be the sin of prayerless lives! Only think how beautifully God has prepared the way for prayer. How much wisdom has he lavished upon this gracious arrangement! How safely and how gently has he contrived to carry you step by step to his throne of grace! The precept tells you that you must obey. Even God himself cannot release you from that. It is a painful lesson; yet is it not well to know it, while hope yet remains, that it may become a practical lesson? It is mercy in God to speak out ere all hope is gone. The precept tells you of your helplessness and convinces you of this experimentally when you attempt to obey it, and find that you cannot 'make a new heart and a new spirit'. Surely it is good to know this truth also. Your ignorance of it would not make it less true, and your knowledge of it will at least turn you away from a fruitless source of labour, and should make you willing to try a 'more excellent way' if it can be shown you. And that this can be done you need not doubt; for the promise now comes in to show that all may yet infallibly be well, pledging immutable things to your full deliverance and your eternal safety. 'What could have been done more to my vineyard, that I have not done in it?' (*Isa.* 5:4). Will you turn it all into contempt? Nay, rather, I should say, will you yourselves become a contempt and a hissing to all passers-by, through indolence, or pride, or unbelief, or any other miserable habit of your wretched hearts, the very presence of which should only add wings to your haste, and fervour to your prayer? What! shall God do so much for miserable guilty rebels, and will you do nothing, absolutely nothing, for yourselves? Will you not even arise and call upon your God for mercy? How *can* we persuade you? What arguments remain wherewith to ply you? To the authoritative voice of the taskmaster, and the pleasant voice of the charmer, ye are alike deaf. Ye are like sullen 'children in the market-place'. By the precept we 'have mourned unto you and ye have not lamented'; by the promise we 'have piped unto you and ye have not danced'. One word more, and may the Lord bless it to your souls. Your guilt is now tremendous, because your case is now made so hopeful; and your case is thus hopeful because you have so little to do. Yea, you have only to plead with God to do *all* the work for you. Will you cast away eternal joy and court eternal agony by refusing *that?*

How calculated are these imperfect meditations to encourage the hearts of those who are Israelites indeed, princes with God, in prayer! Let the precept, and the promise, and the prayer, be alike precious to you, and have your souls disciplined by a due attention to them all. Never think you can obey the precept in your own strength. Never think that your interest in the promise sets you free from the authority of the precept. Never think that prayer can supersede either the precept or the promise. Prayer is presumption except when grounded on the promise. Prayer is hypocrisy except with a view to the obedience of the precept. In all thy ways, diligently search for the pure precepts of thy God, crying evermore, 'Lord, what wilt thou have me to do?' Fear not for thy weakness to know thy duty, though it should be thine in divine command to remove mountains, 'Who art thou, O great mountain? before Zerubbabel thou shalt become a plain:

and he shall bring forth the headstone thereof with shoutings, crying, Grace, grace, unto it' (*Zech.* 4:7). His 'grace is sufficient for thee' (*2 Cor.* 12:9). His promise is, that 'as thy days, so shall thy strength be' (*Deut.* 33:25). But 'I will yet for this be enquired of by the house of Israel, to do it for them' (*Ezek.* 36:37). Therefore, let thy duty, and thy weakness, and the cheering promise, send thee to the throne, for 'grace to help in time of need' (*Heb.* 4:16). 'Put him in remembrance' (*Isa.* 43:26), saying, 'Remember the word unto thy servant, upon which thou hast caused me to hope' (*Psa.* 119:49). Then 'Fear not, thou worm Jacob . . . thou shalt thresh the mountains, and beat them small' (*Isa.* 41:14–15).

∽ 9 ∾

The Plague of the Heart

'Which shall know every man the plague of his own heart' *(*1 Kings 8:38*)*.

Sin is here called a plague. It is a very awful and alarming designation: a plague, a pestilential disease, a pestilence! 'The city of the plague' is an expression that fills the mind with pictures of deepest horror. The heart of man is here virtually called 'the city of the plague'. The king of Israel, in communion with God at the dedication of the temple, had been speaking of literal pestilence and he is led thereby to think of the far worse, the spiritual pestilence in man's depraved nature. 'If there be in the land famine, if there be pestilence, blasting, mildew, locust, or if there be caterpillar; if their enemy besiege them in the land of their cities; whatsoever plague, whatsoever sickness there be; what prayer and supplication soever be made by any man, or by all thy people Israel, which shall know every man the plague of his own heart, and spread forth his hands toward this house: then hear thou in heaven thy dwelling place.'

Sin in general is a disease, a pestilential disease; and the Saviour is called a physician – 'They that be whole need not a physician, but they that are sick.' 'Is there no balm in Gilead; is there no physician there?' But this pestilence, raging as it does in the whole human family, assumes different forms and symptoms in different persons. Hence the text speaks not of every man having a general acquaintance with the symptoms of this disease common in all cases, but of every man knowing the plague of his own heart. This plague assumes a special form or becomes a special plague in each man's case. It is the heart which is the seat of the disorder. Radical, organic heart complaints are peculiarly alarming, inveterate and dangerous. They are with great difficulty reached by the physician and his healing art. They are frequently declared incurable, and nothing more than mere alleviation is possible. Hence it is a very solemnizing thing when we are called upon to recognise each of us spiritually the plague of our own heart.

In dependence on the divine blessing I would speak of some of these plagues, of the difficulty of knowing them, of the danger of not knowing them, of the means of knowing them, and finally of the cures.

1. I would speak of some of these plagues. They are very various, and each individual man has to make himself acquainted with the plague of his own heart. For the great all pervading plague of spiritual depravity – enmity to God – assumes different forms in different men according to their different constitutions, bodily or mental, according to their education or upbringing, their position in society, their various callings, their companionships, their former habits and the vast variety of their influences. The consideration of these diversifying influences would lead us into endless and inexhaustible particulars. It is only certain leading features of the plague that can be pointed out.

One very common plague of the heart is *covetousness*, frequently indicated in Scripture and very specially condemned. It is a great mistake to fancy that this is a vice of the heart peculiar to the wealthy. It rages often among the poorer classes of society with a destructive violence not seen among the rich. It is a very direct offshoot from the great leading plague of ungodliness – alienation from God and dislike of communion with him. The godly man rests on the promise, the providence, the power and faithfulness of a reconciled Father. 'Bread shall be given him; his waters shall be sure.' He seeks first the kingdom of God and he knows that all other things shall be added to him. His citizenship and treasure are in heaven, and much store of earthly good he little covets. His future through all the unending ages he has reposed into the gracious hand and keeping of him who sent his own Son to save him when he was lost, and the brief future of a few uncertain years on earth he reposes in the same faithful keeping of his God. Social and commercial calamities therefore may give him a fair and rational anxiety, but they cannot overwhelm his equanimity, nor drive out his soul from her home of trust and peace. Ungodliness on the other hand tends very directly to lead a man to desire so much of this world's good as he thinks may keep him safe, and keep his mind at ease, without a lively trust in God as the source of his peace. He puts his worldly possessions, be they great or small, in the room of God. Hence covetousness is in Scripture, more than any other sin, directly condemned as idolatry.

Another plague, somewhat similar but yet distinct is *over-burdening care* about worldly things and the duties of our callings. Diligence in business is never condemned by the Word of God, nor inconsistent with the true spirit of Christianity, very much the reverse. The Fourth Commandment is 'Remember the sabbath day, to keep it holy. Six days shalt thou labour, and do all thy work.' The grand description of a true Christian serving his generation and glorifying God in his local calling is given by the apostle in the celebrated words, 'Not slothful in business; fervent in spirit; serving the Lord.' Worldly duties and difficulties are to be faced in the spirit of thoughtfulness, vigilance and energy. And anything like inferiority or imbecility in a Christian in his calling is not creditable to his profession nor fitted to commend his religion. That a man should be more weak and less wise in the discharge of ordinary daily duties because he is a child of God is dishonouring to his Father in heaven, and a stain upon the glory of his adoption. But it is too certain and too frequently exhibited that even Christian men do not bring their religious principles – the principles and the power of their communion with God – to bear upon the regulation of their minds and hearts in worldly duties. They do not carry these duties sufficiently into the sphere of their duty to God and their fellowship with him. They do not adequately commit them in prayer to the divine blessing; they do not aright seek from him the wisdom and serenity of mind for discharging them in peace and with effect, and very specially they do not leave the care and burden of them on the Lord at the right point, but continue frequently to lie under the pressure of them themselves after they might safely, and ought dutifully, to leave them on him.

If you in your worldly cares and difficulties seek wisdom from God who giveth liberally, and in that wisdom discharge just the responsibility that lies upon you, having acted for the best, ought there not immediately to ensue a quiet trusting of the result unto the Lord? But alas! is there not too often an utter want of quietness, with no rest until the issue is seen? As if the issues were in our own hands, as if we were the ultimate disposers of results, as if the whole responsibility of God's providence were lying on our shoulders and crushing us down into the dust! Who among us displays the tranquillity of spirit and the strength of character such exhortations as the following are fitted to confer: 'Commit thy way unto the LORD; trust also in him; and he shall bring it to pass.' 'In all thy ways acknowledge him and he shall direct thy paths.' 'Sufficient unto the day is the evil thereof.' 'Rest in the LORD, and wait patiently for him: fret not thyself in any wise to do evil.' Alas! how much unnecessary soul-weakening care even Christian men burden themselves with from not believing and trusting in the good hand of God for the issue of their labours. While positive duties still remain to be done, an anxious sense of responsibility is not to be condemned, and a light and thoughtless tone of mind concerning them is to be abhorred. But here is the grievous evil. When the necessary action has been taken and when the issue is now gone from our own hands and is afloat upon the scheme of God's own providence and management, we still are burdened, weighed down, full of a thousand thoughts and cares, exactly as might be natural enough if we with our poor faculties and wisdom had the final overruling of all things in our own hands. It is as if every passenger on board a ship were to fancy himself charged with all the care and anxiety of the governor of the vessel who, with a very small helm, turneth the ship whithersoever *he* listeth. How little is there of the Christian faith and wisdom which, in matters of responsibility and care, can say, 'I have now done the part allotted to me and the issue I now quietly leave with the Lord.' But where this is not practised, what obedience can be rendered to the divine command, 'Be careful for nothing; but in everything by prayer and supplication with thanksgiving let your requests be made known unto God'? Or what realisation can there be of the promise that is conjoined, 'And the peace of God, which passeth all understanding, shall keep your hearts and minds through Christ Jesus'? Yet our very plague of earthly care disfigures and weakens the Christian character of those who disobey this injunction so reasonable, and defraud themselves of this promise so precious.

Another heart plague – alas too common – is that of *vain thoughts*. These defile the soul as with the plague of leprosy. 'Wash thine heart from wickedness . . . how long shall thy vain thoughts lodge within thee?' The hearts of men are full of thoughts. Thoughts flow from the heart as sparks from a fiercely blown furnace, as rays from the mid-day sun. The mind of man is a thinking principle. The exercise of its faculty of thinking is inseparably bound up with its existence. A vast proportion of its incessant flow of thoughts is altogether vain and useless. Multitudes do not see any sin in this. They can spend hours in useless empty vain thinking and yet never take themselves to task as if they had done anything blameworthy. An immortal being created for glorifying God, endowed with a soul which in its capacities is more precious and wonderful than all the starry heavens with their countless hosts of worlds, can expend itself in revolving the most frivolous, useless and unprofitable imaginations, such as fancying oneself possessed with wealth and devising how to spend it, or fancying oneself in positions in which one will never be placed and devising how to act in these situations. It were in fact a waste of time and an exemplifying of the very evil which is now condemned were we to attempt to set forth the countless imaginations of utter vanity which are allowed to course their uncontrolled career through the chambers of the minds of men. But I am sure that there is not a single person present who, on reflecting on the manner in which when alone he mentally spends his time, is not conscious that a spiritual chart of his thoughts could not be spread out for his fellow men without large portions of it being such as to cover him with ridicule and shame in the eyes of his neighbours. This is a sore plague of many a man's heart. It is a feature of the heart which no true Christian can be ignorant of or can fail frequently to be pained with and to deplore. The multitude, the variety, the ceaselessness, the impertinence, the incessant interference, the pertinacity, the force of these vain thoughts are all most distressing to the believer. The continual invasion that they make on his most sacred hours and holy duties. The unblushing return and fresh presentation of themselves after being rebutted and resisted; the strange power they have of withstanding all exposure of their shameful uselessness and of continuing to solicit our regard and entertainment of them; the length to which the mind can go in prosecuting them when they once have engaged us in the foolish, profitless chase: these and many other deplorable features or results of them make them to every Christian a hateful plague; make his life by reason of them a greater burden than many bodily diseases could make it. Some have much greater determination than others in fighting against, overcoming and keeping in check these hateful birds of prey, but the best are humbled by them perpetually, and filled with shame in the sole reflection that they do not provide for Christ a better temple than a heart so frequently invaded and defiled with what to an infinitely wise God must be so unspeakably abominable.

Another heart plague is the *great difficulty of maintaining a spiritual savour in the mind of those divine things which the soul really loves.* How hard does the Christian find it to cherish a sweet and sanctifying sense of his privileges in Christ. He may have learned to glory in the righteousness of Christ, have chosen Christ as the pearl of great price and the portion of his soul, delight in the liberty wherewith Christ makes his people free, and love to contemplate and prove with gratitude and wonder the access to God which Jesus has obtained for believing sinners by his blood-shedding and priesthood. He may have often said in sincerest joy, gratitude and admiration, 'Behold, what manner of love the Father hath bestowed upon us, that we should be called the sons of God.' And he may have experienced the heavenly blessedness of placing himself at the disposal of a reconciled Father. And yet, sincerely desiring that these experiences may absolutely mould his character and rule his heart continually, he finds that heart bent on a perpetual backsliding and greatly averse to the spirituality of always living in the love of things divine. As for the command, 'If ye then be risen with Christ, seek those things which are above, where Christ sitteth on the right hand of God. Set your affections on things above, not on things on the earth. For ye are dead, and your life is hid with Christ in God' – how painfully difficult is it to be rendering habitual obedience to it! Carnality of mind comes continually into conflict with it. The soul cleaveth to the dust. Heavenly-mindedness and holy meditation are not to be maintained without a continual effort, as of one who is rowing against the stream and stemming the current; and spiritual indolence and sloth too often give over that effort, and the things that are upon the earth obtain the mastery.

Take these as a few specimens of heart plagues: covetousness or inordinate love of the world, carefulness and inordinate anxiety about worldly duties, vain thoughts, and carnality of mind. And how many subordinate forms may these plagues assume: pride, envy, indolence, self-seeking. Ah! who shall reckon up the plagues to which men's hearts lie open and exposed?

2. But it is time to consider the difficulty of knowing and ascertaining each man the plague of his own heart. This difficulty arises from several causes. Thus, in the first place, it arises from the fact that *the plague of the heart has affected the very faculty by which its presence can alone be detected.* It is the eye that detects or perceives colours; but if the eye be colour-blind the man may go on for years making continual blunders in the matter of colour and not knowing it. A system of painstaking comparison and reasoning will be needed, and he must draw upon the testimony of others and compare it with his own perceptions and frame certain rules for his future guidance before he can trust his own experience. It is precisely the same with the eye of the soul. Its perceptions are deteriorated and deranged by the very plague which it ought to be able to detect. Instead of being able to pronounce by instant and immediate intuition, it will fatally err unless it adopts a system of comparison and defers to external testimony. There must be comparison with the law of God, and deference paid to the testimony of God. Nay, the eye of the soul must itself be put under a remedial process before it can appreciate even the very standard of judgment, or put a just construction on the divine testimony itself. For while the colour-blind may in soundness of reason conduct the necessary system of comparison and intelligently weigh the testimony of other observers – the spiritual eye and the spiritual reason are identical and the plague has exerted a universally deteriorating influence over all the inner man. Hence, there is a way that is right in a man's own eyes, though the end thereof be death. The grey hairs of spiritual declension and unbelief may be upon a man yet he knoweth it not. The powers of perception are themselves damaged.

Then *the blinding influence of self-love* is proverbial. A

due self-respect is becoming in the Christian. A child of God is bound to have a certain respect for his own person; and by that self-respect is kept instinctively aware of an unbecoming element in many things, which for that reason alone he ought to eschew. A man justified by faith and living on terms of friendship with God, adopted into his family and having access to his throne and presence, renewed in the whole man after the image of God, and cherishing the hope of being for ever with God, ought to cherish also a certain self-respect, justified by such divine declarations to him as this, 'Since thou wast precious in my sight, thou hast been honourable.' But this holy and humble self-respect is utterly removed from self-love and self-complacency. It is in fact built upon the ruins of these spiritual vices. And where these vices have not been mortified and overthrown self-esteem will always be found to exercise a blinding influence, hiding from the knowledge of the soul its own character and leaving it ignorantly a prey to the plague that is in the heart. Self-esteem in such a case cannot be maintained except at the expense of hiding from view the real humbling evils that rank in the soul. And hence the painful spectacle so often seen of a man actually fostering and inflaming as a praiseworthy feature in his character what others of quicker moral and spiritual perception see to be his foible – his spot – his plague.

Then also *the singular deceitfulness of sin* is to be taken into view in accounting for the difficulty of knowing the plagues of the heart. Against this, Scripture frequently and very solemnly warns us. 'Exhort one another daily . . . lest any of you be hardened through the deceitfulness of sin.' And the deceivableness of unrighteousness is spoken of as exerting a dreadful influence on them that perish. It were a long and laborious work to speak of the various methods by which sin deceives the sinner. But consider how plausibly does it represent itself in false colours; so that the covetous man appears in his own eyes to be merely prudent and cautious, sloth puts itself forward as claiming merely what is due to reasonable relaxation, worldly-mindedness shields itself beneath the obligations of a lawful calling, uncharitable suspiciousness passes itself off as powerful penetration, and moral blindness as the charity that thinketh no evil; while reckless passion calls itself righteous indignation, and conformity to the world pretends to be merely softening down the asperities which religion should not present to others and conciliating the regards of them that are without.

3. But thirdly, if the difficulties of discovering the plague be great, the dangers of not discovering it are as great. A plague is infectious and so are heart plagues. They spread. They spread to others and contaminate them. No man liveth to himself and no man dieth to himself. Insensibly but inevitably we influence one another. We do so when we know it not ourselves. We do so when it is not known by those we influence. Our manifestations of character are regulated by the state of heart-health or disease within. And he who knoweth not the plague of his own heart knoweth not the sore, injurious spiritual influence which issues forth from him incessantly upon his fellow men. There may be those who in keen spiritual sensibilities and careful self-discipline are habitually so walking in all vigilance as to guard themselves against the infection. But the vast majority are not so: and the evil – the plague – that a Christian carries with him is peculiarly damaging, in as much as he is the object of a confidence that tends to disarm watchfulness. Meantime, the plague spreads, both

among others, and deeper into the man's own heart and nature. Its tendency is to gain strength by continuance, to advance by stealth upon the very fountains and springs of character, and to gain possession of them. Hence a man under a predominant lust or heart plague is weakened in every Christian grace, and declines in every Christian duty. Many a believer thus fades and withers, brings no honour on his profession, does no good service among his brethren, faints through disinclination for duty, sinks beneath trial and the cross, wearies in well-doing, becomes heartless and remiss in prayer – the great feeder of the Christian life – and all through the unnoted reign of some spiritual plague. Regarding iniquity in their hearts, their prayers are not heard. The new creature within them, if they are indeed Christians and therefore born again, languishes and pines, the evidence that they are born again is clouded and in abeyance, spiritual comforts are unattainable, for the Spirit, the Comforter, is grieved; and, in the absence of his protection and invigorating grace, enemies find the soul an easy prey. For the Christian heart is besieged by enemies. It is fearful when a besieged, beleaguered city becomes the city of the plague. The efforts of the garrison are paralysed, and the efforts of the foe are redoubled, animated by fresh hope and fresh malignity. Oh! what Christian would not tremble to have his heart in this dangerous estate!

4. Let us then in the fourth place consider the method and means of becoming acquainted with the plague of our own heart.

And first of all, this cannot be attained if we have not *a just sense of the great general plague of sin.* Unless we know the exceeding sinfulness of sin as sin, as rebellion, opposition, enmity to God, we cannot know or adequately appreciate the special forms or symptoms that this great evil takes on in our own case. Sin is opposition to the will of God, contrariety to the nature of God; and he who sees not in this an evil greater than he can express, and which he is lost in shame and wonder in contemplating as radically fixed in his own nature, is assuredly ignorant of the particular plague of his own heart. Full half the cause and reason of unwatchfulness, imbecility, backwardness and backslidings among believers will be found in their ceasing to entertain solemnizing views of sin. All sin is enmity to the holy and blessed God, and what can be more alarming than to have in the heart a rooted element, a living, powerful root and principle of enmity to God? The carnal mind – the flesh – is 'enmity against God: for it is not subject to the law of God, neither indeed can be.' Whatever form sin puts on, in whatever direction this baneful tree, from its root upwards, branches forth, to whatever side the streams of this pestilential, polluting fountain flow forth, the quality remains unchanged, the horrible feature of enmity to God abides continually. It is a deep insight into this enmity to God, the very essence of what the Scripture calls the flesh, which renders the believer an enemy, a sworn enemy, to the flesh, and all its lusts and all its plagues. The moral disease is one, unchangeable in its essence, and wherever it is, in any form, in any position, in any of its symptoms or actings, there it is rebelling, resisting, opposing the good and holy will and government of God. No man will know the plague of his own heart who knows not this and is not duly affected, humbled and alarmed by the knowledge of it. This is a disease which makes its patient a criminal under the terrible charge of treason and rebellion and enmity against God. For every manifestation of this disease which is in his moral nature, he is responsible and blameworthy.

God is entitled to prosecute his quarrel with him down even to the lowest hell. Everything short of eternal perdition is divine patience and mercy. The fact that it may not break forth into glaring and embodied and announced rebellion is not to be pleaded in extenuation except to the insult of God's omniscience and his heart-searching prerogative. He is the Father, the Sovereign Lord, of the spirits of all flesh. He made the heart for himself. He is entitled to claim it as his own property, his own dwelling place and temple. He has so claimed it, and taken up his dwelling in it, in the case of all who have repented and believed the gospel. And they above all others are criminal and blameworthy when they defile the temple of God by plagues and lusts, all whose essential nature and operations are exerted in hostility to God, and put forth for the purpose of expelling him from his own house by making it uninhabitable for his holiness and glory.

It is a deep persuasion of this which must lie at the foundation of our seeking to obtain a knowledge of our own heart-plagues. Nothing short of this will lead us to do other than trifle with this momentous matter. Nothing short of this will engage us to the work with that moral earnestness without which our failure is sure before we begin.

But if we are impressed with a deep sense of the vileness of all sin in the sight of God, with a true grief and hatred of it, then we may undertake the work of *examining our own hearts to detect their respective plagues* with some hope of success. Let us then bring our spiritual state to the test of Scripture characters. Let us compare ourselves with the saints of God, as we find their hearts opened to us by the light of God's Word. And let no man say that this is setting up a superhuman and unnecessarily high standard of spiritual character. Were Abraham and David and Paul more holy than they, and consequently we, are bound to be? Had they exceeded the standard of righteousness which was set before them? Did they ever count themselves other than unprofitable servants? Did they go beyond what was needful in giving an example to others? And can we be safe, can we be sincere, if we exempt ourselves from the duty of being followers of them as they were followers of God? There is a powerful delusion on the minds of many Bible-reading men, to the effect that it is not expected of them to aim at the marvellous moral excellence to which these Scripture saints attained. Alas! the idea wherever it prevails is itself a plague in the heart. It is a pestilential notion, under whose influence all spiritual good, all grace, must inevitably faint and wither. Is this the recompense due to God for favouring us with a record of the experience, the attainments, the religious character of his friends? When he has set forth the good fight of faith in its many aspects, as conducted by men of like passions with ourselves, in every variety of circumstance, in every stage of progress, in order that we might never be at a loss for a precedent or example, in order that we might always see the footsteps of the flock marked before us in the path of our weary pilgrimage as we escape from the city of destruction – the city of the plague – and make our way to the new Jerusalem, is it a grateful, is it a reasonable, is it a becoming reception to the divine kindness thus exhibited to turn round and coolly decline their example? Remember that this is the example of those who continually lamented that, with all their fidelity and vigilance, still they were but unprofitable servants, and still the law in their members carried them captive to the law of sin and death. The good that they would, even with all their attainments, still they reached not nor accomp-

lished. Ah! if such an imagination ever flit across our
minds as that we can release ourselves from the obligation
of being as holy and spiritual and watchful unto prayer as
they were, let us bear in mind that there is an even higher
pattern set before us than they, the Son of God himself,
manifested in the flesh, always about his Father's
business, counting it his meat and drink to do the will
of his Father, always doing those things that pleased
him, pleasing not himself, instant in season and out of
season, going about doing good. Far from pitching our
point of attainment lower than what was by Scripture
saints attained, the call is, 'Be ye holy, for I am holy.' Be
in the world as Christ was in it. All short of this is
sin – blameworthy disobedience to the will of God,
blameworthy and offensive contrariety to the nature of
God. If we mentally rise against this standard of re-
quirement, can we have any difficulty in detecting in that
very feeling the great plague of our inveterate depravity.
And if we bring our hearts to the test, What would Christ
have done? How would Christ have felt in my circumstances – may not each man distinguish the plague
that is specific to his own individual heart? It is the law of
God which is the great discoverer of heart plagues, but
that law was embodied in the life and character of Christ
with a perfect fulness and a marvellous precision of application. It is actual circumstance and duty that renders it,
as seen in Christ, peculiarly valuable and serviceable as a
standard by which to measure ourselves and to discover
the evil that afflicts and spiritually disgraces us. Whosoever then would know the plague of his own heart, let him
study the revelations of Christ's heart as these are given in
the history of his life and the delineation of his character in
the gospel. And seeing that our spiritual blindness is so
great, let us offer the prayer, 'Search me, O God, and

know my heart: try me, and know my thoughts: and see if there be any wicked way in me, and lead me in the way everlasting.'

5. Finally, let me speak briefly of the cure of heart plagues. The discovery of heart plagues may be effected by examining the life and character of Christ. The cure of them will be found in his death. It is the death of Christ alone that has virtue in it to heal our plagues, to mortify and slay our lusts. All your resolutions, all your wise plans of surmounting and expelling your plagues, will never succeed unless you bring them continually to the cross of Christ. You must have believing communion with a crucified Saviour if you are to mortify the deeds of the body, to crucify the flesh with its affections and lusts. Without this you may change one for another, but you will never aright mortify or vanquish any. Christ gave himself for us that he might redeem us from all iniquity. There is a secret virtue in his blood, received by faith alone, which powerfully wastes the energy of every plague and sinful habit. Our old man is crucified with him, that the body of sin might be destroyed, that henceforth we should not serve sin. Engrafted into his death we become dead to sin, and sin reigns not in our mortal bodies, that we should obey it in the lusts thereof. Whatever heart plague you have discovered, bring it to the cross of Christ. Despite all deceitful efforts it may make to escape the fiery ordeal, compel it to face and confront the cross of Christ. Tie it down to be dealt with in the light and under the power of the sacrifice and death of Christ. And if the Holy Ghost has indeed enabled you to come to the cross and look there for healing, as the Israelites stung with the flying fiery serpents looked, and if he enables you there to hold up your plagues to that searching holy light of dying love and

dreadful expiation, you will find that under it they wither into the powerlessness of shame, and you arise to the energy of holy hatred against them. While nailing them to that cross by faith, in new-born loathing of the evil they do to the love of Jesus, you will feel that, in washing your heart from their pollution in the fountain that flows from the wounds of him who was crucified for these hated sins, you rise to renew your warfare against them as one refreshed with wine. Bearing about in the body the dying of the Lord Jesus, the life also of Jesus will be made manifest in your mortal body.

∾ 10 ∾

Heart Plagues Cured

'Which shall know every man the plague of his own heart' (1 Kings 8:38).

On a former occasion we considered the subject of heart plagues, specifying certain of them, such as covetousness, over-carefulness, vain thoughts and carnality of mind generally, pointing out also the difficulty of knowing them, the danger of not knowing them, the method of ascertaining them, and the cure. On the last of these topics there was room for little more than a few brief observations. But it is manifestly the point of the greatest practical importance, in the light of which alone the others are really valuable. We propose therefore to return to it now, and to point out how these plagues may be cured.

1. In the first place, it is essential that you should *cherish a deep sense of the evil of these plagues.* A predominant and powerful heart plague carries in it a vast amount of varied evil. It indicates evil, it invokes evil, it spreads and perpetuates evil. And if you are zealously and per-severingly to seek a cure you must foster a lively sense of the evil from which a cure alone can deliver you. Let it be therefore an express exercise of mind to meditate on the varied evil that your heart plague carries with it. And what material of painful reflection will thus be brought before

you! A heart plague, in so far as it prevails, makes you unlike God. To that extent it defaces, mars and rejects his blessed image. It counteracts and transgresses the law of God. It thwarts the design of Christ's work which is to redeem you from all iniquity and purify you wholly unto God. But to thwart the end for which a loving divine Saviour died, what ingratitude must this involve, what heartlessness and base indifference to his wishes and his will! A heart plague uncured grieves the Spirit of God, weakens you in your communion with God, hinders you in prayer, makes you averse from God's holy fellowship, and hides the light of his countenance from you. It hinders you also in your work, to which you address yourself with the conscious weakness of a sick man and with a lethargy which promises no valuable result, withholds from you all encouragement, and tends also to confirm and strengthen and perpetuate itself. It leaves you open to Satan, for every heart plague is just a weak point at which Satan has you at advantage, a handle by which Satan can hold you and use you in his service. I need scarcely say that a heart plague must inevitably interfere with and intercept your consolations, for it will indispose you for that spirituality of mind to which alone spiritual comfort can address itself and commend itself, while it will at the same time cloud your evidences of adoption and conceal from you your title to the consolations and privileges of the children of God. Moreover, if you are in any measure enlightened and awake, you cannot but be kept in perpetual bondage and terror by the apprehension of this plague breaking out in terrible external manifestations, this heart evil manifesting itself in your character and conversation, which it is con- tinually tending to do unless kept down and crucified and cured, even as, for instance, Peter's heart sin of vain self- confidence broke out in treachery and falsehood and denial of the Lord.

Finally, of every heart plague, if we would see the full evil involved in it, we must remember its continual and urgent tendency to infect the whole soul, and possess itself of the entire man, on the principle that a little leaven leaveneth the whole lump. It must be so. You cannot have a heart plague uncured and uncorrected in one corner or chamber of the soul, and all the others free and healthful. For strictly there are neither corners nor chambers in the soul at all. It is not as a house in which may be many compartments. It is not as the body which has many members. The soul is one. It is a living unity. A plague in it anywhere pervades it. It is all darkened, diseased, enfeebled, polluted, when any polluting and enfeebling principle acts within it. It is not some fragment of you that is rendered weak, or guilty, or helpless or unclean, but you. It is you – your entire self – whom the plague affects. You will be what a heart plague uncured will make you. I say, cherish a deep sense of the evil which is involved in heart plagues. If you would be delivered from them, if you would keep up a lively desire and effort to be delivered from them, be not dead to the deadly evil which they carry in them. They must be cured else you never can embody, in your own soul, the law and image and character of God. You never can realise the design of Christ's work, nor avoid thwarting the object for which he died, and grieving the Spirit whom by his death he obtained for you. You will go on weak and growing weaker in communion with God, and weak and even weaker in the work of God. You will lie exposed and a prey to Satan, with little evidence of your adoption and still less comfortable feeling of its privileges. You must subsist under the constant and too-well-grounded apprehension of your heart sin bursting out in some eruption of flagrant iniquity, and, even though it be not so, you cannot stay the operation of the sure law by which a little leaven leaveneth the whole lump and by which even one sin indulged will transform you wholly into its likeness and move you entirely in its service.

Let the consideration of evils such as these keep up in your mind an anxious desire to have your heart plagues cured, whatever they may be, for without this there is no prospect of their being cured at all.

2. Be persuaded that no heart plague can be cured unless you *take your position decidedly within the covenant of grace* and act upon its constitution and arrangements. If your heart plague is to be cured, or your besetting sin mortified, it is absolutely indispensable, it is the great and indispensable preliminary, that you should be under the covenant of grace and observe its order and provisions.

For the covenant of works can afford you no help or encouragement whatever. On the contrary there is nothing more adverse to this work, nothing more replete with power to hinder and prevent the cure of heart plagues. It condemns you under the guilt of sin, the curse of the law and the wrath of God. And it follows up this sentence of condemnation by shutting you up as a prisoner, concluding you under sin – a prisoner of hope indeed so long as the gospel is preached to you, but a hope set before you only in the gospel, and that new covenant which it reveals and proclaims. The law – the covenant of works – gives you no promise and holds out no prospect of help or grace. It requires an absolutely perfect spotless obedience, a pure, spotless, unplagued, undiseased heart, and does so under an awful penalty if its demand is refused, offering no help whatever to enable you to meet that demand. It leaves you cut off from the divine blessing, shut out from divine help, a prey to Satan. When he finds you in this forlorn estate, the covenant of works makes no attempt to frighten him away when he seizes on you as his prey and works in you as a child of disobedience. By this covenant you have no advocate, no deliverer, no captain of salvation, no destroyer of the works of the devil, no shield, no fortress, no high tower nor shadow of protection. Nay more, the strength of sin is the law. It strengthens and confirms your heart plague, nourishing it into masterful virulence and hopeless power.

Under this covenant you have no aid provided to you, no encouragement, no hope in the struggle with sin. While under its bonds, in unbelief, your heart plague is hopeless, incurable. It will finally and surely cut you off. It is solely in the covenant of grace that all hope is to be found. But how abundant the hope, the encouragement, the aid which it provides. It removes your condemnation, delivering you from the curse of the law and the wrath which is to come. It delivers you with divine and unappealable authority from the standing of a criminal and from the treatment due to such. It throws wide open the doors of your prison and brings you forth into the sweet light of day, into the freedom that belongs to the soul and that refers to eternity. It says to the prisoners, 'Go forth; to them that are in darkness, Shew yourselves.' It makes express promises of help to you in your efforts against sin. It says with great decision, explicitness and authority, 'Sin shall not have dominion over you: for ye are not under the law, but under grace'. 'For this is the covenant that I will make with the house of Israel after those days, saith the Lord; I will put my laws into their mind, and write them in their hearts'; 'I will put my spirit within you, and cause you to walk in my statutes'; 'I am the LORD that sanctify them'.

Now, when commanded to work out their salvation in fear and trembling, it is on the hopeful ground that God himself is working in them to will and to do of his good pleasure. With advantages and encouragements such as these, the covenant of grace conjoins others which give it a character of great completeness. It defends you from Satan, answering and repelling all his accusations through the righteousness and intercession of an all-prevailing Advocate, and putting you in a position to repel also all his temptations and assaults in divine strength. It removes all that was fitted to strengthen sin, for it removes that paralysing sense of guilt upon the conscience, in the face of which no man ever truly set himself to serve the living God or to cure his heart of evil. It condemns sin in the flesh, it dethrones the old man, weakens him, saps and mines his citadels and is mighty through God to the pulling down of his strongholds. It reveals holiness in its true beauty and loveliness as seen in the character, and especially the death, the loving death, of a Friend and Elder Brother. It plucks off the mask of sin, unvarnishes its pictorial illusions and throws a steady light upon its baits and snares, exposing them to view and enabling you to shun them. It provides you in this work with a loving, compassionate, considerate, faithful and unchangeable Companion and High Priest, even one who, in that he himself hath suffered being tempted, is able to succour them that are tempted. It provides and secures God's affectionate and fatherly acceptance of your sincere though imperfect efforts after holiness, and all these and many other glorious advantages it crowns with the final assurance that perfect victory shall at last reward these efforts, and perfect spotlessness and moral beauty at last shall shine upon you when your whole heart shall be without plague or spot or blemish or any such thing.

Surely if such and so great is the difference between the two covenants as bearing on the matter now in hand, it concerns you greatly to mark this difference and to entertain no expectation of the slightest success save as shutting yourself up in faith, consciously, resolutely, continually in the covenant of grace.

Observe also the order of its arrangements. The provisions and privileges of that covenant are not only in their respective natures valuable to you and productive of your welfare, but the order and succession of these privileges is to be attended to, for there also your interests have been consulted wonderfully. In particular, remember that justification goes before sanctification, and this holds good not merely in the order of the catechism or of instruction, but also of experience and consciousness. The unjustified man has no claim on God for sanctifying grace. It is as lying under no condemnation that you will walk not after the flesh, but after the Spirit. Your entire redemption is a redemption both by price and by power. But it is as redeemed by price that you have a right and title or claim to obtain the power to resist your enemies. It was as redeemed by price – the blood of their passover – that Israel had power to defy Pharaoh, to abandon Egypt, the house of bondage, to face the dangers of their flight, and confront even the waves of the sea and pass through. It is not as a criminal, either really so or consciously so, it is not as an apostate, an outcast, an alien that you can receive grace and strength from God. It can only be as a friend, a son, justified freely and adopted in the Beloved. The entire rectifying of your relation to God must precede the rectifying of your heart.

Now this leads you into growing gratitude and praise for a free justification, a free reconciliation, a free adoption. With all the plagues of my heart – notwithstanding them all, burdened and blackened with them all – I am free as a sinner, by faith alone, without one single qualification or good thing to show, to accept Christ, to enter into Christ and stand steadfast in him, God's righteous Servant, God's beloved Son. Sharing this position with him, sharing his relation to God, in him and with him, righteous and a son, justified and adopted, I am also counted God's righteous servant and beloved son, with all my holy Sovereign's approbation resting on me and all my heavenly Father's love. And from this position, with all its glorious securities and immunities, all its privileges, all its hopes and prospects, I am placed in circumstances now to wage a hopeful, healthful, victorious war with all my plagues and sins and foes. Is not this precisely Christ's doctrine when he says, 'Abide in me, and I in you. As the branch cannot bear fruit of itself, except it abide in the vine; no more can ye, except ye abide in me'? But when, by faith, we abide in Christ, sharing his position and drawing on his grace, we then act in his authority and by his power. In a word, we then act in his name. 'All nations compassed me about: but in the name of the LORD will I destroy them . . . They compassed me about like bees; they are quenched as the fire of thorns: for in the name of the LORD I will destroy them.'

Be it yours then, if you would rise above the power of indwelling sin, to study the provisions of the covenant of grace in their nature and order, and to abide in that covenant by faith.

3. If you would cure your heart plagues, *study universal sincerity in all duty and in resistance to all sin*. Remember the profession which David made: 'I esteem all thy precepts concerning all things to be right; and I hate every false way.' Remember the prospect which he indulged: 'Then shall I not be ashamed, when I have respect unto all thy commandments.' This is a point of vital importance and you will assuredly find it so in your experience.

It may be that you find some heart plague specially predominant, injuring you grievously, fighting against your spiritual welfare and your peace, tempting you, misleading you, weakening you, defiling your conscience, interrupting your communion with God, and hindering you in all your work. And you may seriously set yourself to seek the cure of this evil, the destruction and removal of this foe. Meantime, however, there may be others which are not plaguing you at all, plagues which you do not feel to be plagues, for which you have no sorrow, no humiliation, no real sense of their evil and injuriousness and therefore no desire to be healed of them. Your duty in respect of the Holy Scriptures for instance may not be utterly neglected, and yet you may be failing grievously in that continuous reverential believing study of them which their divine Author has enjoined in passages like these: 'Search the Scriptures'; 'Let the word of Christ dwell in you richly.' Or you may be secretly cherishing revenge against an enemy, tolerating in yourself feelings of malignity towards him, or even plausibly justifying yourself therein. Now, do not imagine you can have any success in ridding yourself of plagues that really plague you while there are others you are so thoroughly reconciled to that they are no plagues to you at all. There are two considerations fitted to show you the reasonableness of what I say. In the first place the heart plague which you cherish weakens you out of power to deal rightly with that which you hate; and in the second place God is displeased with you on account of that which you cherish and chastens you by leaving you a prey to the influence and dominion of the hated plague. This latter consideration is peculiarly solemn and one which is perhaps little attended to. Besetting sins are often painful enough and yet contrive to hold their ground. In such cases it is surely open to enquiry whether God is not using them as scourges and chastisements, making their painful prevalence the punishment of the tolerated prevalence of others that are not painful but beloved.

There is often something ominous and judicial in the continued power of a lust which the Christian is vainly striving to quell. Israel of old would not thrust out the Canaanites, and God made them pricks in their eyes and thorns in their sides, vexing them in the land that ought to have been unto them one of eminent tranquillity and gladness. Even so, a heart plague may resist many efforts and prayers and tears and strong cryings, work for you many a sorrow, extort from you many a sigh, and fill you with many a doubt whether it ever will be cured at all, or whether you shall not yet one day fall by the hand of Saul. Under this perplexing experience you may be only suffering the righteous chastisement which God appoints to be the means of drawing your attention to some other plague to which you are ministering nourishment and strength as if it were the right hand of your dexterity, or sheltering with the assiduous care with which you might protect your organs of vision. That right eye must be plucked out, that right hand cut off, and only then shall grace be given to subdue the enemy you hate, and raise you victorious and peaceful and pure and strong above the sin that besets you.

4. If you would cure your heart plagues you must *remember that all your success is from the Holy Spirit,* according to the rule and leading oracle on this theme, 'If ye through the Spirit do mortify the deeds of the body, ye shall live.' It is the Spirit that is the real agent in all successful action against beloved sins and idols. The whole work of sanctification and this particular department of it are his.

i. In the first place, it is to him that you are indebted for a true sight of the evil, the hatefulness, the injuriousness and the sinfulness of these plagues. It is his function to convince of sin and righteousness and judgment, and when he is come he will fulfil his office. He will tear away every veil and mask which hides from view the malignity of your heart plague. He will correct all your false judgments and estimates. He will show you the bearing of the disease on your relation to God and your whole spiritual state and prospects. Your soul's real condition and interests, the Spirit makes plain before you.

ii. Secondly, he withdraws you from the first covenant and brings you under the second. Not only does he do so at first, at your first conversion, but when the heart would fall back again, as through unbelief it is always prone to, into legalism, the Spirit leads you forth again into the covenant of grace in fresh renewed actings of simple faith. Indeed, as a Spirit of sanctification, he acts uniformly in connection with the covenant of grace. All his saving, sanctifying work is within the compass and rule of this covenant. It is not by the works of the law that we receive the Spirit, but by the hearing of faith. The gracious gospel and not the law is the chariot in which the saving Spirit of God goes forth in his glory. The everlasting covenant, not the broken covenant, is the vehicle of his saving grace and power. The second covenant, not the first, promises and conveys the Spirit, and is indeed called the ministration of the Spirit. And if, as we have seen, it is only under this gracious and better covenant that you can wage a successful warfare against heart sin, then the Spirit, who alone can bring you under this covenant, is the only real Author of your success.

iii. Then also, in the third place, it is he who bestows and maintains in you a universal sincerity of purpose in your walk with God. We have seen that without such sincerity you cannot succeed in curing a heart plague that may be grieving you, and it is to the Spirit that you must be indebted for it. He renews the heart and gives truth in the inward parts. He searches and humbles and cleanses you. He puts the law in your heart and writes it in your mind. He writes it all and he writes it correctly. He maintains your integrity. He teaches you to judge yourself in the judgment of God.

Thus revealing the evil of sin, bringing you under the second covenant, and giving you thorough sincerity, he fulfils in you all those conditions without which your efforts to cure your heart plague must fail. But he proceeds further and renews in you a positive success. He leads you to pray for the healing balm that is in Gilead. He helps your infirmities. He is a Spirit of grace and supplications to you. He reveals to you the great Physician in all his fitness and fulness to heal and cure you. He especially brings into your clear view the infinite grace of the High Priest that can have compassion. He shows you that so long as a heart plague really plagues you, so far from looking askance upon you because of the spiritual evil it implies, the pain you suffer from it renders you an object of the High Priest's special care and love and gives you a peculiar interest in that intercession which procures for you all supplies of saving, sanctifying, healing grace. For all this you are indebted to the Holy Spirit. Oh, then take no step in this work without him. Through the Spirit, mortify the deeds of the body and be healed of the plagues of the heart.

5. Finally, I must again ask your attention to what was

briefly noticed in the former discourse, namely that *it is by a believing use of the cross that you are to slay your corruptions or cure your heart plagues.* In proportion as you wander in spirit from the cross your plagues and besetting sins will revive. Your right and adequate return to the cross weakens and mortifies and kills them. All sanctification is from participating in the power of the cross. It is from communion in the death and resurrection of Christ. It is by being made conformable unto his death. If the body of sin is to be destroyed and you are not henceforth to serve sin, your old man must be crucified with Christ. You must be baptized into his death. You must make his death your own. You must drink of the cup which he drank of and be baptized with the baptism wherewith he was baptized. Humiliation and holiness can be found by a sinner nowhere but at the cross. And they cannot be carried away from the cross. You must make the cross itself yours if you are to make humiliation and holiness yours. He gave himself that he might redeem you from all iniquity. He loved you and gave himself for you that he might cleanse you with the washing of water by the word. He redeemed you by his blood unto himself that *he* might – that no iniquity might – have dominion over you. His name was called Jesus because he should save his people from their sins.

All efforts after holiness and holy self-control apart from the cross will issue in proud self-righteousness or in a paralysing sense of failure. Ah! how very much the most advanced among us needs to search the treasures, not of peace only, but of sanctifying power with which the cross is replete! Perhaps we know it as the place of peace but we know little of its power of sanctification. The sin-killing power of a Saviour's death – would that we adequately knew and felt and exemplified it! Would that it were unto us, not less, indeed, a theme of meditation, but more a power to purify. It possesses this power, else were it weak indeed. But it is the power of God. Through its glorious vicarious righteousness the Spirit comes, and he is honoured in coming thereby. To achieve its purposes, the Spirit comes. To make good and guarantee the ends for which that cross was endured, the Spirit comes. And when he comes he wields on his people's souls the virtue and energy of Christ's death and resurrection. And you partake increasingly by appropriating faith of that death and resurrection of your Head, making them indeed your own, and so yourselves also dying unto sin and living unto God. Reckoning yourselves dead indeed unto sin but alive unto God, even as your living Head, the power and purpose of his death will be manifested in you and your conformity to the Son of God promoted. It is thus that you will have your heart plagues more and more cured and your besetting sins crucified, till at last you are, through the infinite power of Emmanuel's blood and Spirit, holy and harmless and undefiled and separate from sinners, without spot or plague or any such thing.

Those that are Christ's: A Pre-Communion Address

'They that are Christ's have crucified the flesh with the affections and lusts' (Gal. 5:24).
'Knowing this, that our old man is crucified with him, that the body of sin might be destroyed, that henceforth we should not serve sin' (Rom. 6:6).

A few remarks on the subject we have under notice may serve, with the blessing of the Spirit of Christ, for the part of this day's duty now before us. We are to indicate the state and character of those who are respectively invited to the Holy Supper, and debarred and discharged from partaking of it.

In a word, those that are Christ's are welcome; those that are not are forbidden.

Now those that are Christ's have crucified the flesh with its affections and lusts. Those that are not Christ's have not. They are still in the flesh and cannot please God. They are carnally minded, which is death. They are under the reign and unbroken power of sin. They may not live in the practice of the more scandalous and gross works of the flesh, yet do they in some respects, and deliberately, make provision for the flesh to fulfil the lusts thereof. If they should say that they have fellowship with God, they lie and do not the truth. They walk in the darkness of enmity to God and neglect of God's Word and will, in self-will, impenitence and unbelief. They imperil their happiness in following their own projects, in seeking their own pleasure, in converse only with the things that are seen and temporal, giving their soul in exchange for the world. They have resisted the strivings of the Spirit to convince them of sin, of righteousness and of judgment to come. Their only fear of God is dictated by a heart that condemns them, and it prompts only to a terrified desire to escape his wrath – to get off from reckoning righteously with him concerning their sin. It is imbued with no desire for his fellowship and love and holiness and service. Their thoughts of Christ are not those of a heart weary and longing to be interested in him, hungering and thirsting after him. Their worship of God is outward, formal, unfilial and dead. All their heart service is given to other lords that have dominion over them. They are in the flesh, and cannot please God, nor discern the Lord's body, nor receive the Lord's Spirit, because they see him not, neither know him. All such, in the name of Christ, the Master of the feast and King of the Church, we debar from coming to his holy table, his supper of reconciliation, friendship and love. All ignorant, scandalous, profane persons living in the works of the flesh which are manifest, living in any sin or offence against their knowledge or conscience, unbroken in their hearts, untroubled for their apostasy from God, unconscious of, and undismayed by, their guilt of being without Christ, of slighting and rejecting the Son of God, of disesteeming and despising his sorrow and his sacrifice for sinners, we debar. And because the body and blood of Christ are really and truly, though spiritually, present in the supper by Christ's word of institution and promise, very near to be received and fed upon by the faith of believers, and very near to be with special guilt dishonoured and rejected by those who, uncleansed and in their sin and unbelief, discern not the Lord's body, we warn them that their presuming to come to the table of the Lord will be the occasion of their eating and drinking the wrath of God and judgment unto themselves.

On the other hand, in the name of Christ, who spreads this table and presides over all its feast and fellowship, we invite those that are Christ's, those who have crucified the flesh with its affections and lusts. You are to come to the table of the Lord for special communion in him and in his death, 'knowing this, that your old man is crucified with Christ, that the body of sin might be destroyed, that henceforth you should not serve sin.'

1. I remark then, in the first place, that *if you are Christ's you will feel deeply interested in 'knowing this'*. It is an arrangement on God's part that will commend itself to your lively study and attention. It is an arrangement in which you are most vitally concerned. You cannot be Christ's without having come to know in some measure the exceeding sinfulness and the exceeding strength of sin. And here is God's method of ultimately freeing you from sin's presence, and enabling you in the meantime and henceforth to rise superior to sin's power. Surely it is a very marvellous scheme, coming forth from him who is wonderful in counsel and excellent in working. It is worthy of your deepest regard. Nor is anything more precious in it, to those that are Christ's and the subjects of this privilege, than the perfection of its unity and its freedom from all perplexity. It provides for all details, but it goes directly and completely to the root of the evil. It lops not off branch after branch. Alas! this principle and root of sin within is of wondrous vigour, vitality and

fertility, and all mere dealing with branches in detail leaves the evil in its strength and reign as before. But, while dealing with the various members of the body of sin, this arrangement on God's part grapples with the old man himself – with the vigorous principle of our corruption, the old man in his unity and principle of evil life – and nails him to the cross to be destroyed. The Holy Spirit, coming for the sake of the cross, to fulfil its purpose, to realise its purchase, to wield its power, dethrones, dishonours, condemns, breaks and crucifies our old man with Christ. Is it possible that sin can be your burden, that sin can be your chiefest affliction, that the plague of your own heart can be really a plague to you, that you are convinced that in you, that is, in your flesh, dwelleth no good thing – nothing but enmity to God, subjection to worldly lusts, uncharitableness towards man, selfishness, self-will, insubordination to the authority of God and disinclination and disability for his fellowship and service – is it possible that you can be awakened to all this without taking an interest in knowing this also, that your old man is crucified with him?

2. Secondly, *if you are Christ's you will joyfully acquiesce in this arrangement.* They that are Christ's have crucified the flesh with its affections and lusts. They have fallen in voluntarily, actively, gladly, decisively with this arrangement. They are of one mind with the Spirit of God concerning it. It pleases them. It commends itself to their acceptance. They struggle not against it, but embrace it with joy. Any struggling against it of which they are conscious is not theirs – it is the old man not yet destroyed, struggling against the destruction to which he is given over. But they that are Christ's do themselves give him over to it. They put off 'the old man which is corrupt

[174]

according to the deceitful lusts.' They through the Spirit
do mortify the deeds of the body. They rejoice in the
prospect of its ultimate extinction. They rejoice in the
present release from its reign. They know that, but for its
presence and remaining power, all things would be with
them, even in this weary world, wholly according to their
desire, promoting and securing therefore their unbroken
happiness. For they know that all things work together for
their good. They know therefore that, were it not for the
remains of their depravity marring their unbounded trust
in their Father's unerring wisdom, his perfect righteousness, his infinite and unchanging love, they could
amidst all outward evils so bear up in faith, in patience, in
meekness and filial confidence that they should never
stumble, nor be troubled, nor be afraid for the terror by
night, nor for the arrow that flieth by day, nor for the
pestilence that walketh in darkness, nor for the destruction that wasteth at noonday. Quietly waiting for the
salvation of God, they would rest in the knowledge that,
whatever their lot or their affliction, no evil should befall
them nor any plague come nigh their dwelling. They
know also that, but for the remains of this depravity, this
enmity to God, this dislike of and rebelliousness against
their own reconciled God, they would serve him with
unlimited obedience, even as his own Son, Jesus Christ
their Saviour; for they consent unto all his law, that it is
holy and just and good; and they know that in the keeping
of it there is great reward; that in the doing of it they are
blessed in their deed.

And how then can they but rejoice in the prospective
destruction and the present dethronement of an evil so
altogether and continually injurious? Nor will their joy be
otherwise than greatly enhanced by remembering that it is
by the cross of their Redeemer, that it is the purpose of his

death, the purchase of his pain, the travail of his soul, the gratification and satisfaction of his heart, that their old man, their perplexing enemy, is fastened and nailed down beyond the possibility of being king over them again. Power may remain to vex often, and much to hinder and hamper and humble, nay, humiliate them, but with no remaining right to claim their service or compel it, or to keep them in the bondage of corruption. Every view of this is joyful, and doubtless there is an undercurrent of joy in the apostle's heart when he declares the text, and in the heart of those who enter into sympathy with him in adopting it, as if he and they should say, 'Knowing this, thanks be unto God that our old man is crucified with Christ, that the body of sin may be destroyed, that henceforth we should not serve sin.' They habitually act by faith in the cross, in Christ's death, in Christ crucified, for the actual obtaining of the benefit of this arrangement. They do not once and for all accept of it and acquiesce in it and then neglect it. They do not expect that, having once acquiesced in this arrangement, it will act on them as a spell and emancipate them without any effort of will or putting forth of intention and exertion on their part. They have to work out their salvation from the old man, from the body of sin, with fear and trembling. They may be apt to neglect this in first committing their souls to the infinite love and the all-varied and boundless sufficiency of Jesus. Amidst the clearness of a first decision and the warmth of a first love, they may feel as if the old man were destroyed. But they will soon learn that this is not the case; that all that is guaranteed and provided for in this life is, not that the body of sin is destroyed, but simply that they should not serve sin. And there is no greater risk of falling into some device of sin than to imagine that the body of sin is destroyed.

To the cross of Christ therefore they must again and continually come, to exercise fresh and lively faith, and for fresh communion with him in his death. Then once more in believing contemplation, in quiet dependence on the Spirit by that cross, they set before them Jesus Christ manifestly crucified for them. They meditate on the glory of his pardon, the matchless marvel of his love, and his purpose to redeem them from all iniquity and set them free from their love of and bondage to sin. They meditate afresh on the purchase that he has made of all-sufficient grace to conform them to himself, and on the right he has earned as their Saviour to reign as king, to subdue them to himself, to give them repentance unto the acknowledgement of the truth, to deal at his pleasure by his Spirit with their spirit, and to maintain in them a broken and a contrite heart. When they mix all these meditations with faith, and by faith lay their hearts open to receive all that they thus see Christ's cross obtaining for them, submitting to the power they see that cross fitted and designed to wield over them and in them, then this lively acting of their faith will be found weakening the energy of the old man, and enabling them, in the name of Jesus, in the constraints of his love and in the power of his Spirit, to put sin with its instigations away, to keep themselves from their iniquity, to deny ungodliness and worldly lusts, to put off the old man and to die more and more unto sin, serving not sin but righteousness and God.

3. In the last place, let it now be observed that they that are Christ's not only take a deep interest in this arrangement, joyfully acquiesce in it, and habitually improve it by faith, but they do *actually find and verify its sufficiency, so that in point of fact they do not serve sin.* The flesh is in them, for the old man, though crucified, is destroyed only in

commencement, in design and in prospect. But though the flesh is in them, they are not in the flesh, but in the Spirit. Sin is in them, yea, a body of sin, a sadly complete and well-organized system of many mutually-supporting lusts, the desires of the yet undestroyed old man which is corrupt. Nevertheless they fight a good fight of faith, and this is the victory by which they overcome, even their faith. Much hampered, sorely pressed, often in heaviness through manifold temptations, they are yet not the followers of sin, but of God, not the servants of sin but of righteousness. They have to work with fear and trembling. Sin is their trial, their burden, their sorrow. But repentance is their choice, and a contrite spirit is sweet to them. Their delight is in the law of the Lord, and his communion and service are better to them than all that this world can give. A day in his courts is better than a thousand. They love the habitation of his house. His precepts are their heritage and their song in the house of their pilgrimage. His children are their friends, and the advancement of his kingdom gladdens them. The perplexities and pains which their remaining sin occasions they hide not from their Father. They take brokenhearted and believing counsel with him concerning them. They find cleansing from the guilt and shame of them in the blood of Jesus. And always, when anew they are so washed and purified, humbled, chastened and refreshed in spirit, they serve the living God with reinvigorated ardour, with lowlier self-renunciation, with a deeper sense of what the holiness of their God requires, and hence with appreciation of what his combined authority and love demand of a believing and guileless walk with him.

The difficulties to which they are subjected and their experiences of sin's malignity all constrain them to a distrust of self. They confess, 'In me, that is, in my flesh, dwelleth no good thing.' These things simplify, strengthen and establish their faith in Christ alone, and shut them up more and more to him as made of God unto them wisdom, and righteousness, and sanctification, and redemption. Their gradual deliverance from sin amidst experiences such as these secures in them a deeper holiness than the immediate abolition of the old man on their conversion could secure, and their light affliction which is but for a moment worketh for them a far more exceeding and eternal weight of glory. For in the meantime God opens to them, in holy ordinances, wells of refreshing and salvation. He gives them to drink of the brook in the way, brings them to his banqueting-house, and spreads over them his banner which is love. He displays before their gladsome faith the fulness of his Christ and the unswerving faithfulness of his covenant. In particular, in the holy ordinance of the supper, he gives them a gracious seal of his promises that are yea in Christ, and in him Amen. He gives to their faith communion in Christ's death and victory. By the working of his Spirit he nourishes their souls and mortifies their sin, feeds them with unseen bread such as even angels do not eat, and gives them to know that, even compassed though they be by this earthly tabernacle in which they groan, and compassed still more painfully with a body of sin, they are nevertheless in the house of God and at the gate of heaven. He assures them that they are the sons of God and a spiritual priesthood, sealed by the Spirit till the day of redemption.

In Christ's name therefore we invite to the table those who have examined themselves, whose hearts respond to the views that have now been expressed, and who, acquiescing by faith in the truth of God, are fleeing in the fear of righteous wrath to the blessed reconciliation that is by the blood of Christ – who are burdened with sin as their greatest sorrow, and who desire to devote themselves wholly to God in Christ as a living sacrifice, holy and acceptable, which is their reasonable service. And we assure you in his name that, according to your sincerity, according to your faith, Christ will feed you on himself – his flesh and his blood, the passover sacrificed for you, the paschal feast prepared for you – to your spiritual nourishment and growth in grace.

The Risen Life: A Communion Sermon

'If ye then be risen with Christ, seek those things which are above, where Christ sitteth on the right hand of God' (Col. 3:1).

Brethren, we have now shown forth the Lord's death. Death at all times and in all forms is a solemnizing thing. How especially so is the Lord's death. It is the death of him who is the Life, who remained the Life even in dying, and who by death became to us the Resurrection. 'O the depth of the riches both of the wisdom and knowledge of God!' The Life becomes by death the Resurrection. This death we have been showing forth. Is it not worthy of our highest efforts to show it forth well, and now to show forth in ourselves its sanctifying power? For if we have intelligently shown it forth for what it really is, the death of him who is the Life, and who has by death become the Resurrection, then surely that animating call of an apostle is to the point, 'If ye then be risen with Christ, seek those things which are above, where Christ sitteth on the right hand of God.'

The apostle does not mean by the word 'if' to cast any doubt on whether those who believe on Christ now are risen with him. He has, in the former chapter, absolutely asserted, 'Ye are risen with him through the faith of the operation of God, who hath raised him from the dead.'

This is the value and the power of his resurrection, even that it is the resurrection also of his believing people, according to his own word, 'I am the resurrection, and the life: he that believeth in me, though he were dead, yet shall he live.' While this is the sure fruit of faith, it indicates one very solemn ground of our obligation to believe, to be always believing, on his name. For otherwise we incur the fault of doing what in us lies to make his resurrection fruitless. By union with Christ through faith the power of his resurrection enters into us and quickens us to newness of life. The privilege of his resurrection also becomes ours, and we stand before God related to him now even as the risen Saviour does. Mark well what that privilege is – the fundamental privilege of Christ himself in his risen life. For what right Jesus asserted and made good, claimed and had the claim thereof acknowledged in his resurrection, that most surely and first of all must be ours if we are risen with him.

Consider, then, that in rising from the dead, Jesus divested himself of the covenant of works, purged his relation to the Father from every element of obligation, and claimed his Father's love and promises as all most fully earned. He had nothing more to suffer now in order to the covenant assurance being fulfilled unto himself, 'He shall see of the travail of his soul'; or the covenant assurance being fulfilled to his people: 'I will put my laws into their mind, and write them in their hearts . . . and their sins and their iniquities will I remember no more.' He had nothing now to suffer and nothing now to do in order to obtain the ends of his covenant with the Father. All the stipulated service, the obedience unto death, had been rendered; all the legal element removed by the law's being wholly satisfied. It remains now for the Father to be ever fulfilling unto him the now sealed promise, to divide him a portion with the great, and that he should divide the spoil with the strong. He enters on the Father's unclouded favour and unconditional love.

And so also do ye if ye are risen with him. Like him and in him you divest yourselves of the covenant of works. You take the promise 'their sins and their iniquities will I remember no more' as being free to you without money and without price, without condition or works on your part, as much so as the risen Christ at God's right hand is free from obligation to suffer any further penalty or pay any further price for the glory in which he dwells with the Father. You too, like Christ, with Christ, in Christ cast out the element of legality. You enter unconditionally into absolute and free favour with God. You enter freely on a covenant with him ordered in all things and sure.

And you do so because you rightly understand, appreciate and personally embrace Christ as the Resurrection. You feel that by not believing on him so as to rise with him, you make his resurrection void. You reduce it to an empty pageant. You make it powerless and profitless to you. For this and this alone can be its profit and its power, namely that, in virtue of it, you cast off that covenant of works which makes you guilty and cast out that legality which straitens you with the spirit of bondage. You are no more now a servant, a slave or a criminal but a child, accepted and adopted of the Father, declared to be, not a servant who trembles at a hard taskmaster's tasks, but a son of God with power according to this resurrection. For the God and Father of our Lord Jesus Christ has begotten you again to a lively hope by the resurrection of Christ from the dead, to an inheritance that is incorruptible, undefiled and fadeth not away. And if so, how powerful is the call to seek those things which are above!

Those things which are above are now yours. This is the

privilege of the risen life. It is a life in which a right to the things above has been made yours. It is not a life which is spent in seeking to make good a title to the things above, but a life to be spent in seeking them and enjoying them as your own.

Do not think that your having to seek them is inconsistent with the truth that in Christ they are yours. They are Christ's by purchase, a purchase most complete, ratified by his resurrection, yet he seeks them: 'I will pray the Father, and he shall give you another Comforter.' And listen to the oracle that assigns to Jesus the very course that is assigned to you, 'Ask of me, and I shall give thee the heathen for thine inheritance, and the uttermost parts of the earth for thy possession.' No, your seeking the things which are above is not inconsistent with the privilege of claiming them as yours. It is in prosecution of that privilege, it is in actual acceptation of it that you seek.

What shall you seek above as yours?

1. First of all the Father, at whose right hand Jesus sits. It is true that the apostle's phraseology, when translated into our language literally, does not seem to include persons at all. It speaks of the *things* that are above. But the usage of the original makes it quite admissible to include persons, for in John 8:23 Jesus, speaking of his own divine origin and heavenly home, says, 'I am from above.' This is literally, 'I am of the things above.' Let this then be your habitual course. Be it yours to seek the Father who is above; our Father which is in heaven. Seek the Lord and his strength, seek his face evermore. Seek the Father's love, the love that gave the Son and with him the Spirit, yea, and with him freely all things. Seek filial fellowship with the Father, and do so in the constant faith that Christ sits at his right hand as your advocate, maintaining the

permanence of your adoption and the perpetuity of your peace with God, that you may enjoy with him a truly risen life. This is a life of filial confidence and filial security, even such life and fellowship as you may anticipate with One who has begotten you to a lively hope by the resurrection of his Son from the dead, who rejoices over you with singing, saying, 'This my son was dead and is alive again' and who has declared you to be his with power, according to the Spirit of holiness, by the resurrection from the dead. Seek the Father in the faith of the resurrected Christ who is the Resurrection. In spirit may it be yours to say with the risen forerunner, 'I ascend to his Father and my Father, to his God and my God.' In so ascending you shall share in Christ's ascension even as you share in his resurrection. For he ascended on high carrying captivity captive, receiving gifts for men. Your ascension in spirit to the Father shall burst the bonds of all your captivity, secure for you enlargement and liberty in the Spirit of adoption and communicate the very gifts which Jesus has received for you.

2. Seek the Lord Jesus himself. It is his own express assertion, 'I am of the things above.' Seek ye the Lord Jesus; seek and ye shall find. Being risen in him, living the same life with him, living in the same world or sphere in which he lives, your seeking him surely will be a successful seeking, for Jesus fills that sphere or kingdom with himself. He ascended far above all heavens that he might fill all things with himself. Every where, in the sphere of risen life, you meet with him, Jesus Christ, the all in all. Surely your seeking must be followed with finding. To others indeed, to those who believe not on his name, it cannot be so. 'Ye shall seek me,' he said to the unbelieving Jews, 'and shall not find me: and where I am, thither ye

cannot come.' Their unbelief put a fatal gulf between him and them. Unbelief is from beneath; Jesus is from above and faith is from above. It is of that new birth which is from above. Hence to them that are of faith Jesus says, 'Whither I go ye know, and the way ye know.' The way was by the manger, the cross and the empty grave, and the path of life which, at that empty grave, he saw stretching out before him, on even to the Father's presence where there is fulness of joy, where he now sits above at the right hand of God. By this way your faith seeks and finds, seeking by no deceitful light but by the light of the Word and Spirit of the Lord. And your hope thus enters within the veil, whither Jesus has already entered as forerunner. Your faith and hope enter there and you find Jesus. 'I found him whom my soul loveth . . . and would not let him go,' and even as anew you find him, you will find something more in him. You will find him something more to you than you ever found before. For out of his fulness have we all received and grace for grace.

3. Seek the Spirit. If ye be risen with Christ, seek the Spirit who is from above. It is a risen Saviour who has received the promise of the Father, the promised Spirit, and who sheds abroad the life of the Spirit on the church. As risen with Christ you specially share with him the promise of the Father. Declared to be the son of God, according to the Spirit of holiness, by the resurrection from the dead, you have a personal and acknowledged interest in the outpouring of the Spirit. He is the seal of your adoption, the earnest of your inheritance, the first fruits of your glory.

4. Seek the wisdom which is from above, for 'wisdom is the principal thing; therefore get wisdom'. In one view,

wisdom embraces the entire Christian character. It is the
embodiment of all Christian graces. Study that wisdom
that is spoken of and so highly and variously commended
in the book of Proverbs and seek to be able to manifest in
growing measure its various excellencies. It is the wisdom
which comes from above. It is the wisdom which Christ is
made by God to them that believe. Oh! if being risen with
Christ you seek the things that are above, give a first place
to that wisdom which comes from above and which is 'first
pure, then peaceable, gentle, and easy to be intreated, full
of mercy and good fruits, without partiality, and without
hypocrisy.' Well may you seek that wisdom if you are
risen with Christ. If you are risen with Christ you need
wisdom. You need to 'walk in wisdom toward them that
are without,' those that are not risen, wisely remembering
that they may yet rise with Christ, and wisely seeking that
their intercourse with you and your bearing towards them
may contribute to their being led to count all things but
loss that they may win Christ, the Resurrection and the
Life. If you are risen with Christ, you need manifold
wisdom to walk worthy of your high calling from above,
which is of God. Your being risen with Christ renders this
wisdom in a thousand lights absolutely indispensable.
Your being risen with Christ brings it within your reach,
places it at your full disposal by faith.

5. If you are risen with Christ seek the good of Jerusalem –
that Jerusalem which is from above and which is free,
which is the mother of us all, named the Church of Christ,
the Kingdom of Christ, the city of the great king, of which
glorious things are spoken, the one family in heaven and
on earth. Seek the good of that portion of it which our
prayers or services may profit. Specially as risen in Christ
may we do so. For being risen with Christ we must

CHRIST FOR US

naturally and inevitably feel a world like this to be a
foreign shore, a land wholly uninhabited save for what of
the Jerusalem which is from above is in it, and feel the
hope of being at last translated from it to Jerusalem above.
A world of sense and sin and sorrow and separation surely
cannot be a home to one risen with Christ. 'In the world ye
shall have tribulation,' but, saith Jesus, 'In me ye shall
have peace.' By sense you dwell in the world, there is
tribulation there. By faith you dwell in me, the Resurrection, in me and in your new home, the home of your risen
spirit, in Jerusalem to which, risen with me, you ascend
and have peace. For there is no cause of sorrow in the
kingdom of Christ. All sorrow is from that outer sphere
from which you are not yet wholly disentangled and
emancipated. In the kingdom of Christ there is no
adversity, no evil, no death, no bereavement, no separation. In Jerusalem there are included all the faithful of
every age, the whole family in heaven and on earth, an
innumerable company of angels, and the spirits of just
men made perfect, and God the Judge of all, and Jesus the
mediator of the new covenant, and the blood of sprinkling
that speaketh better things than that of Abel; and all who
by that new and living way have found boldness, though
tabernacling still on the earth, to enter into the holiest. In
this church of the Resurrection and the Life, there are no
real deaths, no real separations, no real bereavements and
no real losses. There are transpositions, transferences and
translations. But bereavements, strictly speaking, and in
the language of faith, which is the language of the
kingdom and the Word of the Lord, there are none. 'He
shall not return to me,' said David, therefore his heart was
heavy. 'But I shall go to him,' therefore his glory rejoices
and his flesh shall rest in hope.

Oh, if you are risen with Christ seek first the kingdom of

God, seek the good of Jerusalem, bind in your heart the church of the Resurrection and the Life. You will get nothing there to wound your heart. Jerusalem is the mother of us all, full of consolation, even as one whom his mother comforteth.

Brethren, we are led to draw upon consolatory reflections such as these at a time when it has pleased God to deal solemnly with us as a congregation. The Lord who giveth not account of any of his matters has been pleased very suddenly to take away from among us one whose position among us was very prominent, his character very exemplary, his services very valuable and his desire for the welfare of this congregation very great. We mourn not on his account, because we mourn not as those that have no hope, for we know him that has said, 'Them also that sleep in Jesus will God bring with him,' and we know that our departed friend was a man of faith and prayer. On his account we mourn not, not even because of the swiftness of the last messenger's flight to him, nor the haste with which the earthly house of this tabernacle was taken down. Why mourn for the righteous being swiftly rapt away into their Saviour's rest? Shall we complain because their journey through the valley was abbreviated and they found a joyful surprise in crossing Jordan at a step?

But while we mourn not on his account we may rightly mourn on our own, for surely this solemn dispensation carries somewhat of chastisement in it towards us. The less cause we have to mourn on his account, the more have we on our own. The more the Lord hurried the last messenger and cut his work short in righteousness and love to his servant, the more startling is the voice of the swift rod to us. Brethren, let us try to lay it solemnly to heart when we are deprived so unexpectedly of one who went out and in among us in all the confirmed appearances of fullest health and vigour; of one so valuable to his own home circle, now grievously bereaved and yet so greatly sustained and comforted; of one so valuable to us in this congregation and also to this great community in which on all sides and with such depth and unanimity we hear his removal deplored. Surely in all this a lesson is read to us of the utterly uncertain tenure by which we hold this present perishable life and how solemnly it behoves us, if we would not perish in very folly, to see to it first of all that we be found in him who is the Resurrection and the Life. For when we see that in the midst of life we are in death, what possible comfort can we have unless we are seeking to be able to add the glorious counterpart and counteractive, 'In the midst of death we are in the Resurrection and the Life'? Secondly, how impressively are we warned, in the words of our Lord, 'Be ye also ready, for in such an hour as ye think not the Son of Man cometh.' 'Whatsoever thy hand findeth to do, do it with thy might; for there is no work, nor device, nor knowledge, nor wisdom, in the grave, whither thou goest.' We have reason to be grateful that not the departure only of our friend but his life and example also enforce this solemn exhortation.

This is not the place for eulogy. We are showing forth this day the Master's death, not his servant's. But in the Master's death, in which the Life became the Resurrection, we see the bond by which the Master's brethren, whether in earth or heaven, are beyond the power of death to separate them from him. We have shown forth the Lord's death until he come. His coming will be the coming of his saints also. Them that sleep in Jesus will God bring with him. That forms part of our high anticipation concerning that blessed hope and that glorious appearing of the Lord. Oh! brethren, if we share in Christ, in his death (and we have been professing communion therein), if we share in Christ, in his resurrection, let us share with him in his ascension. 'If ye be risen with Christ, seek those things which are above.' Let our conversation be in heaven. Forget the things that are behind, reach forth to those that are before. Press toward the mark for the prize of the calling which is from above. Purge away from your souls the wisdom that is from beneath. Keep yourselves unspotted from the world. Be not of it. Live above it. And having fellowship in Christ, in his death, in his resurrection, in his ascension, ye shall have fellowship with him in his reappearance: 'When Christ, who is our life, shall appear, then shall ye also', and all your brethren in Jesus, 'appear with him in glory.'

๑ 13 ๑

The Hidden Life

'Your life is hid with Christ in God' (Col. 3:3*).*

The believing child of God is in possession of eternal life. He is in *present* possession of it. He does not tarry till he enters into glory to be put in possession of everlasting life. He possesses it already. 'He that believeth on the Son of God hath', even now, while sojourning in this estate of trial and probation, 'everlasting life' (*John* 3:36).

He has already emerged from the region and shadow of death, and entered on the realm of life genuine and true, life that is real and endless. The domain of death is behind him, not before him. He has not to die: that is past. True, indeed, he has to fall asleep in Jesus. He must put off this earthly tabernacle. But as to death in its high and awful meaning, as to death in its constituting essence and real power, regarded in the light of penalty on sin, he is done with it for evermore. That is past, not to come: it is behind him, not before him; he is not advancing towards it, but triumphantly escaping from the very shadow of it. 'Ye are dead, and your life is hid with Christ in God.'

The believer is thus dead, in and 'with Christ', in Christ's death, and as proprietor and inheritor of *it*. The death of Christ is imputed to him, and received by faith alone. Now, Christ's death was a death-conquering, death-extinguishing death. It was death in its perfection; death up to the full limits of its power and reign; a death which, as it passed away in its perfect consummation, swallowed up death in victory, and left the field in undisputed possession of death's enemy – in possession of the life everlasting.

'By one offering' Jesus has 'perfected for ever them that are sanctified' (*Heb.* 10:14). He has perfectly reconciled us to the Father, perfectly satisfied the law, perfectly vanquished Satan, perfectly extinguished the curse, perfectly abolished death, and brought life and immortality to light – clear from every taint of the region and shadow of death and darkness. And now, you who believe on him, have, by him, the Resurrection and Life, passed through death's realm in your living Head, and are numbered among the living in Jerusalem. His perfect death is your death, already past, and over, and gone. 'Ye are dead, and your life is hid with Christ in God.'

The believer, then, is in present possession of everlasting life. And how great are the glories which this one fact implies! He stands personally in the favour of heaven; he stands well with God – Oh, how well! – even as God sees his shield and looks on the face of his anointed one. And in this favour of God – in this good understanding between him and his God, the very life of his soul consists. 'In his favour is life', and 'thy loving kindness is better than life.' He is a son of the King of glory, he is an heir of God, a joint-heir with Christ. He is a member of a spiritual priesthood, of a general assembly of worshippers, officiating daily before the God of the whole earth. He is a king and priest. There is no end of the glorious things that are spoken of the city of God and its citizens. They have a life which, in its character, and functions, and privileges, and history, and prospects, is altogether full of glory.

But these declarations cannot be made of the present dignity and glorious estate of the sons of God, without an apparent contradiction, or objection, coming to our remembrance. Were it not for our familiarity with the fact, it would strike us as a strange incongruity – indeed, a strange presumptive argument against the truth of those exalted representations of the Christian's estate and privileges – that he does not carry with him in the world any obvious and unmistakable stamp and evidence of his high pretensions, such as even the world's carnal eye could not fail to perceive, and dare not profess to overlook. If it be really true that the believer stands in the endearing and exalted relation of a son to the God of heaven and earth – if the King eternal, immortal and invisible speaks with him in peace and love, and calls him 'My son' – 'My son, despise not thou the chastening of the Lord', 'My son, give me thine heart' – it might almost be expected that living, as he now lives, a life of such near, and blessed, and glorious relationship to God, some gleam of glory should shine upon his forehead; that some stamp and seal of heavenly majesty should sit enthroned upon his countenance; that some spell or talisman of power to command disease, and poverty, and grief, and trial far away should be at all times his. No wonder, one might almost say, meditating on the high rank of a veritable son of the living God, and labouring in thought and feeling to do justice appreciatingly to what the simple but sublime designation must imply, no wonder if, when such an one walks abroad, the Mahanaim of Jacob, the angelic hosts of God should meet him manifestly, and throng around him, to secure his inviolable safety, to constrain acknowledgement of his princely name – more high than any name, higher than the kings of the earth. No wonder if his face should shine with palpable irradiation of heavenly glory, as once, with one noble son of God, from the mount of communion with his Father (*Exod.* 34:1-29). Nay, no wonder (for it were but in keeping with, it were only in seemly celebration of an heir's infeftment[1], infeftment in all nature, in all things as his own) though, on his moving forth beneath the canopy of heaven, and amidst the loveliness of earth, the very music of the spheres should break forth, and greet, with exulting welcome, the child of God – though the hills were heard rejoicing on every side, and the forests clapped their hands.

But it is not so. Nature greets alike the righteous and the wicked, as they move amidst nature's mighty elements, and nature's rich adornature. And no lambent flame tarries on the Christian's brow to tell the world the secret of his high adoption. And no talisman is his, by which to charm suffering and sorrow far away. Nor is there any visible display afforded, giving over-powering evidence of the life and the inheritance incorruptible and undefiled to which he has been begotten, by the resurrection of Christ from the dead.

And our text prepares us to expect this. It says, Look not for any carnal, constraining index of the glory that pertains to your new life in Christ, so long as you are here. Expect not that your life, glorious, everlasting, blessed though it be, should overflow into obvious manifestations of its surpassing glory. On the contrary, in any such sense, it is to remain altogether secret; it is to remain, while you are here, a hidden life. 'Your life is hid with Christ in God'; and only 'when Christ, who is your life', shall himself no more be hidden from this world, within the veil, but 'shall appear' again and every eye shall see him –

---

[1]Infeftment is the action or deed by which a person receives the right to lands, property, etc.

only then shall your life break forth in palpable, unbounded, and constraining evidence of its glory. Then
only shall ye also 'appear' or be made manifest 'with him
in glory' (*Col.* 3:4).

Viewing the life of faith then as a hidden life, there are
three of its characteristics which seem to court our
attention.

1. Being hidden, it is secure. 2. Being hidden, it is
secluded. 3. Being hidden, its manifestation is delayed.

1. The hidden life is a *secure* life, it is safe. And oh, how
safe, considering where it is laid up – considering with
whom we share it! It is laid up in God: 'Your life is hid in
God'. It is shared with Christ: 'Hid with Christ in God'. It
is hid in God, in the inaccessible depths of Godhead –
inaccessible to every eye save the eye of faith, which,
seeing in the light of God's Word and God's Spirit, enters
with safety and penetrates among the things and thoughts
of God only wise. This life is hid with God; for 'with thee is
the fountain of life', and 'in thy favour is life'. Yea, it is
that secret life in God – that unspeakable favour of God –
possessed by Emmanuel himself, which believers share.
Their life is bound up with Christ, 'hid with Christ in
God'. Yea, more, Christ is their life; for we read that he
'who is our life shall appear'. Christ himself is our life. For
all the fulness of the Godhead dwelleth in him, and the
fountain of life which Godhead only yields. And seeing
that God the Son, in mediatorial fellowship with the
Father in our name, enjoys in our name the favour of God
– surely, if divine favour is life, Christ, the eminently
favoured one, the beloved, must be our life. God has given
us eternal life, and this life is in his Son. Oh, then, draw
near, and by Christ, the open door – the door into the deep
things of God – the door into the Father's opened heart of

love – the door into the otherwise hopelessly concealed mysteries of Godhead unapproachable – behold the over-flowing, the exhaustless fulness of your life! Let faith, seeing by the lamp of God's Word, as it testifies of Christ, not shrink from looking into the opened recesses of the mind and love of Godhead – into the rich and sovereign favour of God, wherein all our real life standeth – into the lovingkindness which is better than life.

Behold where that love, that life, hath its ceaseless, ever-flowing fountain! Behold who drinks the rivers of these pleasures! Deep as the depths of eternal, all-sufficient Deity, boundless as the infinite loving heart of God, appropriated and enjoyed by Christ himself, your elder brother, is that hidden life in the favour of God, which, believing on his Son, you unfailingly can call your own.

Within this veil your life is hid. And how glorious the life that is here, though as yet not breaking out in glory perceptible to sense – accessible, as yet, only to your faith! Are you ready to complain of the difficulty of getting to your own life, because it is so hidden? Yea, but consider how safe it is. Outside that secret veil, within which your life abides – and it is realised, consciously enjoyed, only when ye yourselves, by faith, are within the veil – outside, the tumult of sin, of Satan, of worldly foes, of sad temptations, fightings and fears, may rage; but within, your life is safe. The waves may dash themselves on the bulwarks by which your life is protected, but not even a tinge of their broken, baffled spray can light within. The sound of war may prevail around, but within, immeasurable peace broods evermore; sounds of sweetest love and joy alone are there: you shall call its walls 'Salvation', and its gates 'Praise'. Did you ever enter in by faith within the veil and get a new view and new enjoyment of your life, 'hid with Christ in God'; and did you ever on any such blest occasion, find your life damaged, or diminished, or endangered? You never did. You always found that it was safe. Outside, while you tarried perversely from your secret home, your soul may have withered, cleaving to the dust; the heavenly life may have seemed to be waning to extinction; your actual sense and enjoyment of it may have been greatly diminished. But when you came again, in self-condemning, self-renouncing faith, within the veil; when you came again with Christ to God, to dwell with Christ in God, to live with Christ in God, you found your hidden life all safe, altogether unviolated, without deterioration, and without decay – without spot or blemish, or any such thing. For within that glorious asylum, where your new life in Jesus is concealed, no evil ever reaches to prey upon the vitals of your life, to dry up its fountain, to embitter its ever-flowing streams, to taint those waters that flow forth from the throne of God and of the Lamb. No adverse influence dwells there, and you can carry none in along with you. On the very threshold, sprinkled by the atoning blood – and 'the life is in the blood' – you do, by virtue of that blood, leave behind you the guilt that entails death; you pass in, delivered from all condemnation; and, in your renewed believing view of that precious blood, your love of all known sin as well as the guilt of all your sin, vanishes utterly, and you pass in with a true heart and an upright mind, not regarding iniquity in your heart. And no enemy of your salvation can accompany your believing heart within, or follow to disturb. No enemy can find that door. Your enemies may grope for it, as the blind, but they find it not. You have a safe retreat, where your life is safe. 'Come, my people, enter thou into thy chambers, and shut thy doors about thee: hide thyself as it were for a little moment, until the indignation be overpast'!

How often, in holy Scripture, do we hear the Lord assuring his people of the perfect, inviolable security of their life, which is hid in him! 'No weapon that is formed against thee shall prosper.' 'When thou passest through the waters, I will be with thee; and through the rivers, they shall not overflow thee.' And how often do we find his people triumphing, with songs of exultation, in the hidden security which with Christ in God they enjoy! 'Thou art my hiding place; thou shalt preserve me from trouble; thou shalt compass me about with songs of deliverance.' 'Surely in the floods of great waters they shall not come nigh unto him.' 'Hide me under the shadow of thy wings, from the wicked that oppress me, from my deadly enemies that compass me about.' 'For thou hast been a shelter for me, and a strong tower from the enemy. I will abide in thy tabernacle for ever: I will trust in the covert of thy wings.' 'Yea, in the shadow of thy wings will I make my refuge, until these calamities be overpast.'

Most blessed privilege! To have a spiritual, secret, near asylum, a strong tower, into which the righteous runneth and is safe! Shall tribulation, or distress, or persecution, or famine, or nakedness, or peril, or sword endanger the hidden life? Nay; for all evils, all enemies stand without; while, within, the believing soul is altogether safe – safe as Christ is safe, safe with Christ in God. It is from *within* this hidden retreat that the voice of limitless defiance of all evil, the bold assertion of limitless security, issues: 'In the time of trouble he shall hide me in his pavilion . . . and now shall mine head be lifted up above mine enemies round about me.' It is from *within* that David, looking upon the trials and evils in his house, as being all *without*, exclaims: 'Though my house be not so with God, yet he hath made with me an everlasting covenant, ordered in all things, and sure; this is all my salvation, and all my desire.' It is all right *within*. It is as standing *within* that Habakkuk looks abroad; but the mournful desolation he beholds is all *without* – no blooming fig-tree, no fruit in the vine, the labour of the olive failed, the fields yielding no meat, the flock cut off from the fold, and no herd in the stall. But turning inwards, with his life hid in God, and safe, he can cry, 'Yet I will rejoice in the LORD, I will joy in the God of my salvation.' This gives peace, this gives courage. 'Though an host should encamp against me, my heart shall not fear: though war should rise against me, in this will I be confident . . . for in the time of trouble he shall *hide* me in his pavilion: in the secret of his tabernacle shall he hide me.'

2. But the hidden life is *secluded*, as well as safe. It is a secret life. Of its ongoings, no stranger is cognisant; with its joys, no stranger intermeddles.

The believer, indeed, is not to keep his spiritual life a secret. He is not to hide his light under a bushel. His life, in that sense, is not to be secluded or stealthily concealed from human knowledge. Rather must he let his light shine, and so shine that men, seeing his good works, may glorify his Father which is in heaven. In this respect, by patient continuance in well-doing, his life will be manifested, even as ointment in the hand betrays itself. Yea, the life also of Jesus ought to be made manifest in our mortal body. But in its spring and source, and chiefest ongoings, it is essentially a life of seclusion, in which the soul is alone with God. Perfect seclusion with God, perfect confidential intercourse with God, not only with none to make him afraid, but with none to witness the intercourse, none to mar the perfect stillness of its repose, this is the heritage of him whose life is hid with Christ in God. He has not only a retreat of safety, a rock, a fortress, a high tower, but he has a retreat of seclusion, a life in God, and with Christ in God, on which no creature may intrude, which no power anywhere may interrupt. This is the rest and this is the refreshing wherewith he causes the weary to rest. He takes them alone with himself. He composes their souls into peace. They sit under his shadow with great delight. 'He that dwelleth in the secret place of the most high shall abide under the shadow of the Almighty.' No more does such an one need to long for 'a lodge in some vast wilderness, some boundless contiguity of shade'. Nor does he need to adopt the cry: 'Oh that I had wings like a dove; for then would I fly away and be at rest. Lo, then would I wander far off, and remain in the wilderness. I would hasten my escape from the windy storm and tempest.' Nor is he in danger any more of seeking to throw aside all the cares and duties of this life, or to abandon his post in the world, because of the many besetting harassments that may encompass it. Amidst bustle and business he has a life into which no din of business, no tumult of affairs may intrude. The true life that he lives in the flesh is not in worldly interests and business. In that case he might be fretted hopelessly and irritated and annoyed habitually, worried and wearied out of his very life by the adverse circumstances, the failures of hope and effort, the disappointment of cherished desires, which, even in most flourishing worldly concerns, are continually occurring. But his real and very life is not in that sphere at all, that he could be fretted and worried out of it. He has a life whose seclusion cannot be violated; a life that has its dwelling in another sphere, and that a sphere so distinct, so high, so separate, so secret, that the shocks of worldly disappointment do not reach it to effect continual collisions there, and even the echo of them cannot enter. The

CHRIST FOR US

secret presence-chamber of the Eternal Majesty is the dwelling-place of the life of faith. The eternal peace of the heavenly places belongs to the life in which the believer is raised up together with Christ, and made to sit together with him. He enters there by faith; and therefore he may enter at all times, in all places. And he may go forth into the world still dwelling in the secret home of his hidden life; he may bear it about with him in the body. The pride of man may be passing painfully before him, in its thousand-fold forms and pretensions; the strife of tongues may be going on around, with its thousand-fold arrows that cut like spears; but the presence of the Lord he can set over against the pride of man, and the pavilion of the Lord against the strife of tongues. And though his Lord's presence and pavilion both be secret, this does not mar, but makes for, his quiet: 'Thou shalt hide them in the secret of thy presence from the pride of man: thou shalt keep them secretly in a pavilion from the strife of tongues' (*Psa.* 31:20).

3. The third characteristic of the hidden life is that *its manifestation is delayed*. It is not always to be hidden. But the revelation of its full excellence and glories tarries for the revelation of Christ himself. His own life in the days of his flesh was concealed from the world. He was despised, and we esteemed him not. There was no beauty in him, no dazzling splendour to draw the carnal eye. The infinitely blessed life which he led of peace and favour with God was never rendered palpable to the world. The world knew him not. The glory which the Father had given him was a spiritual and hidden glory, perceptible alone to the eye of faith; and even when he tabernacled with men upon the earth, Christ's spiritual, glorious life was as much concealed, even then, from the carnal men of that generation

as his person has been concealed from all generations since at the right hand of the Father within the veil. The afflictions that pressed upon him, the humiliations he endured, the death of shame in which, to carnal understanding, he and his cause seemed to expire together, constituted a continual obscuring cloud through which no force of human wisdom could pierce, to see the hidden glories of his soul's life in God. And as it was with Christ, so with Christ's members. The called of the Father are predestinated in this, as in other respects, 'to be conformed to the image of his Son, that he might be the firstborn among many brethren.' A continual cross buries out of sight the life everlasting with which they have by faith been invested. A lowly condition, replete with many a trial, spiritual and bodily, militates against the supposition of their high rank and dignity, and seems altogether inconsistent with the claims and pretensions made on their behalf as the sons of God. The apparent antagonism between their possession of an everlasting glorious life in the love of God, and their subjection to many a wasting, lasting humiliation is a trial of their faith which has often staggered them. Asaph's memorable seventy-third Psalm turns wholly on this palpable and painful incongruity. The whole agony which the prophet endured arose from overlooking the fact that the believer's life is a hidden one; from expecting that it should not be hidden but palpable and manifest; and from disappointment at finding it stamped with no obvious and undeniable seal, to distinguish in outward dispensation the righteous from the wicked. The want of this made him, for a moment, in his infirmity, exclaim, 'I have cleansed my heart in vain, and washed my hands in innocency.' And his restoration to tranquillity of mind, was it not achieved simply by his recognising the believer's life once more as a hidden life, by retreating in faith into its secluded secure abode in God, by leaving all trials behind him, as it were, as pertaining to the things of the outer court or ante-chamber, and retreating into the holy refuge, the sanctuary where the life is hidden in God: 'Until I went into the sanctuary of God' (*Psa.* 73:17)? For in comparison with the inwardness and secrecy of that hidden life, one's own very flesh, yea, throbbing heart itself, are things that are *without*. 'My flesh and my heart faileth: but God is the strength of my heart, and my portion for ever' (v. 26). This is the continual and true relief from all doubts, from all apparent contradictions, from all that a present state of manifold trial and much corruption would seem to argue against the believer's present possession of eternal life and exalted rank with God. Let him retreat by faith to a life confessedly hidden. When he can *see* no evidence of his high estate and dignity let him remember that the very supposition *is* that he does not and cannot see it. Let him know that he is to hold to it by faith – by faith in his Father's word – even when all things that he can *see* appear to go against it. Let him grow strong in the knowledge that this is faith's very office – to penetrate to a life which is hidden, buried under the weight of the earthly tabernacle, oppressed by a remaining body of sin and death, obscured by countless clouds of darkness, which oftentimes return after the rain. The hidden life is a glorious Alpine summit – itself bathed in sunlight's utmost splendours, but utterly concealed from the inhabitants of the plain beneath by seas of mountain mists, that roll their ceaseless fleecy waves in mid-ascent. 'Command these mists aside', says sense; and weeps, and groans and toils to obey its own command, ever craving for its own devices, and leaning to its own understanding. But all the armies of all the monarchs would retire baffled from the effort to expel the fleecy clouds, and reveal the glorious scene beyond them and above. 'Let me rise through them', says faith, 'as on eagle's wings; let me ascend above them; be it mine to live in the realm to which they cannot come.' And what all earth's armaments and engineering never could effect, the eagle can: it can procure a prospect of the sun-lit scene beyond. For what is it that faith really achieves when, against hope, it believes in hope but the very prerogative of the eagle – to transcend the realms where obscurity rests, and rise to the elevation where the mists and the tempests and the lightnings cannot come?

But all obscuring clouds are one day to be swept aside for ever. Till then, the believer must expect nothing but the discipline of a state in which, confessedly, it is not designed to bring his hidden life out to the gaze of others or himself, as in his impatience and infirmity he might oftentimes desire. Till then, the clouds of trial that intervene between him and his very life are not by any effort whatsoever to be rolled away; neither by impatience are they to be murmured at, as if some strange thing happened to him. It might be comfortable and delightful to see and enjoy here the unbroken felicity of eternal life. One may even ask, in agony, Why should it not be so, why, if I am a child of God, why, if I am alive for evermore, why, if I am not only a prospective heir but a present possessor of eternal life? Why are so many things, if not all these things, against me? Why is it with me thus? Why cannot I do the things that I would? Why cannot I compel the acknowledgement of my high estate, my heavenly credit and renown? Why should I be in heaviness through manifold temptations? Why should I have to groan within myself, oppressed continually with anomalous and seemingly irreconcilable conditions?

It is a state of feeling of which thousands of Christians

have been conscious, an agony that multitudes have never spoken of but suffered from most intensely. More apostles than one respond to it and soothe it. Evidently Paul has this very state of mind in view when he says, Yes, we are saved, but it is 'in hope'. We have eternal life, but as yet it is a hidden life. 'We are saved by hope: but hope that is seen is not hope: for what a man seeth, why doth he yet hope for? But if we hope for that we see not, then do we with patience wait for it' (*Rom.* 8:24–25). John also answers this difficulty with striking exactness when he says, 'Beloved, now are we the sons of God'; and if our outward estate seems to argue against our claim it is granted that 'it doth not yet appear what we shall be'. The glory that pertains to our relationship and rank is not yet manifest. Yet we only share in this with the Eternal Son himself: 'The world knoweth us not, because it knew him not . . . but we know that, when he shall appear, we shall be like him; for we shall see him as he is' (*1 John* 3:1—3). And thus also Paul testifies in our text: 'When he shall appear' – when he shall no more tarry within the veil but shall come forth and be manifested to the world, and every eye shall see him – then our life shall no more be hidden. *It* also shall appear. How, indeed, could it be otherwise? Christ himself 'is our life', and when he who is our life is hidden from the world our life must be hidden also. But when he who is our life is no more hidden but shall appear, then shall we also 'appear with him in glory'. Then shall full justice be done to our adoption. Then shall it become obvious. We shall be heirs-*apparent* then.

Meantime all nature, sympathizing with the children of God in the present concealment of their identity and delay of their high estate, 'groaneth and travaileth in pain together until now.' 'The earnest expectation of the creature waiteth' wearily 'for the *manifestation* of the sons of God' (*Rom.* 8:19). But when that shall at length take place, when obvious glory is assigned them, adequate to the rank they now possess, all nature shall welcome the sons of God. 'For ye shall go out with joy, and be led forth with peace: the mountains and the hills shall break forth before you into singing, and all the trees of the field shall clap their hands.' 'Because the creature itself also shall be delivered from the bondage of corruption into the glorious liberty of the children of God.'

If your life with Christ is a hidden life, consider what you must hide and what you must not hide.

1. Consider what you must not hide. You must not hide sin. And there are two respects in which you must not hide it.

i. You must not hide sin in the love of it. If you regard iniquity in your heart, the Lord will not hear you (*Psa.* 66:18). And if the Lord shut out your prayer, are not the springs of your hidden life deranged immediately, at least your conscious enjoyment of it and all its aspirations and exertions?

ii. You must not hide sin in the guilt of it. 'When I kept silence, my bones waxed old through my roaring all the day long . . . I acknowledged my sin unto thee, and mine iniquity have I not hid. I said, I will confess my trans- gressions unto the LORD, and thou forgavest the iniquity of my sin' (*Psa.* 32:3, 5).

2. Consider what you must hide. 'Thy word have I hid in mine heart, that I might not sin against thee' (*Psa.* 119:11). For the hidden life is a life of faith; and faith lives,

and moves, and has its being in the Word of God. Faith's light is from the lamp of the Word, kindled by the Spirit; and by this lamp, faith penetrates, with unfaltering, unquailing gaze into the things which eye has not seen, nor ear heard, nor reason grasped, nor imagination bodied forth. The 'Word-and-Spirit' is a combination with whose glory we might well make all heaven ring in celebrating it. The 'Word-and-Spirit' is the *life of God*, and whoso has it is hidden, because God is hidden, hidden not for defect of light, but for excess of splendours, dwelling in light that is inaccessible and full of glory. Amen.

∽ 14 ∽

Blessings in Christ

'Blessed be the God and Father of our Lord Jesus Christ, who hath blessed us with all spiritual blessings in heavenly places in Christ' (Eph. 1:3).

The language of the believing soul is, 'The lines are fallen unto me in pleasant places; yea, I have a goodly heritage.' There are other texts of Scripture which also speak of the Christian heritage in its unity, a 'pearl of great price'; 'a kingdom that cannot be moved'; a 'portion'. But this text speaks of the heritage in its multiplicity, as made up of or branching out into a multitude of blessings. 'Blessed be the God and Father of our Lord Jesus Christ, who hath blessed us with all spiritual blessings in heavenly places in Christ.'

We may consider the subject under the following six heads: 1. The origin of these blessings; 2. The end, the final purpose of them; 3. The locality of these blessings; 4. The depository or treasure-house of these blessings; 5. The method, and 6. The means of participating in them. Or grouping them in pairs we have, 1. The origin and end; 2. The locality and treasure-house of these blessings; and 3. The method and means of attaining them. May this subject, by the divine blessing, be profitable to all among us who sincerely desire to be enriched with spiritual good.

1. The origin and end of these blessings. First consider the origin. What is their source? Whence do they take their rise? The context very emphatically answers the question and very steadily keeps the answer under our attention. They originate in the mere grace and good pleasure of God, his unfettered, undeserved sovereign love. In the fifth verse they are said to be 'according to the good pleasure of his will.' In the seventh verse they are said to be 'according to the riches of his grace.' In the ninth verse, 'according to his good pleasure which he hath purposed in himself.' In the eleventh verse, 'according to the purpose of him that worketh all things after the counsel of his own will.'

In the second chapter of the epistle the same truth is very frequently and forcibly presented, the apostle losing no opportunity of asserting it, till the declaration that 'by grace are ye saved' becomes almost the refrain or sacred chorus of his lofty theme. In the fourth verse of that chapter these blessings are traced to their origin, namely 'his riches in mercy', and to his 'great love wherewith he loved' – so great, so free, that it embraced us even when we were dead in sins. In the fifth and sixth verses the apostle, impatient to celebrate this rich mercy as the alone fountain of our salvation, without pausing for the close of his sentence and the completion of his sentiment, interjects parenthetically a burst of gratitude and admiration: he 'hath quickened us together with Christ (by grace ye are saved) and hath raised us up together' with him. In the seventh verse his expression for this infinitely precious truth becomes still more emphatic and intense and he testifies of 'the exceeding riches of his grace in his kindness toward us'. Finally, as if he never could make this truth sufficiently emphatic and impressive, he returns again to the expression and celebration of it: 'For by grace are ye saved through faith; and that not of yourselves: it is the gift of God.'

Surely it argues the deep depravity of the human heart that this doctrine should have been so frequently and so fiercely assailed. Do you dislike the sovereignty, the free unfettered sovereignty of God in salvation? Would you fain find some other origin for spiritual saving blessings than the good pleasure, the rich mercy, the free, royal, sovereign love of God? Would you have more hope of them and better liking to them, and greater readiness to repair to and partake of them, if their fountain-head were other than the good pleasure and the free love of God? Oh, can you fail to see what base ingratitude, what black suspicion towards God, this state of mind implies? Can you shut your eyes to the clear demonstration of your haughty independence and unsubdued pride which such feelings afford? You cannot brook the overwhelming dependence on God to which this doctrine summons you; the overwhelming obligation to his matchless love under which this doctrine would put you. Then, let it be the means now of revealing to you your dislike of God, your proud opposition to his supremacy. Let it lay the finger on the very plague-spot of your corruption. Let it show you your natural face as in a glass. Surely you may willingly submit to this when it will also show you a salvation which makes a proposal from God to love you notwithstanding all your corruption, with a sovereignty of love that freely loves, that prevails to love still against all your enmity, and a sovereignty of purpose and power that provides for curing it.

Ah, if you knew aright your just condemnation and your entire depravity, you would object no more to God's righteous sovereignty. If you knew the cruel dominion of sin you would rejoice in the free supremacy of grace. Were you but convinced that sin reigned in and over you unto death, you would hail it as the herald of hope that grace reigns through righteousness unto eternal life by Jesus Christ. Yes! by grace are ye saved through faith, and that not of yourselves; it is the gift of God, according to the good pleasure of his will.

Second, the blessings thus originating – to what do they ultimately tend? What is their end or final purpose? To this the answer is, they aim, they tend, they are designed to promote the manifestation of the glory of God and especially of his grace. This is the end that God has in view in blessing us with all spiritual blessings. His glory shall thereby be made great. The apostle in the context keeps this distinctly in sight. In the sixth verse of this chapter he says we are made partakers of these blessings 'to the praise of the glory of his grace.' In the twelfth verse he says in like manner that the inheritance is conferred upon us 'that we should be to the praise of his glory.' In the fourteenth verse he states the same doctrine in the same terms when he says that we are sealed with the Spirit which is the earnest of our inheritance 'unto the praise of his glory.'

Such is the Lord's ultimate object in saving us. He designs thereby to make his own glory manifest, to make it resplendent and conspicuous. He proposes to give an eternal exhibition of the greatness and glory of his grace, 'that in the ages to come he might shew the exceeding riches of his grace in his kindness toward us through Christ Jesus.' He means to give a revelation to angels of his wisdom, 'to the intent that now unto the principalities and powers in heavenly places might be known by the church the manifold wisdom of God.' Thus there is glory to God in the highest, peace on earth, and good will toward men. 'All the promises of God in him are Yea, and in him Amen, unto the glory of God by us.'

Can anything be more encouraging? Can anything be more engaging or constraining? Waking up to think at last of the authority and claims of God, and dimly seeing a very little of his majesty and glory, I ask, can it possibly consist with the honour, the infinite dignity, the glory of God that I should be forgiven, accepted, adopted, renewed, sanctified and made an heir of glory? Ah, says the gospel, it may not only consist with the glory of God but may promote it, illustrate it, advance it, make it real. Do I really understand this? Do I understand that God provides for it and proposes to take occasion in me of glorifying his great name? Of claiming and of calling forth from the principalities and powers in heavenly places, and all throughout the ages to come, adoring exclamations of wonder, joy, surprise and praise? In *me* as the object of his redeeming love and purpose, the subject of his regenerating grace and power? And does not this constrain my wonder, joy, surprise and praise, that I should be called not only to receive freely an infinite, sovereign, undeserved love, but that my reception of it should be the means of throwing light, to the angelic beings, during the eternal ages, on the glorious character and perfections of God? Oh, let the Spirit but teach me this, let him subdue and mould my heart to it and constrain me to acquiesce in a proposal so marvellous. Who am I, O Lord God, and what is my father's house that thou hast brought me hitherto? Who am I, O Lord God, that thou shouldst propose to wash and justify and sanctify me freely, without money and without price, and that with such traces and signatures and implications of thy glory as that thou shalt challenge in me and in thy handiwork in me the holy surprise and admiration of all the heavenly hosts through all the unending ages? And now, O Lord, I believe, help thou mine unbelief. Be it unto me according to thy Word. O Lord, do as thou hast said.

2. We may consider now the locality of the blessings, where the apostle places them, the heavenly places. Now, this same expression occurs other four times in this epistle. In the twentieth verse of this chapter it is ident-ified as the locality of the risen Redeemer. The Father has raised him from the dead and set him at his own right hand in the heavenly places. In the sixth verse of the second chapter it is assigned to believers also, as equally their home, they being risen with Christ: he 'hath raised us up together, and made us sit together in heavenly places.' In the third chapter and the tenth verse it is described as the habitation of the holy angels, the name given to those glorious hosts of light who are called 'the principalities and powers in heavenly places'. And finally in the sixth chapter and the twelfth verse the apostle says, 'We wrestle not against flesh and blood, but against principalities, against powers, against the rulers of the darkness of this world, against spiritual wickedness in high (or heavenly) places.' From these words we learn that into this spiritual and holy place the believer is pursued by the powers of darkness that fight against his salvation. We have an instance of this in the case of Job, when the sons of God came before the Lord and Satan came also.

The heavenly places, then, are the seat of the risen Christ and of believers in him where he dwells bodily and they by faith, the home also of the holy angels, the arena of the good fight of faith where even the wicked spirits have access. In one word, it is the true holy of holies, where the Advocate sits at God's right hand; where he sits bodily and in the name of his clients, and where his clients, spiritually and in faith, sit and worship with him; where the angelic hosts surround the throne and study God's wisdom in the church, finding it a school for heavenly knowledge; and where the hosts of darkness being suffered for the exercise and trial of the godly, find an arena in which to show their malignity, but where, unlike in their own proper kingdom, they may always be repelled successfully and do always come off with loss. This same locality is described by the single word 'above'. When writing to the Colossians, Paul says, 'If ye then be risen with Christ, seek those things which are above, where Christ sitteth on the right hand of God.' It is the secret of the Lord's presence, it is his special pavilion, the region of the spiritual life, the new world into which the new birth ushers us, where we look not at the things which are seen, but at the things which are unseen and eternal, where all old things are passed away and all things are become new. Yes, it is a holy home into which, by faith, the believer enters as soon as he is reconciled to God and transformed in the renewing of his mind. 'For in the time of trouble he shall hide me in his pavilion: in the secret of his tabernacle shall he hide me.' 'Thou shalt hide them in the secret of thy presence from the pride of man: thou shalt keep them secretly in a pavilion from the strife of tongues.' In that region of the new life the believing soul is with Christ already by faith at the right hand of God, the ward and the admiration of the unfallen angels, the envy and the target of evil ones. Such is the home in which the children of the kingdom dwell and in which they are enriched with all spiritual blessings.

In the second place consider the depository, the treasure-house, the trustee of all these blessings. It is Christ. He hath blessed us with all spiritual blessings in heavenly places in Christ. They are all deposited and treasured up in Christ. Hear what Jesus himself says: 'All things are delivered unto me of my Father.' 'All that the Father hath is mine.' 'The Father loveth the Son, and hath given all things into his hand.' Christ is the heir of all things. The blessings in all their fulness are in him. The

Father has kept back nothing from him. As it is said in another place, 'In that he put all in subjection under him, he left nothing that is not put under him.' So, in that God the Father made him the heir of all things, there is no blessing that is not made over to him. The God and Father of our Lord Jesus Christ has blessed HIM with all spiritual blessings in heavenly places. It has pleased the Father that in him all the fulness of the blessings should dwell.

'How then', says unbelief – jealous, querulous, discontented, isolated unbelief – standing apart on its own and proudly standing its ground against grace and Christ and the Lord's salvation, 'how can he bless me with them if he has given them all to another, to Christ? I cannot see how they can be to me when they are all given to him. If they are all his I must be poor indeed.' 'But', says humble faith with a mind exactly the reverse, 'it is enough if he has given them all to Christ. He has not thereby given them past me but given them unto me. He has given them all to me if he has given them all to Christ. He has given them all to me because he has given them all to Christ, for the Christ who contains them all, him has he given to me freely.' Lowly-hearted, full-contented faith, loyal to her bridegroom and embracing her husband's estate as her own says, 'The Father hath blessed me with all spiritual blessings in giving them all to my husband. My beloved is mine and I am his. All things are mine, whether Paul or Apollos or Cephas or the world or life or death or things present or things to come, all are mine for I am Christ's and Christ is God's. They are all mine because they are his.'

Yes, if God had gathered up all his love and all its fruits and gifts and bestowed them in all their fulness on Christ, and then withheld from us this rich and all-embracing Christ, we were indeed left destitute and empty. But

[216]

Christ himself is God's great and unspeakable gift. 'And this is the record, that God hath given to us eternal life, and this life is in his Son.' This is his record, that he has given us all spiritual blessings, and these blessings are in his Son. If he gives you the treasure-house, he gives you all its contents.

Let us go then into this great store-house of blessing, this living depository, the trustee himself being ours by the gift of God! Whatsoever we find in him is our own.

i. First of all, we find election in him for he is the elect of God. 'Behold my servant, whom I uphold; mine elect in whom my soul delighteth.' Where, then, shall the believer find and read his election of God, if it be not in Christ who is the elect of God? Oh, why should anyone wander amidst insoluble perplexities in the region of the hidden purposes of God? Go not to the secret decree of election but go to the revealed elect one, Christ. Embrace him! Make your calling sure by embracing him. Make your calling and election sure by making sure of Christ. All the sovereign, distinguishing, electing love of God is yours in him for the taking. Every difficulty of the humble, sin-sick, earnest soul may be removed. The obstacles that the proud raise disingenuously, no gospel of any kind ever would remove. But look thou to Christ. He is the chosen one of God. In him there is no mystery at all about election. Nor in him is election that cold, arbitrary, repulsive thing it often seems to many. It is the Father's warm loving choice, alighting first on the Son of his love. And in Christ, you also, on receiving him, are gathered by the Father into the same embrace. So you find that you have not chosen him but that he has chosen you. Such is the first of the spiritual blessings which Paul enumerates. He 'hath blessed us with all spiritual blessings in heavenly places in Christ:

according as he hath chosen us in him before the foundation of the world, that we should be holy and without blame before him in love.'

ii. We find sonship in him: for he is the Son. The adopted sons have this privilege in the eternal Son. To bring saved men into a filial relation to God required a Saviour standing in that relation himself. Hence when the fulness of the time was come, God sent forth his Son that we might obtain the adoption of sons. 'But as many as received him, to them gave he power to become the sons of God, even to them that believe on his name.' This, accordingly, is the second of the spiritual blessings which Paul specifies: 'Having predestinated us unto the adoption of children by Jesus Christ unto himself' (*Eph.* 1:5).

iii. We find acceptance in him, for he is the accepted, the beloved. He is himself infinitely acceptable to the Father. His person is beloved and his work admired of God. In him the Father is well pleased. Oh! how unutterably is it true that he finds grace in his sight. In him therefore we have justification, acquittal, acceptance, the approbation and favour of God. Paul says, mentioning this third blessing, 'he hath made us accepted in the beloved' (verse 6).

iv. We find redemption in him, for he is the redeemer, and his blood is the ransom, and the forgiveness of sins is its direct immediate result. This is that redemption of which, in another place, Paul testifies so emphatically that it is in Christ, 'Being justified freely by his grace through the redemption that is in Christ Jesus.' Or as Paul here states the blessing, 'In whom we have redemption through his blood, the forgiveness of sins' (verse 7).

v. We find heirship and the inheritance in him: for he

is the heir. 'In whom', says Paul, mentioning this fifth blessing and finding it, as all the others, in Christ, 'In whom also we have obtained an inheritance' (verse 11).

vi. And finally we find in him the anointing and the seal of the Spirit, for he is himself the anointed one whom the Father has sealed. In him alone the Spirit dwells without measure. Hence the apostle says, 'In whom also after that ye believed, ye were sealed with that holy Spirit of promise, which is the earnest of our inheritance until the redemption of the purchased possession, unto the praise of his glory' (verses 13–14).

How rich and glorious, then, is Christ, considered as the treasure-house of all spiritual blessings; and what an import may the spiritually taught soul learn more and more to find in that promise, 'My God shall supply all your need according to his riches in glory by Christ Jesus', or that other declaration, 'And of his fulness have all we received, and grace for grace.' He is the Elect, the Son, the Beloved, the Redeemer, the Heir, the Anointed and Sealed of the Spirit. In him we find laid up for us election, adoption, acceptance, redemption, inheritance, the Spirit's unction, seal and earnest. We are elect in Christ the Elect One, sons in Christ the Son, accepted in the Beloved, redeemed in the Redeemer, heirs in the Elder Brother, anointed and sealed in the Christ. This same principle, thus copiously illustrated and applied in the context, pervades all the chapter to the end, for, while Paul speaks of the hope of his calling, of the riches of the glory of his inheritance, of the exceeding greatness of the power of grace working in them that believe, he makes it apparent that all these are in Christ and that it is only in Christ that they can be found. The greatness of the power is that very power which the Father wrought in him when he raised him from the dead and set him at his own right hand in the heavenly places. The riches of the glory of the inheritance are just the 'all things' that are put under his feet. And the hope of his calling is the sum of what may be hoped for from membership with him who by his own fulness filleth all in all. Thus, having election in the Elect, sonship in the Son, acceptance in the Beloved, redemption in the Redeemer, inheritance in the Heir and the Spirit in the Christ, you have all in him who is all in all.

3. The method and the means of attaining the blessings.

First, as to the method of our participation with Christ in these blessings. Manifestly, if they are all concentrated in him our participation in them depends on our being united to him. This is indicated very gloriously in the tenth verse of this chapter, where the apostle, explaining the purpose which God purposed in himself, asserts its object and aim to be, 'that in the dispensation of the fulness of times he might gather together in one all things in Christ, both which are in heaven and which are on earth; even in him.' Doubtless this implies that even the holy angels themselves are brought into a certain subordinate union with Christ and secured thereby from ever falling away as vast numbers of their companions fell away. It is in worshipping the Son of God in our flesh that the angels find themselves confirmed in eternal security in their holy and blessed estate. For even *all things*, not excepting those in heaven – those most permanently heavenly and holy, which need no purging from sin and no redemption from the curse – those things which are in heaven as well as those that are on earth are headed up for their eternal permanence and blessedness in the Word made flesh.

But this applies with special emphasis to the redeemed from among men. We are gathered together in one in Christ. This is the very feature and divine characteristic of the days in which we live. This is the leading purport and design of the times now passing over us. This is the special economy of the fulness of the time. It is an economy, a dispensation of ingathering. This full Christ, come in the full time, is that Shiloh of whom it was of old said, 'To him shall the gathering of the people be.' Emmanuel, throughout the gospel age, is giving the command, 'Gather my saints together unto me; those that have made a covenant with me by sacrifice' – those that have redemption through my blood, even the forgiveness of sins. And the Father gives the promise, 'Yet will I gather others to him, beside those that are gathered.'

This gathering is the special work of the Holy Spirit arresting, convincing, enlightening and renewing the soul to see and embrace in Jesus Christ an all-sufficient portion, an altogether suitable righteousness to the guilty, life to the dead, a Redeemer to the lost, an Advocate with God through whom a sinner may return and be received in love. It is descriptive of this very gathering into Christ when the apostle in the second chapter speaks of our being quickened, raised up, made to sit in heavenly places with Christ (verses 5–6); of our being made the workmanship of God, created in Christ Jesus unto good works (verse 10); of our being made nigh by the blood of Christ (verse 13); reconciled in perfect peace unto God, permitted and enabled to have access to him as a Father; made fellow-citizens with the saints, built on the foundation of the apostles and prophets, framed together into a living shrine of the Godhead, builded together for an habitation of God through the Spirit (verses 16–22).

Thus gathered together in one into Christ, living in him

by the Spirit, and abiding in him, abiding as free sons in the house forever, abiding in the treasure-house and having right and title through grace to all its rich contents, we are blessed with all spiritual blessings in heavenly places in Christ Jesus.

Secondly, if all spiritual blessings are gathered together in Christ Jesus and all spiritual persons are gathered together in him that they may partake of these blessings, by what means is our gathering together into him effected? In a word, it is by means of the gospel. In the eighth and ninth verses the apostle describes this gospel as the revelation in which God has abounded toward us in all wisdom and prudence, having made known unto us the mystery of his will according to the good pleasure which he hath purposed in himself. In similar terms, writing to the Corinthians, he denominates the gospel, 'the wisdom of God in a mystery, even the hidden wisdom, which God ordained before the world unto our glory.' It is 'the wisdom of God' and 'the power of God unto salvation'. In the thirteenth verse of this chapter he calls it 'the word of truth, the gospel of your salvation', as if he would say that if in all the universe there is anything worthy to be believed, any saying faithful and worthy of all acceptation, any word of *truth*, if there be a *word* of truth in anything that was ever spoken by God or any creature, it is the gospel of your salvation. Oh! precious designation: 'the word of truth, the gospel of your salvation'. By means of this word, informed and enlightened of the Spirit by the instrumentality of the gospel, we behold Christ. In him we receive all blessings, redemption from the curse, release from condemnation, restoration to life and favour from the Lord, restoration to sonship and inheritance. We enter into him renouncing ourselves and taking up our position, our life, our home in him. That portion we find infinitely favourable and secure, exactly as this gospel describes. That hope we find ever blessed and eternal, exactly as this gospel pledges. That home we find replenished with all spiritual blessings in heavenly places, exactly as the gospel teaches us to expect. The gospel awakens our expectations. The gospel more than fulfils them.

We close with a word to two classes. 1. To you who believe not. You will not come into Christ, the home of blessings. How infatuated is your folly! How deep-rooted your alienation! How great your contempt of God! How desolate at last will be your condition! The door which your sin had closed is thrown wide open, and within are all blessings – free. You prefer a foreign land, a far country. Ah! you will one day begin to be in want and no man will give unto you. 2. To you that believe. Let me counsel you to watch the working of your faith. Has not its acting been too often expended on catching hold of your warrant and title to the treasure-house rather than searching and appropriating and enjoying its treasures? Alas, instead of quietly, progressively, patiently, as a rightful proprietor and heir, searching the fulness of Christ and daily embracing such particular blessings as your estate may need, you have been frequently and fitfully exhausting the action of faith on what is but preliminary, the appropriating of Christ himself. This too often has contented you. You have not firmly held and retained him. The obtaining of Christ is not the last step but the first. Then, Christ being yours, draw out of his fulness, search and prove his blessings. Press on and prove on. Live on by the faith of the Son of God; while in your experience and enjoyment you are ever learning more and more what riches of grace and truth are laid up in Jesus. Rejoice that they are all your own in Christ and give thanks unto the Father as in this doxology, 'Blessed be the God and Father of our Lord Jesus Christ, who hath blessed us with all spiritual blessings in heavenly places in Christ.'

∽ 15 ∽

The Sons of God

'Beloved, now are we the sons of God, and it doth not yet appear what we shall be: but we know that, when he shall appear, we shall be like him; for we shall see him as he is' (1 John 3:2).

There are included in these words, first, a bold and firm assertion, 'Beloved, now are we the sons of God.' Secondly, we have a candid acknowledgement, a frank admission of an apparent objection, 'it doth not yet appear what we shall be.' Thirdly, there is a triumphant removal of that objection by a bold and firm anticipation, counteracting or counterbalancing it, 'but we know that, when he shall appear, we shall be like him: for we shall see him as he is.'

1. There is here a bold and firm assertion, 'now are we the sons of God.' This is a high claim and it is put forward with much fervour and emphasis. The emphasis is twofold. (i) 'We *are* the sons of God.' We firmly maintain that this is our true rank and our real relation toward the Lord Almighty: we are his sons. It is as if the apostle was protesting, dissenting from some adverse deliverance, as if he were backing up and bearing out his claim in the face of some painful denial of it; as if his spirit were stirred within him fervidly and emphatically to reiterate that

[225]

claim, notwithstanding the incredulity with which in certain quarters it might be met. In point of fact, it is in these very circumstances, and in this very spirit, that he boldly utters this firm protestation and it is against the whole world, as lying in the wicked one, that professedly he now maintains it. 'The world knoweth us not.' The world doth not own us as the sons of God. The world repudiates our claim, recognising no evidence of its validity, blind to all proof of our pretensions and our rank. But, beloved, let not the world's rejection of us shake our confidence in our adoption. Let us not be moved from our position, and let us not retract or refrain from repeating our pretensions: 'Beloved, we *are* the sons of God.'

But this is not the whole emphasis of the claim. For (ii) the apostle not only disavows all denial, he disavows all delay. 'Beloved, *now* are we the sons of God.' Already this is our rank, firmly sealed and secured. It is no prospective honour. It is our present privilege. We are not on probation for it; we are in possession of it. Frankly must we own that although the visible glory adequate to our high rank is indeed prospective, the grace adequate to instate us in our high rank is present. In this grace we already stand. As to that glory we only rejoice in the hope of it. It doth not yet appear what we shall be. But what we are now, even already, we know and maintain. Beloved, now are we the sons of God, *even now*.

Such a claim must be well grounded. A claim requiring to be boldly sustained would require to be grounded well. And so it is. It rests on a foundation laid in Zion, elect and precious and whoso buildeth thereon shall never be confounded. It rests on a threefold basis. First, the love of the Father; secondly, the call of God by his Word and Spirit; and thirdly, our union with the Son.

First, the love of the Father, 'Behold, what manner of

love the Father hath bestowed upon us.' Secondly, the call of the Father, 'that we should be called the sons of God.' Thirdly, our union, even identification, with the Son of God, which accounts for the world's rejection of us, 'Therefore the world knoweth us not, because it knew him not.'

Our claim of sonship, we rest, firstly, on the Father's love; we prove it by his love to us. In that love we glory, as the foundation of our sonship, and to it we call attention, as the explanation of our sonship. 'Behold, what manner of love the Father hath bestowed upon us.'

This love of God of which we make our boast and our song in the house of our pilgrimage is not the general beneficence of the divine nature. It is not the universal paternal indulgence of the Divine Being towards all his creatures. Creation has not told us of this love, no, not with all its myriad proofs of the goodness of him who created all things, whether they be visible or invisible and who, on reviewing all his workmanship, beheld that it was very good. Nor has providence proved it to us, no, even though the eyes of all things wait upon him and he gives them their meat in due season. It is not such a love that the Father has bestowed upon us, and such a love would not suffice to prove that we are called the sons of God, because conscience of sin within us, the ever-growing consciousness of alienation and estrangement from God, would invalidate and overthrow all evidence that nature can afford of a love in God. It is therefore not sufficient to call us, who are miserable aliens and unrighteous rebels, the sons of God. We need another and a new manner of love bestowed upon us ere we can be called or can become the sons of God. The love spoken of in this verse is a very peculiar, distinguishing love, a sovereign, saving love in God, which we need to provide a fountain of sonship to us.

The manner of love in God that nature tells of will not suffice to make us the sons of God. Conscience makes it void and rejects its demonstration as inadequate. And that holy law of God inviolable, of which conscience is the echo, declares its insufficiency. Our own hearts condemn us; and God, in respect of this very condemnation, and in respect of those righteous grounds and the recognition of those righteous grounds on which that condemnation rests, is greater than our hearts and condemns us even more than they.

Shall we essay, then, to enter into the light that is inaccessible and seek to search the unfathomable depth of the divine heart and will, to learn whether in its secret cabinet of everlasting purpose and affection there dwells such manner of love as can bestow adoption on the alien, sonship on the guilty, estranged and heartless rebel? Ah! that light is indeed inaccessible, dark and blinding in its very brightness. How then, if, in ranging over all creation's bounds and reading all the history of providence, we meet with no such love as our conscience, testifying to God's law and righteousness, can own as adequate to constitute transgressors the sons of God? If the eternal purpose of his will is inaccessible, secret and hidden in the blinding light that is full of glory, how shall we ever learn if there be love enough in the Father's heart, love to spare for such as we are?

Behold, from the Father's bosom there cometh forth the Eternal Son, made of a woman. To us a child is born, to us a son is given. In this was manifested the manner of love we need. 'In this was manifested the love of God toward us, because that God sent his only begotten Son into the world, that we might live through him.' Yea, and he came to deal with that invalidating power of conscience and of the law – conscience of sin and the law of righteousness – that made void and insufficient all other kinds of love. Herein is love, the very kind of love that in vain we searched for; the love that consciousness that we loved not God gave us so great ground to doubt of, and no claim at all to hope for, herein is love, not that we loved God, but that he loved us, and sent his Son to be the propitiation for our sins. Not all the plenitude of the beneficence of the Creator toward his creatures which nature displays could prove that a kind of divine love exists which can suffice for sinners. It is the gift of his Son as a propitiation for sins which manifests that. By its very nature it is a free gift of all-sufficient, sovereign, peculiar love to sinners. It answers and counteracts precisely and wholly all the invalidating power of sin, sin as revealed by the law of God and as attested by the conscience of man. It is, with infinite precision, that kind of love to us which alone could suffice for us as breakers of the law. God sent forth his Son, made of a woman, made under the law to redeem them that were under the law. Christ hath redeemed us from the curse of the law and cleansed us from the conscience of sin, being made a curse for us. And the Son of God, made the Son of man, and manifested thus in the flesh, dwelling thus among us, full of grace and truth, having redeemed us from under the law, the way is open for us to receive the adoption of sons. Ah! this is no precarious amnesty; it is a precise redemption. This is no vague paternal indulgence, putting up with the alien's perverseness, compromising, contradicting the alien's conscience. It is a peculiar, sovereign, saving love purging the alien's rebellion, purging his conscience also from dead works, purging his heart from an evil conscience. It is not inscribed on nature's page; no page, no tablet in all nature is strong enough, not even in the palace or throne-room of the king to bear the engraving of its characters in burning light. No transaction of providence is grand enough, or large enough, or full enough, to body forth its glory. This, this alone shall be the sign: You shall find the babe in swaddling dress, and all the angels of God worshipping him. In this was manifested the love of God toward us. Herein is love. Behold, what manner of love the Father hath bestowed upon us.

This is sure enough as the ground of our adoption and, assured by it, we triumph in it. To others indeed, who do not believe, it may not suffice to prove to them that *they* are the sons of God. Doubtless it would embrace them, doubtless it is sufficient for them also, would they only throw down the weapons of their enmity, believe, return, repent, be reconciled. For the very guiltiest of them all, this manner of love were all-sufficient. For them, surely, if for us; for them as well as for us. For do we not know and feel, and every day confess, that we ourselves are the very chief of sinners – the very least of saints – not worthy to be called his sons? But the grace of God, this marvellous manner of our Father's love bestowed upon us, was exceeding abundant. We hold ourselves to be a pattern of all longsuffering to them which shall after believe, and the signatures of saving mercy towards us trace footprints which shall perhaps cause another, seeing them, to take heart again. To the world also, as well as to us, we know this manner of love to be sufficient for adoption. But if their unbelief shall not make void the faith of God or the love of God, shall it make void our faith in the manner of love which God hath bestowed on us in sending his Son to be the propitiation for our sins? Because they believe not and therefore find in that love of God no ground of sonship for them, shall we deny that it is a fountain of adoption and a ground of sure sonship unto us? Nay, whatever others do, we have known and have believed the love which God hath towards us, and his perfect love casteth out fear. We glory in it as all-sufficient. Rejected by the world, it is believed by us, and believing we have the witness our-selves. That love we make our boast and our song. We stand upon it as a rock and our goings are established. We fill our mouth with it as with a new song: 'Behold, what manner of love the Father hath bestowed upon us.'

The second ground of our adoption is the call of God. 'Behold, what manner of love the Father hath bestowed upon us, that we should be called the sons of God.' It is not merely that we are named or denominated the sons of God. But we are called, we are called to be sons, we are called into sonship. This call is the fruit of his love. He has bestowed such a manner of love upon us as to call us sons of God, to constitute us his sons by his call. For his call, when embraced in faith, when heard and credited by us as believing his peculiar manner of love, is an efficacious call, and it constitutes fully and firmly all that into which it calls us. 'Wherefore come out from among them, and be ye separate, saith the Lord, and touch not the unclean thing; and I will receive you, and will be a Father unto you, and ye shall be my sons and my daughters, saith the Lord Almighty.'

And this call is free, free to you while a sinner, while you have not yet come forth and become separate, while you are yet immersed and wallowing in the unclean thing: while the prodigal is yet feeding swine, feeding himself the husks. For hearken to this call as given of God by Jeremiah: 'Thou hast polluted the land with thy . . . wickedness. Therefore the showers have been withholden, and there hath been no latter rain . . . and thou refusest to be ashamed.' What then? Thou art no more worthy to be called a son? Depart from me ye cursed? No, for behold what manner of love: 'Wilt thou not from this time cry unto me, My father?' Ah! surely adoption is an act of God's free grace. To the alien and the rebel, lying under wrath, living in sin, it comes and says, 'How shall I put thee among the children?' And it not only states the problem but solves it, not only raises the question but answers it: 'And I said, Thou shalt call me, My father; and shalt not turn away from me.' And God gives the full warrant for he first calls you 'My son'.

Yes, this is the manner of this love. To the lost and ruined outcast it comes and says, 'My son, give me thine heart.' 'Ah', replies the convicted sinner, the trembling and incipient believer, the stricken heart on the verge of faith, 'But I am no son of God by very token that I have not given my heart to God and that he needs to ask it. I am no son of his.' A conclusive argument it seems – but it is hard to argue against God. For by asking for the heart he takes for granted that as yet it is not his and that you are an alien. But seeing no inconsistency, he says, 'My son, give me thine heart.' But, you say, I am not that son to whom the Lord says, 'My son, give me thine heart.' Be it so. Yea, it is so, if thy heart is not yet given to the Father. It is granted in that case that you are not yet his son: that apart from this call you are not yet his son. But this call is free to you, as not yet a son for it takes for granted that you are not and that your heart is not yet the Lord's. But this call is free and therefore it is to you. Also it is the Lord's call and not the call of man, weak, uncreating, ineffective. Is not the call of God efficient, powerful, creating, calling the things that are not as though they were? Totally helpless would man's call be if you are not yet a son, but is God's call helpless? Does it not prevail to make thee what it calls thee? Does it not call thee out of alienation into sonship? Does it not say unto thee, Live as a son? 'My son, give me thine heart.' I have called thee Abraham, said God, to him

[232]

who had no child. I have made thee a father of many nations. Ah! Lord God, but to me thou hast given no seed. Say not so. I have made thee the father of many nations, said the mighty God to the childless old man. And he believed God. He believed that God's call made him what it called him. Against hope he believed in hope. So let it be with thee, the seed of Abraham, as it was with Abraham, the father of the faithful. Believe into that call. Close with it. Cleave unto it. 'Therefore it is of faith, that it might be by grace; to the end the promise might be sure to all the seed; not to that only which is of the law, but to that also which is of the faith of Abraham; who is the father of us all, (as it is written, I have made thee a father of many nations,) before him whom he believed, even God, who quickeneth the dead, and calleth those things which be not as though they were. Who against hope believed in hope, that he might become the father of many nations, according to that which was spoken, So shall thy seed be.' Even thus be it thine, against hope to believe in hope, that thou mayest be the seed of Abraham and the son of God, according to that which is spoken, 'My son, give me thine heart.' Stagger not at the promise, stagger not at the call through unbelief. But be thou clear and simple and strong in faith, giving glory to him that calleth the things that are not as though they were, being fully persuaded that what he has promised he is able to perform, that what he calls thee he is able to make thee, that what he is now calling thee he is now making thee, even his own son, taking thine heart unto himself, with thine own full consent, with thine own good will in the day and the call of his power. 'Thy people shall be willing in the day of thy power.' 'My son, give me thine heart.' 'Wilt thou not from this time cry unto me, My father?' Yea, because ye are sons God hath sent forth the Spirit of his Son into your hearts crying,

'Abba, Father'. Now, therefore thou art no more a servant but a son, and let as many of us as believe confirm each other, 'Beloved, now are we the sons of God.'

But the third ground of our adoption is our union with the Eternal Son, a union so complete, an identification so exact, that henceforth 'the world knoweth us not because it knew him not.' Thus the world's denial becomes a proof of our call to sonship in union and communion with the Son. 'God is faithful, by whom ye were called unto the fellowship of his Son.' God has called us into the fellowship, not merely of the righteous and blessed one who happens at the same time to be none other than the Son, but into fellowship with him as the Son, into the joint participation of all the nearness to God, all the interest in God, all the love of God which that relation of the Son himself can possibly yield to us. Not only is the Son the pledge of our adoption, but, received in faith, he is the bond of our adoption, his eternal Sonship being the perfect seal and exhaustless fountain of ours. For as Christ's righteous person, justified of God as our substitute and representative, or Christ, God's righteous servant, is our righteousness, the bond and fountain of our justification, so Christ's beloved person – 'This is my beloved Son, in whom I am well pleased' – owned as a Son while standing as our substitute and representative, declared to be the Son of God with power by his resurrection, Christ, God's beloved Son, is the bond and fountain of our sonship.

We were aliens from God on our part, outcast and disowned on his. So that sonship might again be ours, God sent forth his Son. He was numbered with the transgressors, he took the outcasts' place. He loaded and obscured his sonship with the guilt of our alienation from the Father, with the misery of the Father's disavowal and denial of us. Still he abode the Son, the Son eternal and unchangeable. He bore the guilt of our departure from the Father. He bore the misery of the Father's disavowal of us. He was as far separated from God as the Eternal Word could be. He was as much disowned of the Father as the Eternal Son could be. This was the climax of his bitter woe, 'My God, my God, why hast thou forsaken me?' But he expiated all the guilt of our alienation and exhausted all the misery of the Father's disavowal. For us, he cleared his holy person of all our unrighteousness: 'It is finished.' For us he cleared his beloved sonship of all disavowal, 'Father, into thy hands I commit my spirit.' And if in that hour his vindicated righteousness was righteousness for the guilty, in that same hour his vindicated sonship was sonship for us the aliens. 'As many as received him, to them gave he power to become the sons of God,' so that, not merely the love wherewith God gave his Son might be in us, but the love wherewith he loved his Son might be in us also. For us the Son obscured for a time his Sonship, for us he placed its privileges and glory in abeyance, and though he were a Son he learned obedience by the things which he suffered. Was it not for us, then, that he cleared and vindicated and brought forth into light and glory again that eternal Sonship of his own? Was it not for us, in our name, with us as his associates, that he regained and returned to all its infinite riches and resources of interest and love and favour with the Father? Yea, 'I ascend to my Father and your Father, to my God and your God.' 'God hath called us into the fellowship of his Son.' This is the ground of the world's denial of our sonship; this, to us, is the proof of it. The servant is not above his master. The sons of adoption are not above the Eternal Son. He came to his own and his own received him not. Will they receive us, us who, having received him, have received power to become the sons of God?

The Father's love, the Spirit's call, the Son's fellowship are a three-fold cord in one. The love of the Father calling us through the Spirit into the fellowship of the Son. This is the bond of our adoption. 'Beloved, now are we the sons of God.'

2. But secondly, we must make a frank admission. Though we reject and resent the world's denial, candidly and clearly we must own that it does not yet appear what we shall be. What we are, what we are even now, we firmly hold, we humbly but boldly profess. We are already the sons of God. We have good and valid ground to go upon in maintaining this claim. It may be ground of whose validity we alone can be cognisant, our Father's love, our Father's call, his Son's fellowship and communion in the Spirit. To our own faith alone can these attestations appeal. We cannot expect the world to feel the force of them. Our mournful complaint and our Lord's, the Son's own complaint, is that the world will not prove and see their validity. 'O righteous Father, the world hath not known thee,' thy marvellous manner of love they will by no means believe. Thou hast called and they have refused. How gladly would I have gathered them into my fellowship but they would not. These blessed bonds of adoption the world cannot understand. They are spiritually discerned. The natural man, the world, cannot hope to discern them, yet, spiritual and invisible and supernatural as they are, we maintain their irrefragable validity and value. But if, on the other hand, the world expects that we should point to seals of our adoption discernible by them, to external evidences of our sonship such as should draw the carnal eye and satisfy the carnal mind, if they say that, granting we are the sons of God, we do not look like it, we have no visibly fair robe upon us, no garment for beauty

and for glory, no crown of glory sitting on our brow, no palm of triumph waving in our hand to signalise us as the chosen of the king, frankly we admit the difficulty. There is, we own, no such appearance of our rank and our renown. What, in these respects, we shall be is not apparent. We claim to be the sons and heirs-apparent of the King of Glory, but it doth not yet appear what we shall be.

Of course, we own that no perceptible priestly robes, whiter than the snow, adorn us and no fair mitre made after any pattern shown in the mount certifies our spiritual priesthood. No throne, no sceptre, no regalia have we in proof that Christ hath loved us and made us kings unto the Father; and no Mahanaim of the Lord, no angelic hosts, lead us forth proclaiming, 'Thus shall it be done to the man whom the king delighteth to honour.' Nor do the forests clap their hands at our approach, nor the mountains and the hills break forth before us into singing in welcome to the sons and heirs of the King of Glory. Rather, the whole creation groaneth because our sonship is hidden, waiting for the manifestation of it. A cross lies heavy on our shoulder, rather than a diadem shining on our head. No palm of victory is ours, but the trembling and the toil of weary battle. Diseases grapple with us, having no respect for our adoption. Death at last confronts us as the victims of the loathsome grave, as if we must say unto corruption, not to God, 'Thou art my father,' and call the worm our sister rather than that the Son of God should call us brethren.

But what of that, beloved? Shall we therefore recall our bold and blessed protestation? Shall we canvass anew with bated breath the question whether we be indeed and already the sons of God? Shall we tamper with the truth of our high and hidden rank towards heaven because of our lowly and afflicted state on earth? Shall we quail before the world's demand for palpable and natural proof, a proof we cannot give, and doubt the valid supernatural and spiritual proofs and seals which the world cannot see? We own and deeply feel the difficulty which the world rudely and unfeelingly urges on us and which our own faith has oftentimes with growing grief and deepening sorrow to grapple with. We groan in this vile body. We groan in this still viler body of sin and death. We groan in our cares and toils and conflicts and in all God's waves and billows going over us. And we ask ourselves, when the sentence of death is written in us, and the seeds of death are fruitful in us, how can we still bear up and still stand forth and say one unto another, 'Beloved, now are we the sons of God'? Alas, we feel, O wretched men that we are, we feel daily the painful incongruity, the deep apparent contradiction between our high relation to God as his sons and our present state, as if we were the slaves of time and time's mean and sad and vile conditions. But shall we solve the difficulty, shall we seek a door of escape from this sore perplexity, by razing the foundations, by quitting the belief of our adoption? Doubtless this would remove the incongruity; this would relieve the difficulty. Others might arise in its place, greater even, more distressing and very numerous. For if the foundations be removed what have the righteous done? But for this particular perplexity, doubtless, it might be thus summarily got rid of. Say that all things happen to all alike, that all alike are on the same doubtful footing with God, that no certainty of our relation to him can be had, no sure foundation, no adequate proof, then no satisfying seal of our adoption can be found. Discard the prospect, deny the possibility of ever being able in this life to say, 'Now are we the sons of God', and then you might thoroughly get rid at once of the painful question: how can the veritable sons of the living God be left of their Father which is in heaven to conflict with so manifold and over-powerful presumptive arguments against the truth and sureness of their sonship?

It is to be observed, however, that their sonship rests on grounds of its own. It is to be proved and settled by arguments or evidences suitable and sufficient to itself. And it is a general and great truth that there is no style of reasoning so dangerous as that which, leaving the realm of positive and suitable truth, takes up with mere difficulties and objections and assigns to them the weight due only to proofs direct. It was this that holy Asaph for a time forgot (*Psa.* 73). He too grappled with this very difficulty, or this difficulty, rather, grappled with and stumbled him. 'As for me, my feet were almost gone; my steps had well nigh slipped. For I was envious at the foolish, when I saw the prosperity of the wicked . . . Therefore his people return hither: and waters of a full cup are wrung out to them.' Painfully he felt that, if we are the sons of God, it does not look like it; it doth not yet appear what we shall be. Painfully he felt that our condition is distressingly in-adequate to our rank, our earthly state an apparent strong disproof of our heavenly relation. And alas! he took refuge for a time in doubting that relation itself, in doubting the adoption. He questioned whether to such humbled and afflicted ones there could pertain the adoption. Yet he felt that this doubt was no ordinary evil, that on falling on this stumbling block he suffered no ordinary injury and he felt that in proclaiming it to others he would offend and stumble them also concerning sonship. 'If I say, I will speak thus; behold, I should offend against the generation of thy children.' Not thy servants, friends or people merely, but 'thy children', the sons and daughters of the Lord Almighty. For it is precisely and fatally against the truth and evidence of sonship that this sore temptation strikes. Let me warn you, ye sons of God, weary and afflicted, with your sonship hidden, let me warn you against this wrong and ruining relief from apparent incongruity, this relief that the impatience of unbelief is apt to seek. Let me warn you against tampering with the faith of your adoption as if the sad events of this lower earth could shake those deep foundations that rest in a heavenly, spiritual kingdom and which rest secure though earthly hills be cast into the midst of the sea, though the mountains shake with the swelling thereof. Let not even the most powerful of all apparent contradictions, the consciousness and power of indwelling sin itself, let not even the agony of not doing, not being able to do the things that ye would, let not that induce you to distrust the validity and grounds of your adoption. Even when the cry rises in all its bitterness, 'O wretched man that I am,' seek not the explanation of it in the denial of your adoption. Go on, rather, and cry out for a deliverer. 'O wretched man that I am; who shall deliver me?' Go on to accept anew and to glory in the Son of God as that deliverer, all-sufficient and ever-faithful. Go on and cry 'Who shall deliver me?' Go on to cry in gracious faith and gratitude, 'I thank God through Jesus Christ our Lord.' Yes! Let me warn you against this dark door of escape, the doubt of sonship of faith. It leads to darker labyrinths of sorrow, weakness, despondency and despair. Your hands hang down. Your knees are feeble. All elasticity to recover your soul from depressions disappears, and the recuperating cry, 'Why art thou cast down, O my soul?', your lips will refuse to utter. To be strong against all specious grounds of doubt you must stand upon the rock and have your goings established. You must watch in all wisdom of faith, to say with all firmness, 'Now are we the sons of God.' You must

[240]

keep the new song in your mouth, 'Behold, what manner of love the Father hath bestowed upon us,' notwithstanding that it doth not yet appear what we shall be.

Be very sure also that it is on the peculiar love of God, his special call, and personal fellowship with the Son that you must rest your sonship, if you would distance its security and truth clear from this conflict with sense, shame and sorrow, while the glory, the victory and the joy do not yet appear. Vainly will you try to defend your sonship against shame and sorrow, conflict and the cross, merely on the basis of the fatherly benignity of God the Creator which is in no aspect peculiar but embraces all alike, giving rain and sunshine to the good and the unthankful alike. Whatever may be traced to this beneficence is visible in precisely the same earthly sphere of the world's history in which all the pains and griefs of your earthly state reside. These pains and griefs, therefore, meeting with this general benignity of God in the self-same realm and sphere, limit its obviousness and effectiveness and cloud with real difficulties that general Fatherhood of God. If you only rest on such general paternal love, taking no hold on the special sovereign love of God in Christ Jesus, the propitiation for your sins, making no account of God's special call, addressed personally to you, summoning you to special sonship, and not asserting by faith a special union and communion with the eternal Son, then you do not rise from this sphere of dark and complicated providence at all into the higher and unclouded sphere and kingdom of the Son of his love into which no counteracting doubt can come. Alas! you are helpless in the grasp of the trials and the humiliations of time, and conscious, craven weakness will choke your utterance if you attempt the bold and glorious protestation, 'Now are we the sons of God.'

But hold by faith to sovereign, gracious, peculiar love, hear in faith the Father's special, personal call to you, and maintain by faith a personal communion with the Son. Then, though it does not yet appear what you shall be, in that you merely share with the Eternal Son himself as he was in the world, you still may boldly maintain, 'Now are we the sons of God.'

For hiding thyself in the Son, hark to that voice from heaven beside the stream of Jordan, 'This is my beloved Son in whom I am well pleased.' It also testifies of you and your sonship, for in the water of his baptism and of yours, see how truly it does not yet appear what either he or you shall be. He is driven of the Spirit into the wilderness and you in him, to have his sonship and yours tried and tested, on this very point that, if he is the Son of God, and you in him, it does not at all look like it. What, no bread for thy hungry body? No honour from the sacred people? No kingdom from thine attesting Father? If thou be the Son of God, command these stones to become bread and supply thyself. If thou be the Son of God, alight in safety from this pinnacle and constrain the astonishment and admiration of the people. If thou be the Son of God, accept the kingdoms of the world and the glory of them, which thy Father delays to give thee. If thou be the Son of God, make it manifest, take hold on plenty for thyself, honour from thy nation, the kingdom promised of thy God. Else, how canst thou expect to be received as the Son of God? But under all this trial of his sonship and as animating all his conflict and running through all his victory, can we be wrong or are we irreverent if we think we hear as the undercurrent of the Son's deepest thoughts the bold assertion and the frank confession 'No! I am the Son of God, but it does not yet appear what I shall be.' And in this trial of your sonship in the Son, in this very conflict and in this same victory, has not the Father called you into the fellowship of the Son? And, moreover, besides his bold assertion and his frank admission, the Son of God had also the joy set before him, through which to withstand the delay of glory and the present shame, 'When I shall appear in my glory, I shall be seen to be the Son of God with power.' Is not this anticipation yours also in the fellowship of the Son? 'But we know that, when he shall appear, we shall be like him; for we shall see him as he is.'

3. This is our third head of discourse, and a very brief consideration it must still be permitted. What we are as the sons of God shall be manifest when the Eternal Son of God himself is manifested. Then we shall be like him for we shall see him as he is. We shall be like him and the proof is this, we shall see him as he is. We cannot now see him as he is, for we are not yet like him. Flesh and blood cannot inherit the kingdom of God. We can only see, as yet, through a glass darkly, not face to face. With open face, indeed, as contrasted with the dimness of the early dispensation when a veil was on the face of Moses. In those respects we can, with open face, already behold the glory of the Lord. But it is only in a glass and it is, even in these respects, his glory merely as he was that we can see. And we can see that glory solely because, in a measure, we are like him as he was. Already in a measure we are like him as he was, for already, by faith, we can in a measure see him as he was, full of grace and truth, meek and lowly of heart. Our being like him as he was, through the regeneration and indwelling of the Spirit, accounts for our being able to see him as he was, and also for the world not knowing us, even as it knew him not. We are like him as he was spiritually in the hidden essence of our higher, heavenly character, the hidden man of the heart. We are like him as

he was also outwardly, a man of sorrows and acquainted with grief, a root out of a dry ground, having no form nor comeliness, rejected and despised of men, our spiritual character indiscernible to the world, our outward estate accepted in disproof of our heavenly rank. Still, having not seen him as he is, we love him. In him, though now we see him not as he is, yet believing, we rejoice with joy unspeakable. Beholding his glory as in a glass we are transformed into the same image, the image of the lowly, humble Jesus as he was, from glory to glory, glory hidden in us as it was in him. Yet though transformed into this glory more and more, it does not yet appear what we shall be.

But we shall be transformed into his image after another manner, not of what he was bearing the cross and despising the shame, but of what he is wearing the crown and shining in glory. At death our souls shall be made perfect in holiness. At the resurrection he shall fashion these vile bodies like unto his own glorious body. This corruptible shall put on incorruption; this mortal shall put on immortality. The glory of Christ shall be revealed in us, and the first rapturous confidence that we are become wholly like him as he is will be in the plenitude of our first rapturous assurance that we see him as he is. Then shall it appear what we are as the sons of God, capable of walking in the realms of light with the Eternal Son that loved us, seeing him face to face, forever with the Lord. Like him now as he was, sharing now his cross, we are sustained by the prospect of sharing then his crown, the princely crown of righteousness that fadeth not away, like him as he is. Our priestly robes as the first-born, our regalia and throne of the kingdom, our glory as adequate to our rank as sons of the King do not yet appear, for he with whom we share them all himself doth not yet appear. But when he shall appear, we shall appear with him in glory. 'To him that overcometh will I grant to sit with me in my throne.' Meanwhile, resting on our Father's love, our Father's call, our fellowship with his beloved Son, for our present faith; and anticipating the appearance of the Son to bring us to our Father's house of many mansions, for our hope; loving also the Father in the Son through the Spirit and loving all that are begotten of him, for our charity – and the greatest of the three is charity – we labour now to purify ourselves as he is pure, knowing that only the pure in heart shall see God, for they only are like him, they only shall see him as he is.